MW00633221

Localism versus Globalism in Morphology and Phonology

Linguistic Inquiry Monographs
Samuel Jay Keyser, general editor

A complete list of books published in the Linguistic Inquiry Monographs series appears at the back of this book.

Localism versus Globalism in Morphology and Phonology

David Embick

The MIT Press
Cambridge, Massachusetts
London, England

MIT Press books may be purchased at special quantity discounts for business or sales promotional use. For information, please e-mail special_sales@mitpress.mit .edu or write to Special Sales Department, The MIT Press, 55 Hayward Street, Cambridge, MA 02142.

This book was set in Times New Roman and Syntax on 3B2 by Asco Typesetters, Hong Kong. Printed and bound in the United States of America.

Library of Congress Cataloging-in-Publication Data

Embick, David, 1970–
Localism versus globalism in morphology and phonology / David Embick.
    p.   cm. — (Linguistic inquiry monographs)
Includes bibliographical references and index.
ISBN 978-0-262-01422-9 (hardcover : alk. paper) — ISBN 978-0-262-51430-9
(pbk. : alk. paper) 1. Grammar, Comparative and general—Morphology.
2. Grammar, Comparative and general—Phonology. 3. Grammar, Comparative
and general—Word formation. I. Title.
P241.E43   2010
415'.9—dc22   2009054140

10   9   8   7   6   5   4   3   2   1

Contents

Series Foreword

We are pleased to present the sixtieth in the series *Linguistic Inquiry Monographs*. These monographs present new and original research beyond the scope of the article. We hope they will benefit our field by bringing to it perspectives that will stimulate further research and insight.

Originally published in limited edition, the *Linguistic Inquiry Monographs* are now more widely available. This change is due to the great interest engendered by the series and by the needs of a growing readership. The editors thank the readers for their support and welcome suggestions about future directions for the series.

Samuel Jay Keyser
for the Editorial Board

Preface

The research presented in this book came about as a consequence of my thinking about *competition* in the grammar, a topic explored in Embick 2007a and Embick and Marantz 2008. The general picture that emerges in those papers is that the grammar allows no competition among complex objects (words, phrases, etc.); rather, competition is restricted to the allomorphy of individual nodes. This view, motivated primarily by investigations on morphosyntax, is incompatible with the dominant view in phonological theory, Optimality Theory (OT), which posits competition among infinite sets of complex objects. The conflict between these positions reduces to a form of the debate between derivational and nonderivational views of grammar: more specifically, whether the grammar functions in *localist* or *globalist* terms.

Determining how to make empirical comparisons between such large positions like this, and the different frameworks that embody them, is at the heart of this book. The main argument is that patterns of allomorphy implicate general questions about locality, and specific questions about the manner in which (morpho)syntax relates to (morpho)phonology. Allomorphy in general thus provides a crucial test case for comparing localism and globalism.

With its specific focus on allomorphy, this book presents two major results. First, it articulates a theory of cyclic derivation, which is central to understanding patterns of allomorphic interaction, and shows how linear adjacency plays a further role in relationships in phonological form. Second, it shows that this type of localist theory and various globalist theories can be compared directly in the domain of phonologically conditioned allomorphy, and that the localist theory makes the correct empirical predictions.

The arguments presented below will stand or fall on their own. Further comments are in order, however, concerning how to interpret these results. In my view, it would be possible to conclude from the arguments in this book that the localist theory is correct for morphosyntax, but that, at least for certain parts of the phonology, a globalist architecture is required. That is to say, it could be discovered that there are generalizations about phonology outside the domain of allomorphy that crucially require globalism. This conclusion is possible, but it should be treated with extreme caution. The idea that a large part of the phonological grammar operates in ways that are utterly indifferent to or incompatible with the system for generating complex objects is suspicious, or at the least unfortunate. It would mean that part of the way that complex objects receive their phonological form derives crucially from the manner in which these forms are generated, and that another part derives from a system that operates in radically different terms. More precisely, the morphosyntax would generate a structured representation of a complex form, linearize it, give phonological form to the morphemes, and so on; and then another system would start up, generate infinite competitors from this object, and assess them with respect to well-formedness. The empirical argumentation required to motivate this type of hybrid architecture would have to show beyond any doubt that two fundamentally distinct systems like this are required.

In my view, the most productive research program is to meet these issues head-on. Rather than assuming that morphosyntax and morphophonology might be fundamentally different, and ignoring questions about unification, it should be assumed that there is no extreme difference between these facets of grammar.

My hope is that the research presented here provides a basis for future work along these lines. While there are many areas that could be investigated as a follow-up to this line of inquiry, one general type of question for future work is whether the types of arguments developed for allomorphy in this book can be constructed in other parts of phonology, to bring empirical (and not conceptual) arguments to bear on the question of localism versus globalism. These points are particularly relevant given some other directions of recent research. For example, some versions of OT have moved away from full globalism (e.g., stratal OT, in Kiparsky's (2000) sense); other versions of OT that have emerged recently are radically serialist in nature (see, e.g., McCarthy 2008; Wolf 2008). While I do not review the latter approaches in detail here, the move toward the kind of localism that arises from serial ordering certainly deserves to be noted. What remains to be seen is whether the remaining globalism in such theories (comparison of complex forms at individual derivational steps) leads to predictions that can be distinguished empirically from those of the type of theory presented in part I of this book.

Acknowledgments

I am grateful to many people who have discussed these ideas with me during the time I was writing this book.

For detailed comments on manuscript versions of the book, and for numerous discussions of its core substance, I thank Morris Halle and Alec Marantz. Morris deserves special mention for having read/commented on/suffered through innumerable prior versions, always insisting on improvements that made every aspect of the work better. Alec's comments at a key point in the fall of 2008 led to a reformulation of many central proposals in part I of the book and to some significant clarifications and extensions in part II. I hope that the end product is worthy of this attention.

Many people have contributed substantially to the work presented here, both in discussions of this (and related) material and in providing comments on earlier versions of subparts of the book. To name a few, I would like to thank Jonathan Bobaljik, Gene Buckley, Andrea Calabrese, Andrew Carstairs-McCarthy, Aviad Eilam, Bill Idsardi, Tony Kroch, Laurel MacKenzie, Rolf Noyer, Marjorie Pak, and Don Ringe.

Special mention is due to what I will call the Roca group, for arranging a seminar in July/August 2008 in the Maestría en Lingüística, Universidad Nacional del Comahue, General Roca, Argentina, where I lectured on a first version of this book. Thanks to Adriana Alvarez, Moira Alvarez, Mercedes Pujalte, Andrés Saab, and Pablo Zdrojewski for many discussions in the class and outside of it.

Earlier versions of the material found in this book were presented at Cornell University (SPINE III); III Encuentro de Gramática Generativa (Mendoza, Argentina); the University of Maryland, College Park; McGill University; the Spring 2008 morphophonology seminar at the University of Pennsylvania that I co-taught with Gene Buckley; and my Spring 2009 seminar in morphology. Thanks to the audiences at these talks and participants in these seminars for offering comments that improved this work in more ways than I could list easily.

Finally, I would like to thank the MIT Press—Jay Keyser, Ada Brunstein, and Anne Mark in particular—for working with me on this project.

1 Introduction: (Morpho)syntax versus (Morpho)phonology

Theories of grammar (and of language more generally) make specific claims about how the different facets of language are analyzed, often in ways that create partitions that are at odds with descriptive works, and, notably, at odds with each other. Although different theories propose very different models of the grammar at an architectural level, and the questions involved in distinguishing among competing theories are often quite subtle, the ultimate assessment of questions of this type is empirical. For example, there is no way of knowing based on conceptual or a priori considerations whether "phonology" and "morphology" constitute one component of the grammar, or more than one. This is a question that has to be answered by taking specific models that make competing claims about these facets of linguistic knowledge, and comparing the empirical predictions these models make. While conceptual considerations about a particular type of explanation are discussed to some extent below—mostly to highlight why the empirical questions are the most important—it must be emphasized from the outset that the crucial comparisons are always to be found in the empirical predictions made by different theories.

The question central to this work concerns how the system (or systems) responsible for deriving and representing the syntactic and morphological properties of complex expressions is related to the system that computes the phonological form of these expressions. In terms that look ahead to the details examined below, this is the question of whether morphology is computed in the same system as phonology—in which case morphological and phonological computations can in principle interact globally with each other—or whether morphology and phonology are computed by distinct linguistic systems, organized serially in a way that restricts potential interactions.

This book is a sustained argument for the position that phonological form is computed in a way that is directly linked to the generative procedure responsible for creating complex expressions, and that (morpho)-syntax and (morpho)phonology interact in a limited way that reflects the serial organization of these parts of the grammar. In the particular model of grammatical organization that I argue for, phonological computations apply after syntactic structures have been spelled out cyclically and processed morphologically (perhaps with interleaving; see below). Morphological operations—in particular, those responsible for *allomorphy*, in which the phonological forms of morphemes are determined—are constrained by the cyclic organization of the grammar and by the local domains that are defined by syntax and syntactic relations. The derivational properties of this approach thus place significant restrictions on potential interactions between morphosyntax and morphophonology.

This derivational view of grammar differs substantially from what has been the prevailing view in phonological theory, where much recent research has concentrated on developing *non*derivational theories. The specific questions addressed in this book are part of the more general debate between derivational and nonderivational theories, initiated in the recent theoretical context with the development of Optimality Theory and other surface-oriented theories of grammar. This book approaches the general debate between these opposing positions by looking at allomorphy in natural language, a phenomenon that lies at the interface of morphosyntax and morphophonology. The central point is that allomorphic alternations provide decisive empirical evidence in favor of the derivational view.

Before the discussion advances to technical points, a note is in order about the connotations of some of the terms used in this book. The debate between derivational and nonderivational theories has been at the center of some of the most significant and heated theoretical discussions in linguistic theory. In framing the particular questions that are addressed in this book, I will use another set of general terms for describing the opposing theoretical positions to be examined: specifically, I write in terms of *localist* versus *globalist* theories on the one hand, and *serialist* versus *parallelist* theories on the other. These terms are not as charged as *derivational* versus *nonderivational* are. Moreover, they identify differences in theoretical approaches at a finer level of granularity than the *derivational* versus *nonderivational* distinction does. But the concession to greater detail that motivates this terminological choice—and the air of impartiality that might be associated with the new terms—should not mask the main line of argument of this book. The arguments presented here are part of the derivational versus nonderivational debate, and they come down squarely on one side. When morphosyntactic and morphophonological data are examined carefully in the domain of allomorphy, the empirical evidence in favor of the localist and serialist view—that is, for a strongly derivational model of grammar—is overwhelming.

1.1   Localism versus Globalism; Serialism versus Parallelism

This book focuses on two ways in which derivational approaches to phonological form differ from nonderivational approaches. In both types of approach, the phonology characterizes the relation between abstract underlying representations, which consist of morphemes that are grouped into words and phrases by the syntax, and surface representations that are linear sequences of segments. In the derivational approach, this relation is characterized by a *series* of *local* changes, each of which typically involves a single target in an environment that is locally determined. In nonderivational approaches like Optimality Theory, by contrast, neither of these restrictions holds: the relation between underlying and surface representations is not defined as the result of changes that are applied serially in local environments. To highlight these differences between approaches, the derivational approach is referred to below as *localist/ serialist*, and the Optimality Theory alternative as *globalist/parallelist*.

In the contemporary theoretical context, the prevailing views in syntactic theory and in phonological theory offer strikingly different stances on the question of localism/serialism versus globalism/parallelism.

In syntactic theory, the Minimalist Program developed in Chomsky 1993 and subsequent work continues a great deal of earlier research in advancing a theory in which syntactic relations are inherently local. Particular emphasis in this approach is placed on the idea that derivations are serial. Each computational operation is given a step in a derivation, and these computational steps are ordered so that the output of one step is the input to the next. Serial derivation enforces a kind of localism, by restricting the information that is available at any particular stage of computation. This program and the theories that derive from it are *localist* and *serialist* in nature.

The phonological theory worked out in Chomsky and Halle 1968 is localist and serialist in the sense just described. However, phonological theory is at present dominated by Optimality Theory (OT) (McCarthy and Prince 1993; Prince and Smolensky 1993), which takes a *globalist* and *parallelist* view of the grammar. OT dispenses with many of the assumptions of earlier generative phonology, in which an underlying representation is subjected to a serially ordered set of rules that effect local changes to the representation and ultimately derive a surface form. The earlier (localist and serialist) view is replaced by an architecture in which an input form is paired with a set of potential surface expressions, and a system of ranked constraints selects the winner of the competition among them. A defining property of this globalist and parallelist type of view is that the factors that force a change in the output relative to the input need not be structurally close to the locus of the alternation.

Another defining property of globalist theories like OT is that morphology and phonology are not serially related to one another, but are instead computed in the same system. This architectural premise constitutes another departure from earlier models of phonological computation. In Chomsky and Halle's (1968) theory and later versions of generative phonology, morphological processes are followed by phonological rule application. Although these distinct systems are interleaved in some theories (e.g., Lexical Phonology and Morphology, as in Kiparsky 1982), the ways in which they can interact are restricted by their serial organization.

The opposing positions defined by serialism versus parallelism and localism versus globalism are particularly acute in the domain of morphology, where current theories of (morpho)syntax and current theories of (morpho)phonology take positions that are incompatible with each other.

The morphosyntactic theory developed here, Distributed Morphology, takes a localist and serialist view of syntax and sound (and meaning as well), holding that phonology interprets the output of the syntactic derivation. In frameworks like OT, as just mentioned, morphology and phonology are computed in the same system. It is thus predicted that phonological constraints may in some cases outrank syntactic or morphological constraints, such that the morphological properties of an expression could potentially be determined by output phonology or by the global properties of surface forms, in ways that cannot be formulated in localist and serialist theories. This prediction is especially important in the domain of allomorphy, as will be made clear below.

While the theories discussed above differ in practical terms, in the sense that research in Distributed Morphology is more oriented toward syntax, and research in OT is more oriented toward phonology, they overlap considerably in terms of what they seek to explain, and it must be asked directly why they differ so fundamentally. The opposing views of grammar hypothesized by these frameworks make for a sort of schism between (morpho)syntax and (morpho)phonology. To a first approximation, this schism suggests two possible outcomes to the research now in progress. The first is that one of the two theories is simply incorrect. The second is that they are both correct, and that morphosyntax and phonology are distinct and disconnected systems, in some profound sense. These are fundamental points, and progress can be made by comparing the different predictions made by localist/serialist and globalist/parallelist theories in key domains like allomorphy, where each has something to say.

Since the primary issue here is whether grammar functions in local terms or whether at least some global considerations play a role in computation, the terms *localist* and *globalist* are used throughout the book for the two types of architectures just outlined. These terms refer both to different types of architectures and to specific theories that can be framed within them. As the discussion unfolds, the specifics of different proposals are articulated.

In this book, one of the primary questions that is addressed is whether there is a single computation in which the morphological form and the phonological form of morphemes is determined simultaneously, with the potential for global interaction. Different types of globalist answers can be framed to this general question. A *fully* globalist theory of morphology and phonology would hold that the morphology and phonology of entire words is computed in a way that allows for interaction among structure, allomorphy, and sound—perhaps with syntax included in this computation as well (see McCarthy 2002, 142). *Limited* global interaction can also be implemented. For example, in stratal or cyclic versions of OT, only subparts of a given word are subject to simultaneous morphological and phonological computation (Kiparsky 2000 and subsequent work). While theories of this type rule out fully global interactions across entire words, they nevertheless predict that in a given cyclic domain, there should be global interaction between morphology and phonology.

In the course of examining specific theories below, I make the finer distinctions between full and limited globalism when required. The overall point, though, is that theories with even limited global interaction between morphology and phonology make very different predictions from localist theories about how phonology and morphology can interact, and this allows for direct comparison of the different frameworks.

1.2 (Phonologically Conditioned) Allomorphy

This book examines the predictions that localist and globalist theories each make for *allomorphic* interactions. *Allomorphy* in the broad sense is a term that covers any variations in the surface form of a morpheme. Whether all such variations are the result of one type of operation in the grammar, or different operations, is something that different theories make different claims about.

As an initial example of allomorphy, consider the behavior of the past tense morpheme T[past] in English. According to a standard analysis, the default shape of this morpheme is -*d*, as in *play*, *play-ed*. As is well-known, the past tense morpheme has allomorphs besides -*d* that appear when T[past] occurs next to other verbs; putting aside changes in the phonology of the verb stem itself (such as *broke* from *break*), a rudimentary description is given in (1):

(1) Allomorphs of T[past] in English

    a. -*Ø:* hit/hit-Ø, sing/sang-Ø, break/broke-Ø, etc.

    b. -*t:* bend/ben-t, leave/lef-t, buy/bough-t, etc.

    c. -*d:* elsewhere

Allomorphic interactions of this type appear to be highly constrained. Informally, for allomorphic purposes one node sees another only when the two nodes are "close" to each other in a way that must be made precise.

The kind of allomorphy exhibited by English T[past] is *grammatically conditioned*. Knowing whether a particular verb selects a particular allomorph from (1) is something that does not follow from other factors. In particular, it is not predictable from the phonology of the verb. Rather, the conditioning element is a locally visible, grammatical object: in the case of (1), the identity of the particular verb that the node T[past] is attached to.

This kind of allomorphy is called *contextual allomorphy*. Something in the grammar specifies that the pronunciation of T[past] has one of the nondefault forms in (1) (i.e., either (1a) or (1b)) when it occurs in the *context* of a specific verb. Part of any theory of morphology is the theory of the conditions under which elements can show contextual allomorphy in this way. Part I of this book develops a localist and serialist theory of allomorphy, in which linear adjacency and cyclic locality interact to produce a constrained theory of allomorphic interaction.

A second type of allomorphy, which allows for direct comparison of localist and globalist frameworks, is *phonologically conditioned allomorphy* (see Carstairs 1988 and subsequent work). This is a type of contextual allomorphy in which the choice of a particular allomorph of some morpheme is determined by phonological factors. Some examples are given in (2):

(2) a. Korean nominative suffix

Allomorph	Env.	Example	Gloss
-i	/C__	pap-i	'cooked rice'
-ka	/V__	ai-ka	'child'

    b. Seri passive suffix (Marlett and Stemberger 1983)

Allomorph	Env.	Example	Gloss
p-	/__V	-p-eši	'be defeated'
a:ʔ-	elsewhere	-a:ʔ-kašni	'be bitten'

    c. Haitian Creole definite suffix

Allomorph	Env.	Example	Gloss
-la	/C__	liv-la	'book'
-a	/V__	tu-a	'hole'

These examples are chosen to illustrate different types of effects that are found in phonologically conditioned allomorphy, as viewed from the perspective of the output phonology of the affixed word.

In the first case (2a), Korean -*i* and -*ka*, the distribution of allomorphs could be seen as having a phonological motivation. The vowel -*i* after consonants creates syllables that are "better" than those that would be created by affixing -*ka* to such forms, on the assumption that the sequence CVCV is preferred to, say, CVCCV. Similarly, affixing -*ka* to vowel-final hosts avoids the hiatus that would be created by affixing -*i*. In this sense, it might appear that the "morphological" choice of allomorphs is driven by the output phonology, in a way that fits nicely with a globalist phonological theory in which syllable-structure markedness constraints that favor CV- syllables without codas can determine allomorph selection.

The behavior of the Seri passive morpheme in (2b) is ambiguous. The prevocalic form *p-eši* supports the idea that affixation should produce sequences of an optimal kind. However, preconsonantal forms like *a:ʔ-kašni* are not phonologically optimal. In terms of the phonological forms that the language happens to provide for realizing the passive morpheme, however, the distribution of allomorphs could be seen as phonologically optimal; that is, while *a:ʔ-* does not produce optimal syllables with C-initial hosts, it produces better phonological forms than would be created by affixing *p-*.

Finally, the Haitian Creole allomorphy is "perverse" from the perspective of syllable-structure markedness. Affixing -*la* to consonant-final hosts creates syllable codas, and affixing -*a* to vowel-final hosts creates hiatus between syllables. Both of these results are nonoptimal, and both of these problems would disappear if the reverse distribution of allomorphs obtained.

Intuitively, phonologically conditioned allomorphy is important as a case study because it involves the interaction of morphological and phonological factors in determining a form.

In the localist theory developed in part I of this book, all the cases of contextual allomorphy seen above receive the same analysis. The theory says that the phonological realization of a morpheme, which occurs in a process called *Vocabulary Insertion*, can be sensitive to items that are in the local environment of the morpheme being spelled out. While this theory can account for the distributions in (2), it cannot say *within the grammar itself* that these distributions happen for a reason—that is, that they are driven by surface phonological optimization. This theory can generate the forms that it derives mechanically, but it does so without reference to ultimate output forms; in this sense, it is a theory of morphology without teleology.

In globalist theories like Optimality Theory, the architecture allows phonological constraints to determine allomorph selection. The reason for this is that morphology and phonology are one system, in which phonological constraints can outrank morphological ones. It is therefore possible in such theories to say that allomorph selection—part of the morphology—happens the way it does *because* of the way that affixation creates particular phonological patterns. In the Korean case (2a), for example, it is possible to give an analysis in which the competing candidates consist of the host plus each of the different allomorphs, so that both *pap-i* and *pap-ka* are generated for the input "nominative of *pap-*." The constraint ranking—and phonological constraints governing syllable structure in particular—then work together to derive the pattern of allomorph selection. In such a theory, it is possible to say *in the grammar* that the distribution of allomorphs is the way it is for a reason.

1.3 Surface Forms, Competition, and the Schism

Taking grammars to be theories of how sound-meaning connections are derived, one can ask at a very general level what different theories have to say about the factors that may play a role in determining the surface form of an expression.

OT implements global and parallel computation by generating an infinite set of output candidates for any given input, with constraints selecting a winner from these competitors. The output candidates differ from the input in ways that potentially involve more than one phonological "change." This computation of forms is global in at least two ways: first, because it is antimodular, phonological and morphological constraints can interact in a manner that is not possible in alternative theories; and, second, because the constraints can be ranked in such a way that nonlocal interactions take place within a word.

The central principle that allows output forms to be compared for well-formedness is *competition*. Competition is a fundamental concept in grammatical theory. It is implicated in morphological discussions in the study of *blocking* effects, initiated in the modern era in work by Aronoff (1976). According to Aronoff, for example, the word *gloriosity* is derived by the rules of the grammar, but it cannot be the "abstract noun for GLORY" because *glory* exists and blocks it. For this analysis to work, the grammar must supply more than one object for the potential expression of a particular meaning (in this example, both *gloriosity* and *glory*), and it must supply a means of determining the winner of the competition between them.

Part of the OT program is based on the idea that surface forms are the way they are for a reason, and that the grammar must state these reasons directly. For this idea to be implemented, competition is required. From the infinite set of possible output forms, the winner is the one that is optimal with respect to the constraint ranking. If there were not multiple competitors—if the grammar made just one representation available in any given computation—then there could be no "optimization."

The potentially global interactions mentioned above are a consequence of this type of infinite competition. The fact that phonological and morphological constraints interact to select a winner means that in principle, phonological properties of surface forms could determine what happens morphologically, by forcing a particular affix to be selected because of its effects on the phonology of the whole word.

The globalist perspective on phonological form is incompatible with the view of the grammar that is advanced in localist morphosyntactic theories like Distributed Morphology. The prevailing view of "blocking effects" in the broad sense is that they require competition of the type outlined by Aronoff. More recent work argues that there is no blocking of the type discussed above; this is the conclusion presented in Embick 2007a and Embick and Marantz 2008. These papers examine arguments for blocking among words and larger expressions, and they conclude that there is no motivation for a competition-based analysis of such phenomena. Rather, put somewhat simply, what surfaces in the grammar is what is derived by the grammar; other putative competitors for a particular meaning are simply never derived and therefore do not need to be blocked. In particular, on this view, the grammar of English does not generate *glorios-ity* any more than it creates *good-ity* or *bad-ity*.

According to the theory proposed in Embick and Marantz 2008, competition is strictly local: it is restricted to the procedure that determines the phonology of a single node, the Vocabulary Insertion operation mentioned above. A consequence of this view is that there is no competition among complex objects—that is, no word/word, word/phrase, or phrase/phrase competition. In short, complex objects are assembled in syntactic structures, and this fact accounts for both how they are represented and how they are distributed

This localist theory has consequences for phonological relatedness, especially the shared properties of *lexically related* forms like *plays, played*, and so on, where it places a number of restrictions. Specifically, the theory says that the phonological form and phonological relatedness are determined by the following factors:

• Complex, lexically related forms are built in syntactic structures and contain the same Root.
• In a given structure (with a Root and functional heads), a single output is derived; this output is what exists and therefore what must be used in that grammatical context.
• Complex, lexically related forms share phonological material in a consistent way because
— they are based on the same Root, which has a given underlying representation (UR);
— they appear in syntactic structures whose heads have consistent phonological expression (up to allomorphy); and
— the phonology involves the same rules/constraints (up to exceptionality that must be listed).

The particular restrictions imposed by these factors are directly related to the fact that this theory involves no competition among complex objects. In any derivation, only one output object is produced. It is thus not possible to generate multiple competitors and select a winner based on properties of the output. This precludes, among other things, generating a word with all of the different allomorphic possibilities the language allows and then choosing the winner on the basis of, say, phonological well-formedness.

This localist view contrasts sharply with some basic aspects of the globalist program. The essence of globalism as manifested in OT is unlimited competition, and the essence of competition is that there must be multiple possible outputs for any given input. This is exactly what the localist morphosyntactic theory says is impossible. Putting these different incompatibilities into focus, it is clear that these views of morphosyntax and morphophonology define a schism:[1]

(3) The schism

Globalist theories of morphophonology require competition between multiple potential expressions of a given input. According to the localist morphosyntactic theory, this is impossible because the competitors are not derived by the grammar.

This book brings empirical arguments to bear on the large-scale architectural matters implicated by (3). As mentioned in section 1.1, there are two possible outcomes that could stem from focus on the schism, and each of them is significant.

The first possible outcome is that (morpho)phonology is simply profoundly different from (morpho)syntax. In principle, it is possible to construct a theory in which each of the two views above is correct: that is, "no competition" is correct for morphosyntax, and "competition" is correct for morphophonology. In such a theory, the syntax and the morphology operate in terms of local, serial derivations, but the output of this system in some part of the phonological computation involves multiple or infinite competitors, so that global considerations can play a role in determining surface forms. One question to ask is whether this would be a sort of "worst case" scenario, architecturally speaking, since it would divorce the system of combinatorics from the system for computing sound forms in an extreme way.

The second possible outcome of the schism is that either the localist theory or the globalist theory is untenable: that is, either (i) the "generative" localist view of (morpho)syntactic theory is incorrect, or (ii) the globalist, competition-based theory of (morpho)phonology is incorrect.

These are large points, and they resonate with other aspects of grammatical theory in numerous ways.

This book is divided into two major components. Part I develops a localist theory of allomorphy. Part II explicitly compares the predictions of globalist theories with the core predictions of the localist theory of part I. The fundamental results are that the localist theory of part I makes correct predictions about allomorphy in natural language and that the predictions of globalist theories examined in part II are not supported by the data.

1.4   Prospectus: A Localist Theory

Part I of this book articulates a localist theory of contextual allomorphy. The defining property of this theory, a version of Distributed Morphology, is that patterns of contextual allomorphy are restricted by both phase-cyclic and linear notions of locality.

Contextual allomorphy in Distributed Morphology results from the operation of *Vocabulary Insertion*. This is a procedure by which morphemes in a syntactic structure are assigned a phonological form. I assume that morphemes are terminals in a syntactic structure. Some of these morphemes, the functional heads, have no phonological form as part of their underlying representation. Rather, these morphemes receive phonological content in the PF (Phonological Form) component of the grammar. This is the role of Vocabulary Insertion; individual *Vocabulary items* (VIs) compete for insertion at a given node, and the most specific one that can apply gives that node its phonological matrix.

In the example of the English past tense, the syntax generates a structure that contains the past tense node T[past]. In the PF computation, the VIs in (4) compete for insertion into this node:

(4)   Vocabulary items for Tense

$$T[\text{past}] \leftrightarrow \text{-t/}\underline{\quad} \; \{\sqrt{\text{LEAVE}}, \sqrt{\text{BEND}}, \ldots\}$$
$$T[\text{past}] \leftrightarrow \text{-}\varnothing\text{/}\underline{\quad} \; \{\sqrt{\text{HIT}}, \sqrt{\text{SING}}, \ldots\}$$
$$T[\text{past}] \leftrightarrow \text{-d}$$

When Roots like $\sqrt{\text{BEND}}$ and $\sqrt{\text{HIT}}$ are present, Vocabulary Insertion inserts *-t* and *-Ø* into the T[past] node, respectively; in other cases, it inserts the default *-d*.

The general research question that motivates this work centers on the factors that play a role in contextual allomorphy. According to the view developed below, possible patterns of allomorphy are determined by the interaction of two distinct (and independent) sets of locality constraints. The core intuition is as follows. Contextual allomorphy, where one node X can see another node Y for the purposes of Vocabulary Insertion, is possible only when X and Y are concatenated—that is, in the most local *linear* relationship possible. A further set of restrictions on allomorphic locality is imposed by the assumption that syntactic derivation proceeds in terms of *phases* (in the sense of Chomsky 2000, 2001) that are spelled out cyclically. Phase-based derivation places sharp constraints on the amount of information that is available in a particular cycle of PF computation, and it restricts potential allomorphic interactions accordingly.

The key elements of this proposal can be outlined in a few steps, beginning with the cyclic (phase-based) aspect of the theory. For cyclic derivation, the theory presented below assumes with Marantz 2007 and Embick and Marantz 2008 that *category-defining* heads like v, n, and a define phases. According to this view, heads of this type *categorize* the elements that they attach to. For example, a head v that is merged syntactically with a $\sqrt{}$P headed by a category-neutral $\sqrt{\text{ROOT}}$ creates a vP (5); when the Root and the v head are combined into a single complex head as shown in (6), the result is a "verb":

(5) v merged with $\sqrt{}$P

$$
\begin{array}{c}
v\text{P} \\
\diagup\diagdown \\
v \quad\quad \sqrt{}\text{P} \\
\quad\quad \diagup\diagdown \\
\quad\quad \ldots\sqrt{\text{ROOT}}\ldots
\end{array}
$$

(6) Complex head

$$
\begin{array}{c}
v \\
\diagup\diagdown \\
\sqrt{\text{ROOT}} \quad\quad v
\end{array}
$$

The category-defining heads are *cyclic* in the sense of phase theory. What this means is that when they are merged with a structure, they trigger *Spell-Out*: the operation that sends part of the syntactic structure (to be defined below) to the interface components PF and LF (Logical Form). Other heads that appear in complex words, such as tense morphemes and plural morphemes, are not cyclic in this way. This difference between cyclic and noncyclic heads is manifested in many domains, including possible allomorphic interactions.

The example in (5)–(6) shows a single cyclic head v attached to a Root. Category-defining heads may also be merged with structures that are already categorized. For example, a verb like *break*, which is a Root combined with v, may be combined with a "potential" adjective head a to yield *breakable*, an adjective derived from a verb, as shown in (7):

(7) $[[\sqrt{\text{BREAK}}\ v]\ a]$

When a category-defining head is the first that is merged with a Root, as is the case with v in (5) and (7), this head is said to be *Root-attached*, or in the *inner* domain. When a category-defining head is attached to a structure that has already been categorized, like the a in (7), the additional cyclic head is said to be in the *outer* domain.

A central idea in linguistic theory is that cyclic domains define possible interactions in syntax, phonology, and semantics. One proposal that has been discussed in the literature is that syntactic configurations in which a Root is merged with a category-defining head—the inner domain—appears to be special for the purposes of both sound and meaning. In Embick and Marantz's (2008, 11) formulation, the generalizations about what is special about this inner domain are these:

(8) Cyclic generalizations

    a. *Allomorphy:* For Root-attached x, special allomorphy for x may be determined by properties of the Root. A head x in the outer domain is not in a local relationship with the Root and thus cannot have its allomorphy determined by the Root.

    b. *Interpretation:* The combination of Root-attached x and the Root might yield a special interpretation. When attached in the outer domain, the x heads yield predictable interpretations.

For the purposes of a localist account of allomorphy, what (8a) highlights is the possibility that contextual allomorphy could be found only with Root-attached cyclic nodes.

An important discovery in this context is that a "Root-attached" theory of contextual allomorphy is too restrictive. This point was discussed with reference to allomorphy in participles in Embick 2003, and it arises in cases like the English past tense as well. English past tense verbs have a structure consisting of a Root, a v head, and the node T[past]:

(9) English past tense

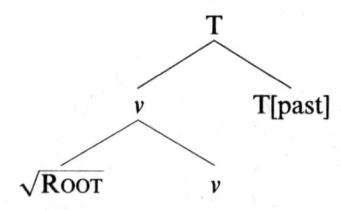

The T[past] node shows contextual allomorphy, yielding the familiar allomorphs in (e.g.) *ben-t* and *hit-Ø* versus the default *-ed* in (e.g.) *play-ed*. Crucially, the T[past] node is not Root-attached; nevertheless, it shows irregular allomorphy conditioned by the Root, contrary to what is predicted by (8a). Importantly, T[past] is not a cyclic head.

The conclusion that emerges from such examples is that the theory of contextual allomorphy must allow at least some outer heads to have their form determined by the Root. The challenge is therefore to present a theory that is capable of accounting for the attested patterns of contextual allomorphy, while being restrictive enough to make strong empirical predictions.

Part of the work presented in part I sharpens the empirical questions that are at the heart of this discussion. While the type of case represented by the English past tense shows that a head outside of the inner cyclic head may show Root-determined allomorphy, the possibilities for allomorphic interaction are still restricted in significant ways. The restrictions are of two types.

First, it appears that a morpheme can show contextual allomorphy determined by another morpheme only when these two pieces are linearly adjacent to one another, that is, when no overt morpheme appears between the two. This generalization suggests a strict linear constraint on allomorphic interactions.

Second, although the cyclic theory based on (8a) is too restrictive, cyclic structure is still relevant for allomorphic interactions. This is clear from another fact: it appears that outer cyclic heads cannot show contextual allomorphy that is determined by elements in the domain of an inner cyclic head. For example, in a "category-changing" structure with two cyclic heads x and y like (10), the outer cyclic head y never shows Root-determined allomorphy:

(10) Structure with two cyclic heads

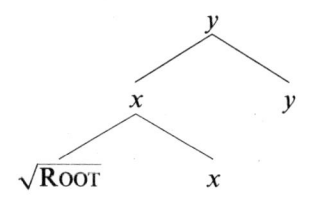

An example of this is provided by English gerunds, like *John's destroying the files*. Unlike special nominals, like *laugh-ter, marri-age, destruction*, and so on, where nominalization involves different suffixes (i.e., a great deal of Root-determined allomorphy), gerunds always take the suffix *-ing: laugh-ing, marry-ing, destroy-ing*, and so on. In special nominals, the *n* head realized as *-ter, -age, -(t)ion*, and the like, is Root-attached. In gerunds, on the other hand, the nominalizing *n* morpheme attaches to structure that is verbalized by *v*. The structures at play here are those in (11) and (12):

(11) *marriage*

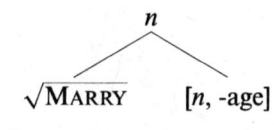

(12) *marrying*

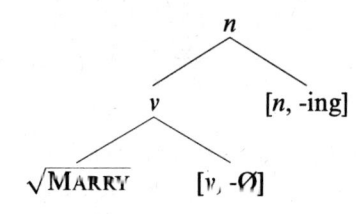

The outer *n* in (12) shows no Root-determined allomorphy: it always has the phonological form *-ing*, even though it is superficially adjacent to the Root. This pattern seems to be completely general: that is, there are evidently no cases in which an outer cyclic head shows Root-determined allomorphy.

There is thus an asymmetry between noncyclic and cyclic heads in allomorphy: outer noncyclic heads can see across an inner cyclic node, but outer cyclic heads cannot; in this way, (8a) is correct, but only for cyclic heads. The important generalizations are schematized in (13), where lowercase *x*, *y* are cyclic heads, uppercase *Z* is a noncyclic head, and α represents the element that conditions the allomorphy:

(13) a. ... α] *x*] *Z*]
      Generalization: Noncyclic *Z* may show contextual allomorphy determined by α, as long as *x* is not overt.
    b. ... α] *x*] *y*]
      Generalization: Cyclic *y* may *not* show contextual allomorphy determined by α, even if *x* is not overt.

The asymmetry in (13) presents a basic empirical challenge for a restrictive theory of allomorphy: not only must the cyclic theory be extended to allow cases like (13a), but also the extension must be executed in such a way that outer cyclic heads as in (13b) cannot be sensitive to elements in *x*'s complement.

The theory of part I proposes that the key generalizations are accounted for by a theory based on the hypotheses (H1) and (H2):

(H1) Contextual allomorphy is possible only with elements that are concatenated.

(H2) Cyclic Spell-Out domains define which nodes are present in a given cycle of PF computation and thus potentially "active" (capable of being referred to) for the purposes of contextual allomorphy. In some cases, superficially adjacent nodes cannot influence each other allomorphically because in terms of cyclic Spell-Out, they are not active in the same PF cycle.

The linear condition in (H1) is straightforward: it holds that one node can show contextual allomorphy determined by another node only when the two are immediately next to one another, that is, when no morpheme intervenes.

The essential properties of the cyclic part of the theory, (H2), can be illustrated with reference to (14) and (15), where lowercase x, y are cyclic heads and uppercase W, Z are noncyclic heads. (14) shows the constituent structure prior to affixation, and (15) the complex heads that are created in the structures in (14):

(14) a. Structure 1

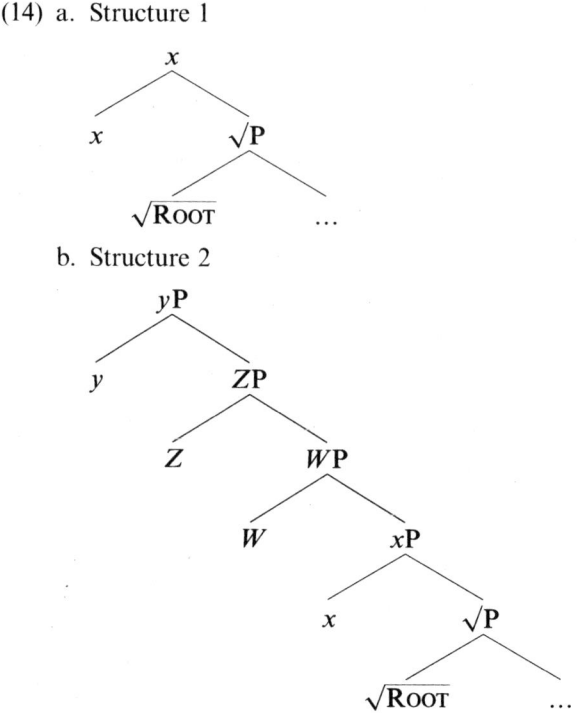

b. Structure 2

(15) a. Complex head created in structure 1

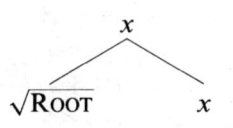

     b. Complex head created in structure 2

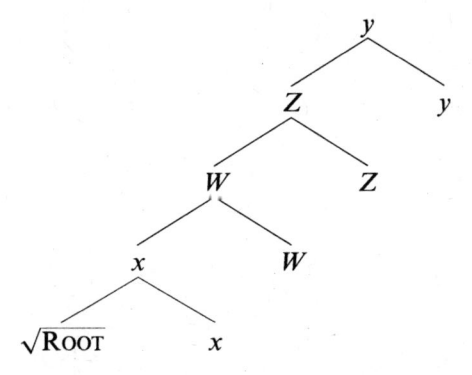

The basic premise of the theory is that cyclic heads trigger Spell-Out; in particular, when a cyclic head is merged, it triggers the Spell-Out of cyclic domains in its complement. With reference to (14) and (15), this means that when x is merged syntactically in (14a), there are no cyclic domains in the complement of x, so that there is no Spell-Out in this particular case.

A subsequent step in the syntactic derivation, (14b), merges noncyclic W and Z. When the head y is merged, the Spell-Out of cyclic domains in y's complement is triggered. In this example, this means that the cyclic domain headed by x is spelled out and, in particular, that a PF cycle is run on this cyclic domain. The cyclic domain headed by x includes the Root, x, and the noncyclic heads W and Z. In this cycle, Vocabulary Insertion occurs at x, W, and Z, giving phonological form to these morphemes. Since all of these heads are co-present in the same PF cycle, any one of them could potentially show Root-determined allomorphy, as long as no overt morphemes intervene.

Later in the derivation, another cyclic head (not shown in (14) and (15)) triggers Spell-Out of material in its complement, which includes the phase centered on y. The elements that are present in this PF cycle are x (the *edge* of the xP phase), W, Z, and y. Crucially, while y could show contextual allomorphy determined by x, W, or Z, it could not show Root-conditioned allomorphy. The reason for this is that the PF cycle in which *y* is given phonological form does not involve the Root; it (and other elements that could be in the complement of *x*) are derivationally closed off.

The principles just outlined account for the asymmetries in (13). This point can be seen by comparing the structure for a gerund with that of a past tense form:

(16) Gerund *marrying*   (17) English past tense

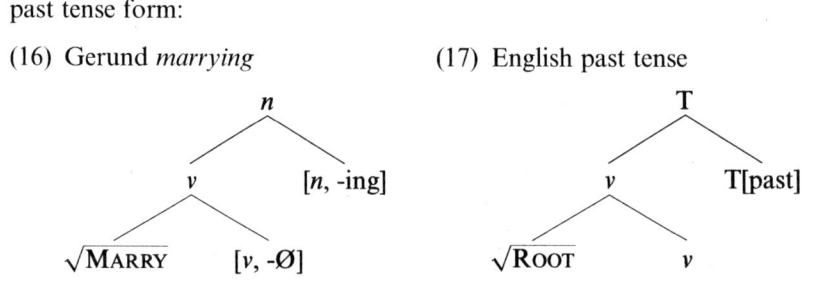

When the *n* head in (16) undergoes Vocabulary Insertion, it is in a PF cycle that does not contain the Root √MARRY. Thus, this outer cyclic head cannot show Root-determined allomorphy. In the past tense structure in (17), on the other hand, the T[past] head undergoes Vocabulary Insertion in a PF cycle in which the Root is present, Thus, this head can show Root-determined allomorphy, as long as it is linearly adjacent to the Root.

The cyclic aspect of the theory restricts the amount of information that is available to condition allomorphy in two ways. First, in a complex word that contains multiple cyclic domains, the computation of the phonological form of inner domains takes place at a stage when "outer" material is not present. This outer material can therefore play no role in determining the phonological form of inner nodes. Second, for computation on outer cyclic domains, certain parts of the inner material are inaccessible, because they are closed off in the way outlined above. As a result, there are cases where outer cyclic nodes cannot be influenced by certain nodes in the inner domain, further restricting potential allomorphic interactions.

In sum, the guiding insight of the theory presented here is that the interaction of (phase-) cyclic domains and a strict linear notion of locality are responsible for possible patterns of contextual allomorphy. Reflecting the interaction of cyclic and linear factors, the approach advanced in chapter 2 is called the $\mathbb{C}_1$-*LIN* theory, where $\mathbb{C}_1$ stands for the cyclicity condition and *LIN* stands for the linear condition.

After developing the details of this theory in chapter 2, I present illustrations and consequences of the approach in chapter 3. This includes a discussion of (linear) intervention effects and cyclic edge effects, along with a series of more complex case studies examining how "the same" pieces of morphology can appear in different cyclic domains. I also comment on how morphosyntax and morphophonology interact in the theory, paving the way for some aspects of the comparison between frameworks in part II.

1.5 Prospectus: Localism versus Globalism

Part II of this book returns to the fundamental tension between localist morphosyntax and globalist phonology outlined earlier in this chapter, by looking at the empirical predictions that these theories make for allomorphy.

Returning to some of the themes introduced in the first part of this chapter, the morphosyntactic theory developed in part I of the book restricts competition in the grammar to allomorphy of a single node: this is the process of Vocabulary Insertion. The theory thus disallows competitions in which multiple competitors like "words" are derived and compared for well-formedness. This effectively restricts the factors conditioning a case of contextual allomorphy to elements in the immediate context of the node being spelled out.

This view differs fundamentally from that offered by a globalist theory of the type assumed in much current work on phonology. In a theory like OT, in which the grammar generates an infinite number of candidate expressions that are potential surface realizations of a given input, the inputs are complex; that is, they involve more than one morpheme. Thus, this theory is responsible for morphology as well as phonology. Since morphological and phonological properties are determined in the same computational domain, this type of framework allows for global interactions in which, for example, nonlocal properties of surface forms play the defining role in allomorphic selection.

The full range of predictions that separate the localist and globalist views on allomorphy emerge from examining these closely interconnected questions:

• *Global morphology/phonology interactions:* Is there evidence that morphology and phonology are computed in a single, global/parallel system (*global-MP*)? Or do the facts on interaction suggest an organization in which phonology acts on the output of allomorph selection, as in the localist theory?

• *Phonological Selection:*   Is there *Phonological Selection*, in which surface phonological well-formedness forces a choice among allomorphs, such that phonology drives allomorphy in ways that are impossible in a localist theory?

• *Global considerations over local:*   Is there evidence that the factors determining allomorphy are global in any sense? That is, are there cases in which localist and globalist approaches make different predictions about which allomorph should be chosen for a particular position, and the globalist considerations win out, in a way that cannot be stated in a localist theory?

Part II of the book begins in chapter 4 with the answers to these questions that derive from globalist theories. The discussion centers on the types of arguments that could conceivably provide evidence for such an architecture. While the emphasis in this discussion is on empirical arguments, some steps are taken to frame the important issues with reference to conceptual arguments found in the literature. As discussed in section 1.2 with regard to examples of allomorphy from Korean, Seri, and Haitian Creole, a localist theory cannot say that a pattern of allomorph selection arises *because of* some output property, phonological or otherwise. To the extent that there are generalizations to be made about surface forms, the localist theory can make them, but they must be derivative of another part of language in the broad sense. That is, the explanations cannot be part of the grammar in the narrow sense; instead, they are the result of diachrony, acquisition, and so on.

As noted in section 1.2, these considerations lead to a kind of conceptual argument that is often advanced in favor of globalist theories. In theories of this type, it is possible to say that patterns of allomorphy happen *for a reason*, within the grammar. For example, the case of Korean -*i*/-*ka* allomorphy can be treated in terms of syllable structure constraints. An OT analysis can then say that the (phonological) grammar forces the attested distribution of allomorphs and, moreover, that the grammar *explains* the distribution by having morphological selection driven by optimization of the phonology of the output. The charge that is leveled against localist theories is that, while they might account for the distribution of allomorphs, they do not provide (within the grammar) a reason for the distribution. This type of argument against localist theories is based on their *putative loss of generalization*. In the domain of phonological rules, the question of whether localist theories are missing generalizations about outputs has been actively discussed since at least Kisseberth

1970. The same kind of considerations about patterns in surface forms motivate globalist views of morphology-phonology interactions, and allomorph selection in particular.

In many cases that have been studied in the literature, localist theories and globalist theories are both able to account for the facts. In such cases, only conceptual arguments, such as appeal to putative loss of generalization, can be deployed against a localist theory; there is no empirical basis for determining which of the two frameworks is to be preferred. Rather, the choice reduces to whatever combination of conceptual, aesthetic, or other factors regulate the intuitions that individual researchers have about what explains what. Such nonempirical arguments are not decisive. A key point that moves the argument presented here from the conceptual to the empirical is that globalist theories predict a number of types of global interaction that simply cannot be expressed in the localist theory. The comparison of frameworks must be directed at such cases.

The decisive predictions are examined here in two steps. Chapter 5 begins by outlining the best-case scenario for globalist theories: the hypothesis that the phonological grammar determines all cases of phonologically conditioned allomorphy (PCA), and nothing more needs to be said about allomorph distribution. This position was shown to be incorrect in early works exploring the globalist research program like Kager 1996. However, the possibility remains that there are *some* instances in which surface phonology drives allomorph selection, in ways that cannot be analyzed in a localist framework.

To highlight the empirical issues, and the motivation behind the globalist program, chapter 5 then examines *systems* of PCA. This part of the discussion is not a formal argument against globalism or for localism. Rather, it examines the intuition that globalist theories are based on: the idea that patterns of PCA are the way they are for reasons that should be expressed in the grammar, and that these reasons should be phonological in nature. The empirical basis for this chapter is provided by systems of case endings found in two Australian languages, Djabugay and Yidiɲ, where there is a large amount of PCA. Although examining isolated subparts of such systems might make it look like there is motivation for a globalist theory in which output phonology determines allomorph selection, this impression is shown to be illusory once the systems are analyzed in detail. The particulars of the analysis show that the case systems in these languages derive from the interaction of stored information about the shape of morphemes with (sometimes exceptional) phonological and morphological rules, in a way that implicates serial organization between morphology and phonology. A further argument, extending this, is that although at first glance Yidiɲ case allomorphy looks as though it might be driven by simple phonological constraints, analyzing the system in surface-based terms obscures key generalizations about other aspects of the language's morphophonology.

Chapter 6 is centered on the fact that theories with even a restricted form of global interaction between morphosyntax and phonology predict effects that cannot be stated in a localist theory. These effects can be seen in cases in which a morpheme X has more than one phonologically conditioned allomorph—say, x_1 and x_2—and X appears in words with other morphemes like Y and Z:

(18) Root-X-Y-Z

There are cases of this type in which the *local* environment predicts insertion at X of the x_1 allomorph, while the *global* environment, because of the phonological properties of the entire word, predicts insertion of the x_2 allomorph.

In a localist theory of the type developed in part I, choice of allomorph at X must be determined by grammatical or phonological information that is visible at the point when insertion occurs. Thus, the localist theory predicts that in cases like (18), the locally selected x_1 allomorph will be found.

On the other hand, in a globalist theory in which morphology and phonology are computed in the same system it is possible for the x_2 allomorph to be inserted, in a way that is driven by the output phonology. This prediction is not the exclusive property of "full" globalist theories. Even restrained, cyclic globalist theories make the same prediction, as long as the affixes in question are not in different strata. That is, the prediction that Z's form (or the form of the entire word) could affect allomorphy at X is made by any theory in which the computation of the morphophonology of X, Y, and Z occurs in the same domain.

The allomorphy of perfect heads in certain Latin verbs, discussed in Mester 1994, provides an example of the type schematized in (18). The perfect head in question has two allomorphs: -u, generally taken to be the default, and -s.[2] Mester argues that choice between these allomorphs is determined by the prosodic structure of affixed words. Specifically, the nondefault -s allomorph is inserted only when the -u allomorph creates a form with an unfooted medial syllable, called a (medial) *trapping* configuration. The idea is that the prosodic undesirability of trapping is what drives the insertion of the nondefault -s allomorph with certain verbs.

The effects of this analysis are shown for the verbs *monēre* 'warn' and *augēre* 'grow' in (19). These verbs differ in the metrical weight of the stem (light *mon-* versus heavy *aug-*), which results in different metrical parses with the *-u* affix. As seen in (19a) versus (19b), these verbs show different allomorphs of the perfect head:

(19) a. Perfect allomorph: *-u* with light Root
       [monu]⟨ī⟩
     b. Perfect allomorph: *-s* with heavy Root
       *[au]gu⟨ī⟩ (trapping)
       [aug]⟨sī⟩

According to the globalist theory advanced by Mester, the perfect morpheme has its allomorphy determined by the output prosody of the word. The grammar generates both *auguī* (with the default *-u* allomorph) and *augsī* (with the *-s* allomorph) and prefers the latter because of its surface phonological form.

In cases of this type, the globalist theory predicts—unlike the localist theory—that the allomorph choice for the perfect may vacillate, depending on the phonological properties of outer affixes. In the Latin example, the globalist theory predicts that in pluperfects like those in (20), the allomorph selected for *augēre* should switch from *-s* to *-u*, because this yields a better prosodic structure (20b). In fact, this does not happen; the grammatical form has the *-s* allomorph as in (20a), even though this creates trapping:

(20) 1sg pluperfect of *augēre*

     a. With *-s* allomorph:
        augseram = [ō̆]ō̆⟨ō̆⟩
     b. With *-u* allomorph:
        *augueram = [ō̆][ŏŏ]⟨ō̆⟩

In this and other cases, the locally determined allomorph is selected, and there is no evidence for the type of global interaction—allomorph vacillation based on output phonology—that would provide evidence for globalism.

The general line of argument in chapter 6 is that any sort of interaction of the type outlined above would be an argument for a globalist view, but that no such interactions are found. In cases where this type of prediction can be tested, languages show local determination of allomorphs of the type predicted by the localist theory.

As stressed above, the differences in predictions between globalism and localism are clearest when a "fully" globalist position—one with interacting syntax, semantics, phonology, and so on—is considered, but cyclic theories with limited global interaction also make predictions that go beyond what the localist theory allows. The arguments advanced in this book extend to theories with even highly restricted forms of global interaction: there is no evidence for global interaction in even the restricted form that could be stated in a cyclic OT theory.

1.6   Implications

Chapter 7 synthesizes the consequences of parts I and II of the book. If the localist theory of part I is correct, then allomorphy is subject to strict locality conditions of a type that derive from a localist syntactic theory.

If the conclusions of chapters 5 and 6 are correct, then there is nothing beyond cyclic and linear locality in the grammar of allomorphy; in particular, there are no empirical arguments for the strong predictions of globalism. This point has implications for the status of generalizations about surface forms, along the lines of what was discussed under the heading of *putative loss of generalization* above. To account for why certain patterns of allomorphy occur, a theory must have global interactions between morphology and phonology. It is only in such a theory that the grammar can refer to properties of output forms in the allomorph selection process. However, theories with this type of globality make formal predictions about morphology-phonology interactions that are not borne out. Taken as a whole, the facts discussed here thus constitute an argument against the globalist architecture *and* an argument against the idea that the grammar itself must say why certain patterns of allomorph selection are found.

A second implication of this argument is that OT is a theory of phonology without a theory of morphology. There are many potential responses to this line of argument, and almost all of them have deep consequences for theories of grammar. One obvious response would be to hold that there are fundamental differences between morphosyntax and (certain aspects of) phonology, and OT is a theory of the latter. Another possibility is that the type of globalist system espoused by OT must be abandoned, or modified in some extreme way. Importantly, since incorrect predictions about allomorphy appear to arise even in systems with a limited amount of global interaction, appealing to stratal or serial versions of OT either does not appear to be an adequate response, or results in a theory that is essentially localist and serialist in nature.

The central importance of cyclicity, locality, and serial organization is a theme that characterizes this entire work. These are, of course, the central principles that emerged in early work in generative grammar, and I take this work to show empirically that these notions must be at the heart of the theory of morphology-phonology interactions, and grammatical theory more generally. The particular emphasis in this book is on allomorphic phenomena, but the results presented here have ramifications that go beyond this area. While it would always be possible to try and avoid the conclusions of this work by, for example, holding that part of phonology is "special," my view—a research intuition—is that the success of the localist theory of morphosyntax and morphophonology motivates a return to a phonological theory in which the sound form of complex expressions is linked as closely as possible to the generative procedure that builds them. This work is a step toward making this intuition concrete.

A Localist Theory

2   A Localist Theory

This part of the book develops a theory of allomorphic locality that is centered on the interaction of cyclic and linear locality domains. This theory is developed as an account of a number of empirical generalizations that are presented in the course of the discussion. If something like this theory is on the right track, then morphology and phonology show the kinds of properties that are expected in a localist view of grammatical architecture. In particular, if the key generalizations about allomorphy in natural language can be explained in a theory with sharp locality conditions and do not require a theory that makes reference to (e.g.) competing forms or to the phonological properties of outputs—things that can be referred to in globalist architectures—then we have support for a localist view. This part of the book presents the details of a localist view; explicit comparisions with globalist alternatives are made in part II.

The theory of allomorph selection that is developed in these chapters is part of a localist, serialist theory of grammar. An important aspect of this theory, a version of Distributed Morphology, is that the syntax generates hierarchical structures that are subjected to further computations in the interface components PF and LF.

I assume that the syntax operates in terms of locality conditions that arise from cyclic derivation. A further assumption, one that is automatic in a syntactic approach to morphology like the one advanced here, is that conditions on locality in syntax also define behavior in the interface components. By reducing at least a certain amount of morphological interaction to cyclic derivation, this theory follows a long line of earlier theories, originating with the theory of the transformational cycle in Chomsky and Halle's (1968) *The Sound Pattern of English* and other pioneering works in generative phonology.

The basic empirical question that is addressed in this chapter and the next concerns the conditions under which a node may have its phonology determined by items in its context. That is:

(1) Locality of allomorphy question

For the contextual allomorphy of some node, what factors in the environment of that node are visible?

Given the architectural premises of the theory that I assume, the key theoretical questions center on how morphological effects are determined in a system that has (i) cyclic derivation, (ii) structural (i.e., hierarchical) relations determined by the syntax, and (iii) linear relations derived from the hierarchical structure (in the PF component of the grammar, by hypothesis). It is important to distinguish (i)–(iii) in this way because conditions stated in terms of cyclic, hierarchical, and linear representations enforce conditions on locality that are in many cases distinct from one another. The relations that are important for different types of effects in morphology broadly speaking could thus be defined in different ways, and, ultimately, empirical evidence must determine which of (i)–(iii) (or a combination) is active for any particular phenomenon.

The theory presented below explores the idea that a kind of strict *linear* adjacency is required for contextual allomorphy, in a way that interacts with a cyclic theory of what is "active" at a particular stage of a derivation. The central idea is that a node can be sensitive to another node for the purposes of allomorphy only when the two nodes are linearly adjacent to one another. There are, however, cases in which surface linear adjacency is not enough, and this is where cyclic structure plays a role: it is only when two nodes are present in the same PF cycle that they may potentially interact. The cyclic and linear notions of locality appealed to in this theory are logically independent of each other. It is an empirical hypothesis of this work that these two distinct types of locality interact to account for attested patterns of allomorphy in natural language.

2.1 Syntax and Morphology

The theory presented here is a piece-based, syntactic theory of morphology: Distributed Morphology, along the lines of Embick and Marantz 2008 in particular. Complex expressions are built out of discrete pieces (morphemes), and it is in the syntax (or in terms of relations derived from syntactic structures) that the composition of morphemes takes place. Another fundamental component of the theory is the idea that morphology is *realizational*. This means that at least some morphemes possess no phonology as part of their basic representation; rather, phonological material is added to such morphemes in the PF component of the grammar, after they have been combined in syntactic structures.

2.1.1 Basics: Types of Morphemes

The syntax creates complex objects out of different types of morphemes, the *Roots* and the *functional morphemes*, corresponding for the most part to the lexical and functional categories of syntactic theory:

(2) Terminals

  a. *Functional morphemes:* Terminal nodes consisting of (bundles of) grammatical features, such as [past] and [pl]; these do not have phonological representations.

  b. *Roots:* Members of the open-class or "lexical" vocabulary: items such as $\sqrt{\text{CAT}}$, $\sqrt{\text{OX}}$, and $\sqrt{\text{KICK}}$.[1]

The Roots are assumed to be category-neutral. They are categorized in syntactic structures by *category-defining* functional heads: *v*, *n*, *a*, and so on, to yield "verbs," "nouns," and so on. A further assumption is that these category-defining heads are cyclic in the sense of phase theory; see below.

The morphemes in (2) are the primitives of syntactic derivations. In the course of such derivations, complex objects are built in the narrow syntax and then spelled out, that is, subjected to a further series of computations in the interface components. While the nature and number of the computations that constitute PF are a matter of ongoing research, at a minimum, the theory holds that certain nodes must be given phonological content via the process of Vocabulary Insertion.

2.1.2 Vocabulary Insertion

As noted above, it is assumed that the functional morphemes have no phonology as part of their basic representation. When such morphemes occur in a syntactic structure, the process of *Vocabulary Insertion* adds phonological material to them in the PF component of the grammar. As an initial illustration, (4) shows the *Vocabulary items* (VIs) for the past tense head T[past] in English, which are competing for insertion into the T[past] node in (3):

(3) Structure

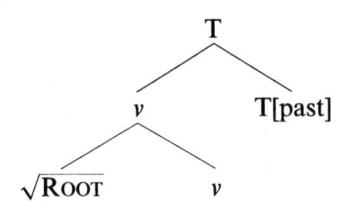

(4) Vocabulary items for Tense

    T[past] $\leftrightarrow$ -t/__{$\sqrt{\text{LEAVE}}$, $\sqrt{\text{BEND}}$, ... }
    T[past] $\leftrightarrow$ -Ø/__{$\sqrt{\text{HIT}}$, $\sqrt{\text{SING}}$, ... }
    T[past] $\leftrightarrow$ -d

The VIs are objects stored in memory. When they apply to a node in a syntactic structure, the phonological matrix that is part of the VI—the *exponent*—occurs in the position of that node.[2]

There are two important assumptions about how this process works. The first is that the items are ordered (see Halle 1997 for one view); the second is that nodes may be phonologically instantiated only once:

(5) Properties of Vocabulary Insertion

    a. *Ordering:* VIs are ordered (according to specificity, in the normal case).

    b. *Uniqueness:* Only one VI may apply to a terminal node.

Taken together, (5a,b) enforce a competition for the realization of the phonological form of functional morphemes. In principle, more than one VI in (4) could apply to a T[past] node, and which one actually applies is determined by ordering. When a more specific VI wins out over less specific ones, the other potentially applying VIs are precluded from having an effect, such that *blocking* occurs.

2.1.3 Linearization

It is assumed for present purposes that syntactic structures contain only hierarchical information. Thus, in a hypothetical structure like [X YP], which results from applications of syntactic Merge, the linearization procedure could produce either a structure in which X precedes YP or a structure in which X follows YP.

When structures like [X YP] are interpreted by the PF component, information concerning the linear order of elements in this phrase marker must be added to the representation. There are different kinds of information that figure in linear order. At the level of categories, information about linear order may be relatively abstract. For example, in a head-initial language, a VP like [V DP] is ordered so that the verb precedes the DP, whereas in a head-final language, the opposite order is derived. Thus, part of what is involved in linearization involves generalizations about categories and their headedness. In linearization representations of this type, the operative factor is a set of statements that encode generalizations that go beyond the properties of individual terminals.[3]

Making this concrete, I assume a linearization procedure along the lines proposed in Sproat 1985 and related work (see, e.g., Marantz 1984, 1988). As an initial example, consider the assignment of linear order to the VP in the sentence *John wants to eat the apple*. Simplifying so that V and N are used in place of v/n-$\sqrt{\text{Root}}$, the syntax generates the structure in (6):

(6) Structure

```
              VP
           /      \
        V            DP
        |         /      \
       eat       D        NP
                 |         |
                the        N
                           |
                         apple
```

When this structure is interpreted at PF, the first stage of the linearization procedure makes use of the information that verbs precede their complements in English (the same thing occurs within the DP as well, where D precedes its complement).[4] It then assigns to the PF representation of this VP a statement that encodes this information in terms of the binary *-operator, which can be read as 'is left-adjacent to':

(7) (V * DP)

As mentioned, there are corresponding statements for the DP, in this case (8):

(8) (D * NP)

In effect, these are representations in which the bracketing provided by the syntactic derivation is retained; the added information in terms of * concerns whether particular elements are to the left or to the right of other elements in the structure. While this information is shown in terms of individual statements above, it could also be presented in one statement like the following:

(9) (V * (D * NP))

As noted above, the generation of *-statements of this type orders elements at a relatively abstract level. By ordering heads with respect to phrases (or phrases with respect to phrases), *-statements contain one type of information necessary for the ultimate linearization of a structure. Many alternatives to the one outlined here—such as deriving precedence relations—could be employed, and these alternatives might have consequences for particular phenomena.[5] However, it is not clear that these alternatives have direct implications for allomorphy, and I therefore do not consider other formulations.

Beyond the information that heads and phrases are next to one another, a more specific type of information must be present in the PF derivation: the terminal nodes must be *concatenated* with one another. In this book, *concatenation* refers to a representation that is exclusively linear. While * encodes that the V is next to the constituent containing D and NP (i.e., that it is to the left of the DP), there must be an explicit statement of which head in the DP the V is immediately adjacent to. Continuing with the example from above, this can be thought of in the following way. The information that V is left-adjacent to the DP is represented, and this must ultimately lead to the statement that V is to the left of the first element of the DP, whatever that may be. What this means is that V is directly concatenated with the first node inside of the DP, which in this example is D. For clarity, I represent the concatenation of terminals with $^\frown$; this is a binary operator that encodes immediate precedence. For the example above, the following statements of concatenation are derived:

(10) V$^\frown$D
       D$^\frown$N

Finally, concatenated elements must be "chained" into a linear representation that can be employed by the input/output system. I will have little to say about the representations implicated in chaining here; I will assume without argument that the chained representation is something like (11c), where the hyphen - is used as a general-purpose boundary symbol. While these statements do not play a role in the discussion below, they have been implicated in other domains, notably, in the locality conditions on "prosodic" phonological rules; see in particular Pak 2008.

Putting things together, then, we have the following linear representations for the VP in question:

(11) a. Linear relations by *: (V * DP), (D * NP)
       b. Linear relations by $^\frown$: V$^\frown$D, D$^\frown$N
       c. Chained: V-D-N

In the localist spirit of the framework, it is assumed that these different representations are derived sequentially in the PF component. It is possible that distinct stages with * and ⌢ operators might not be necessary for the full set of generalizations that implicate linear relations at PF. From the perspective of the present investigation, what is important is that the PF component contain representations in which terminal nodes are concatenated with each other. While other aspects of this concatenation operator might be crucial for, say, postsyntactic reorderings (see the discussion of affixation under adjacency in Embick 2007b), the key relation for allomorphy is immediate precedence, and I focus on this below.

2.1.4 Words/Terminals/Linearization

The discussion of allomorphy below is, for the most part, devoted to "word-internal" cases of allomorphy. This calls for some clarification, since the theory of Distributed Morphology does not have a primitive notion of "word." Rather, the theory makes available an inventory of primitive elements (the morphemes in (2)) and a set of procedures for (i) combining these objects syntactically (syntactic Merge) and (ii) combining heads into *complex heads.*

2.1.4.1 "Words"

I assume that the theory of constituent structure provides a way of deriving objects in which multiple syntactic terminals have been combined into one internally complex head. The "packaging" of heads in this way is something that correlates with standard phonological definitions of wordhood, at least to a first approximation. For example, when two terminals X and Y are not combined in a complex head, these nodes constitute a two-word or "analytic" expression; when they *are* combined, they constitute a one-word or "synthetic" expression:

(12) Analytic ("two words")   (13) Synthetic ("one word")

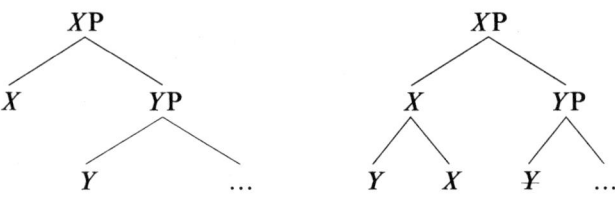

One way of forming complex heads like that in (13) is with the operation of head movement. As has been discussed elsewhere, it appears that, in addition to head movement (assumed for convenience to be part of the syntax), there are operations that affix terminals to each other to create complex heads in the PF component (see, e.g., Embick and Noyer 2001 for one view).

The overwhelming majority of synthetic realizations like (13) show the phonological characteristics of "word-level" phonology.[6] It is for this reason that, informally speaking, when the heads are packaged as one complex head they are "one word," whereas terminal nodes realized as separate heads are "two words."

Overall, then, the theory proposes that the difference between "words" and "phrases" is not architectural; it has to do with how the terminals in a syntactic structure are assembled. Importantly, the "special domains" for various types of interaction, whether involving sound or meaning, do not correspond to the informal notion of "word" employed above. Rather, they are defined in terms of cyclic structure. For one version of this view, see Marantz 2007 and the discussion in section 2.2.1.

In addition to the role played by cyclic structure, it appears that structural relations like "complex head" have some relevance to the phonology as well. As mentioned above, the basic generalization is that objects created by affixation (i.e., by the creation of complex heads) behave as phonological words—or, more cautiously, show "close" phonological connections. Moreover, certain phonological processes, such as "word-final devoicing," target the word boundary in the informal sense intended here, indicating that there is a connection between the "complex head" in syntactic terms and the domains required for phonological rule application. Beyond this rough characterization, however, there are many other cases of interest that must be examined. For example, the phonological behavior of elements inside compounds is not identical to that of non-compounds, despite certain similarities in terms of structural properties. In addition, asymmetries in the morphophonological behavior of certain (classes of) affixes might in some cases reflect important structural differences, while in other cases the phonological differences might result from the diacritic properties of particular exponents (as discussed in, e.g., Halle and Vergnaud 1987).

Looking at the larger picture, the general goal within the kind of approach outlined here is a theory of the connections between domains of phonological interaction on the one hand and structural configurations on the other. A fundamental question is which aspects of phonological behavior are reducible to (cyclic) structure and which are reducible to properties of individual exponents. (For some research along these lines, see among others Marvin 2002 and Oltra-Massuet and Arregi 2005 for "word-internal" investigations, and for larger objects, Wagner 2005 and Pak 2008.)

2.1.4.2 Some Definitions Returning to the PF relations relevant for allo-morphy and other effects, the linearization procedures outlined above are general in the sense that the same operations apply both to heads, as in the examples given, and within complex heads. These points are clear in the context of a hypothetical structure like (14):

(14) Hypothetical structure

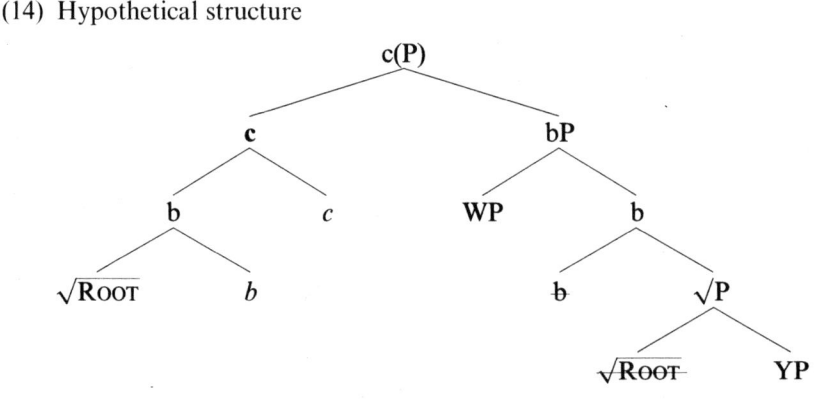

What (14) represents is a structure typical of head movement, in which a Root moves to functional head b, and the resulting complex then moves to functional head c.[7] Structures like this with complex heads im-plicate the manner in which the PF component employs different *types* of objects, such as those defined in the two-level ontology of Embick and Noyer (2001) (see also Embick 2007b):

(15) Definitions

    a. *M-Word:* (Potentially complex) head not dominated by another head projection

    b. *Subword:* Terminal node within an M-Word (i.e., either a Root or a bundle of morphosyntactic features)

Illustrating with reference to (14), boldfaced **c** is an M-Word, while ital-icized *b*, *c* are Subwords. The theory of typing discussed in Embick and Noyer 2001 and Embick 2007b holds that M-Words enter relations with respect to other M-Words, and Subwords with respect to other Subwords.

The concatenation of M-Words was illustrated above. Within a head, Subwords are concatenated with other Subwords. This is illustrated with reference to the word *breakability*, which has the hierarchical structure in (16):

(16) Structure

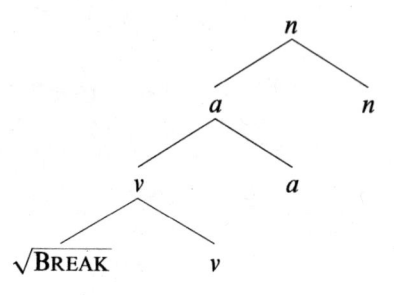

Here *-statements are derived as described above, and then statements of concatenation, so that (16) has the statements in (17) assigned to it:

(17) $\sqrt{\text{BREAK}} \frown v, v \frown a, a \frown n$
     (surface: break-Ø-abil-ity)

Thus, the linear order of M-Words and Subwords is computed in the same way.[8] Notationally, concatenation of Subwords is represented with the operator ⊕ in the works cited above. In the discussion below, it is primarily word-internal allomorphy (i.e., allomorphy internal to the M-Word) that is at issue. Since little hinges on the notational conventions in many of these cases, I will employ ⌢ for concatenation in most of the representations below, making finer distinctions only when necessary.

2.1.5 Phonological Form: Competition and Visibility

As highlighted in chapter 1, what is ultimately at issue in comparing the predictions of localist and globalist theories is the range of factors that may determine the phonological form of an expression. The theory of Distributed Morphology in the form advanced in Embick and Marantz 2008 involves two specific points that are crucial to the comparative discussion to be undertaken: one about *competition*, and one about *visibility*.

Each of these points connects directly with the theory of allomorphic interactions. *Competition* is important for reasons outlined in chapter 1. In order for a theory to implement the proposal that surface forms are optimized phonologically, so that phonological outputs can be compared for purposes such as allomorph selection, it must be the case that the grammar generates multiple competitors and compares them.

According to the localist theory adopted here, allomorph selection cannot make reference to output phonology, or to any factors that would require competition among complex forms. Rather, the relevant factors determining the outcome of allomorphic competitions (and determining phonological form more generally) must be definable in terms of cyclic, hierarchical, and linear notions of *visibility*, within the confines of a single derivation.

2.1.5.1 Competition   Earlier, it was noted that Vocabulary Insertion involves competition that derives from the assumptions in (5), which holds that VIs are ordered and that only one VI may apply to a given node. The status of competition in the grammar in general is the central issue discussed in Embick and Marantz 2008. The theory of blocking presented in that paper allows for extremely limited competition: in particular, it is only the underlying representation of individual morphemes that is subject to competition. In terms of the framework presented here, competition is restricted to the process of Vocabulary Insertion, in which the phonological form of a single morpheme is determined. There is therefore no competition among complex objects in this theory:

(18) No competition (among complex objects)

The theory does not allow multiple potential expressions to be generated for a given meaning. Rather, derivations produce one output per input. No complex objects are in competition; rather, competition is restricted to Vocabulary Insertion at one node.

What this means can be illustrated with the past tense example used to illustrate the basics of Vocabulary Insertion in (3)–(4). When the syntax generates the structure of, say, "past tense of the verb *leave*," this structure involves a complex head like (19) in the PF component; when the list of VIs is consulted, the one with the exponent -*t* must apply to the node T[past], as in (20):

(19) Structure   (20) After Vocabulary Insertion

Crucially, it is only at the T[past] node that competition occurs. The winner of the competition is the VI with the exponent -*t*, and the fact that this VI wins means that the VI with the exponent (orthographic) -*ed* loses. Even though the VI with -*ed* loses this particular competition, this object nevertheless is part of the grammar; it wins (is part of a grammatical derivation) in the case of *play-ed* and the like—the "regular" verbs of English. So, if √LEAVE were not on the list for the VI with the -*t* exponent, the VI with *-ed* would apply. It is in this sense that the VI with *-ed* is blocked by the VI with *-t* when Roots like $\sqrt{\text{LEAVE}}$ are present.

While the VI with *-ed* is part of the grammar, and it is blocked in the derivation of *lef-t*, the hypothetical form **leav-ed* does not have this status. It is not part of the grammar in any form, because the rules of the grammar do not derive it. Another way of putting this is that while *-t* blocks *-ed* in the context of $\sqrt{\text{LEAVE}}$, *left* does not block **leaved*, since the latter is not generated.

The theory presented in Embick and Marantz 2008 advances this "local competition" view of blocking by showing that putative competitions between words and words, or between larger objects (as in, e.g., Andrews 1990; Poser 1992; Bresnan 2001), are better analyzed as not involving competition. This position is defended with respect to "canonical" cases of blocking, such as the *glory/*gloriosity* relationship from Aronoff 1976. Beyond this, moving to the level of what look like "word-phrase" interactions, or *Poser blocking* (Poser 1992), it is not the case that *more intelligent* blocks **intelligenter*, nor is it the case that *smarter* blocks **more smart* (see also Embick 2007a). Instead, the syntax derives a structure that either may or may not provide the structural description for a rule that affixes the comparative element to the adjective. When this rule applies, a synthetic form like *smart-er* is the result; when it does not apply, an analytic form like *more intelligent* is pronounced. In neither case is there any need to block "losers" like hypothetical **more smart* and **intelligent-er*; as in the case of **leav-ed*, the grammar does not generate these objects.

In all of the cases examined to this point, there is one principle that accounts for the derivation of the grammatical forms. The rules of the grammar are set up to generate, for example, *lef-t* and *more intelligent*. There is no way of building the "ungrammatical" objects **leav-ed* and **intelligent-er*. Thus, they do not have to be blocked; they are not built in the first place. The general principle that does the important work in this kind of analysis is as follows:

(21) Apply computation K when the structural description of K is met.

The general principle is, informally, Rules Apply. This principle—together, of course, with the rules of the grammar of the language—defines what exists and what is grammatical.

This view of competition has direct consequences for what may exert influence on the derivation of phonological forms—and thus for the theory of allomorphy, and (morpho)phonology more generally. The theory holds that what exists is what is derived, per (21). In this way, the amount of information that is available to condition the insertion of a contextual allomorph is restricted to what has been produced at an earlier stage of the derivation.

A consequence of this view is that it is not possible to analyze allomorphy by having the grammar generate all possible host-allomorph combinations and then blocking all but one (optimal) winner from among this set. In this way, the theory differs fundamentally from the perspective offered by Optimality Theory (OT), in which complex objects (words, for example) enter into competition. In a standard OT grammar, both *lef-t* and *leav-ed* are "derived" in the sense that they are surface forms that GEN delivers for the input "past tense of *leave*"; the constraint system must then be configured so that *lef-t* wins, rendering **leav-ed* ungrammatical. The general property of this type of theory is that multiple complex competitors for a given input can be derived, so that, most pertinently, different host-allomorph combinations can be derived and compared on a number of parameters. This type of comparison is impossible in a theory that bans competition among complex objects; as discussed in part II of this book, the different types of frameworks (localist, no competition versus globalist, full competition) make a number of distinct predictions about allomorphy that can be tested empirically, predictions that derive to a large extent from the opposing positions such theories take on competition in the grammar.

Within the framework developed here, another set of restrictions arises from the position that derivations are *encapsulated*, in the sense that there are no transderivational relations. Thus, it is not possible to say that allomorphic choice is influenced by other parts of an element's paradigm, by the paradigms of other words, or the like; all such "paradigmatic" considerations are banned from playing a role in well-formedness (this point has been examined with respect to syncretism in Bobaljik 2002).[9]

2.1.5.2 (Local) Visibility A theory with the properties outlined in the last section allows the following factors to play a role in the computation of a complex form's phonology (see also, e.g., Bobaljik 2008, with reference to certain globalist, paradigmatic claims made in McCarthy 2005):

(22) a. Identity/Phonological forms of Roots and morphemes
   b. Locality (phases, linear adjacency)
   c. Phonological processes
   d. Things that have to be listed: allomorphy, exceptions, readjustment rules

In order to interact within the confines of what is allowed by (22), elements in a derivation must be visible to each other. The theory of what is locally visible in PF representations begins with the notion of cyclicity. Two notions of *cyclic* are at play in determining morphological and phonological form in the present framework. The first is an "inside-out" kind of cyclicity, which takes the form of the assumption that Vocabulary Insertion applies first to the most deeply embedded node in a structure and then targets outer nodes successively (see Carstairs 1987; Bobaljik 2000; Carstairs-McCarthy 2001, 2003; Adger, Béjar, and Harbour 2003). The second kind of cyclicity is phase-based in the sense of Chomsky 2000, 2001, and Marantz 2001, 2007 (see also Marvin 2002 and Bachrach and Wagner 2006 for some phonologically oriented proposals).

The first type of restriction can be illustrated in the abstract with reference to the structure in (23):

(23) Structure for Root-*X*-*Y*-*Z*

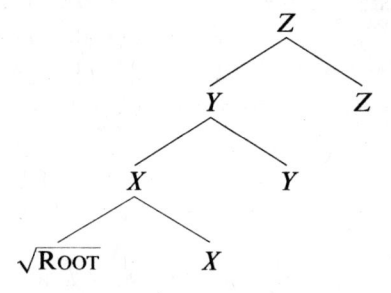

The working hypothesis of "inside-out" cyclicity is that Vocabulary Insertion targets the node *X* first, then *Y*, then *Z*. This ordering has the potential to restrict the amount and type of information available for particular instances of Vocabulary Insertion. For example, insertion at *Y* could be sensitive to the output of insertion at *X*, but not to the output of insertion at *Z*. While the assumption that Vocabulary Insertion functions in this way does not seem to follow from any other aspects of the theory, it is well-motivated empirically and will be retained here (see in this connection Bobaljik 2000).

The second type of cyclic restriction is hypothesized to derive from phase-based cyclicity, in the sense of Chomsky 2000, 2001, and related work. Within a given derivation, objects may interact only if they are active (i.e., co-present) in the same cycle of computation. As discussed below, this type of cyclicity appears to play a role in allomorphic interactions as well.

2.2 Contexts for Allomorphy: Toward a Localist Theory

The theory of contextual allomorphy in Distributed Morphology is, in effect, a theory of suppletion. Contextual allomorphy is found when (i) a single morpheme like T[past] for past tense T, or [pl], for plural, has more than one exponent, and (ii) the different exponents cannot be derived from one another via the phonology. The allomorphs are thus suppletive alternants. This is the case in, for example, the English [pl] head, which has (orthographic) -*s*, -*en*, and -*Ø* allomorphs (this example is employed here instead of the past tense, since an additional point about phonologically derived allomorphs can be considered):

(24) $\#[\text{pl}] \leftrightarrow$ -en/{ $\sqrt{\text{Ox}}$, $\sqrt{\text{Child}}$, ... } __
       $\#[\text{pl}] \leftrightarrow$ -$\emptyset$/{ $\sqrt{\text{Moose}}$, $\sqrt{\text{Foot}}$, ... } __
       $\#[\text{pl}] \leftrightarrow$ -s (= /z/)

The competition for insertion at the #[pl] node is waged among the three VIs in (24). In a given derivation, only one may be employed. A result of this competition—and the fact that there is more than one possible "winner" for the expression of plural when the language as a whole is viewed—is that the node #[pl] has three suppletive allomorphs.

In the kind of competition just described, distinct VIs are at play. This sort of *competition for insertion* can be distinguished from another sense in which the term *allomorphy* is sometimes employed. Continuing with the plural example, it is clear that not all surface realizations of the orthographic -*s* allomorph are phonologically identical; rather, there are /z/, /s/, and /əz/ "allomorphs" that surface in phonologically predictable contexts (in, e.g., *dogs, cats, churches*). This type of "allomorphic" effect is not suppletive, and within the theory outlined above it is not treated via competition between distinct VIs with /s/, /z/, and /əz/ exponents. Rather, this pattern is found when (i) the morphology (Vocabulary Insertion) inserts -/z/ and (ii) the (morpho)phonology derives from this single exponent the different surface forms seen above.

As a general point, I use the term *allomorphy* (or *phonologically conditioned allomorphy* when the conditioning factor for suppletion is phonological) for cases that involve competition among VIs.

The general theme of this work is that allomorphic relations are constrained to obey certain locality conditions. This means that while VIs must be specified so that they make reference to objects in their context, not just any object in the syntactic structure may be referred to. Put somewhat abstractly, the initial question that must be posed is as follows: for a

VI like (25), which encodes contextual sensitivity of the morpheme [α] to X, what can the relation represented by ∼ be?

(25) Locality

$$[α] ↔ -z/X∼\_\_$$

In a framework like the one assumed here, (25) asks which structural or linear relationships can appear in a VI. The theory proposed below holds that the relation symbolized by ∼ in (25) is *concatenation*, ⌢ in the discussion of linearization in section 2.1. In addition to this, the cyclic component of the theory restricts possible allomorphic interactions further, by circumscribing the set of cases in which nodes like [α] and X are actually operated on in the same cycle of PF computation.

2.2.1 Cyclic Structure and Allomorphy

I assume that the syntactic component of the grammar is derivational and that derivations operate in terms of cyclic domains in the sense of Chomsky 2000, 2001, and related work. The natural move in a theory with cyclic locality domains is to assume that the significant domains for (morpho)phonological and semantic interactions are identical to syntactic "phases"; this is the type of theory presented in Marantz 2001, 2007, which takes category-defining heads like v and n to define cyclic domains in this sense:[10]

(26) Category-defining heads such as n and v are *cyclic* heads.

This means that the functional vocabulary of a language—that is, the non-Roots—consists of two types of heads. There are cyclic heads, the category-defining ones in (26), and there are noncyclic functional heads. Into the latter category fall all other functional morphemes: tense nodes, number nodes, and so on.

On this type of theory, the generalizations for sound-meaning connections that are hypothesized are as follows, in the formulation of Embick and Marantz 2008, 11:

(27) Cyclic generalizations

    a. *Allomorphy:* For Root-attached x, special allomorphy for x may be determined by properties of the Root. A head x in the outer domain is not in a local relationship with the Root and thus cannot have its allomorphy determined by the Root.

    b. *Interpretation:* The combination of Root-attached x and the Root might yield a special interpretation. When attached in the outer domain, the x heads yield predictable interpretations.

Root-attached in (27) refers to the first category-defining head that appears in a structure.[11] The idea behind (27) is that being in the Root or *inner* domain correlates with effects both in terms of interpretation and in terms of form—in other words, that structures in which a category-defining head x is merged with a Root are (potentially) special, in the senses covered by (27). A further motivation behind (27) is that the special domains should not be stipulated; rather, they should be defined as a consequence of the way that Spell-Out works. The idea that, for example, *outer* heads cannot show Root-specific interactions would follow from the fact that in a cyclic theory based on (27), such heads are not present in the same cycle as the Root.

Patterns of nominal formation illustrate some of the basic properties of this type of cyclic theory. In some well-studied examples from early work on derivational morphology, it appears that patterns of allomorphy correlate closely with interpretive properties in a way that is congenial to the perspective of (27). The relevant data here center on *derived* or *simple* nominals like *destruction* in (28a), versus *gerundive nominals* (gerunds) like *destroying* in (28b) (this discussion draws on Chomsky 1970 and subsequent work):

(28) a. John's destruction of the city...
     b. John's destroying the city...

According to an analysis that, with different variants, has been given in the framework under discussion, the derived nominal involves Root-attached *n*, as in (29), whereas in the gerundive *n* is attached to a verbal constituent, shown as *v*P in (30), although there could in fact be motivation for additional noncyclic structure between *v*P and *n* (see Marantz 1997; Alexiadou 2001; and related work):

(29) *n* Root-attached   (30) *n* not Root-attached

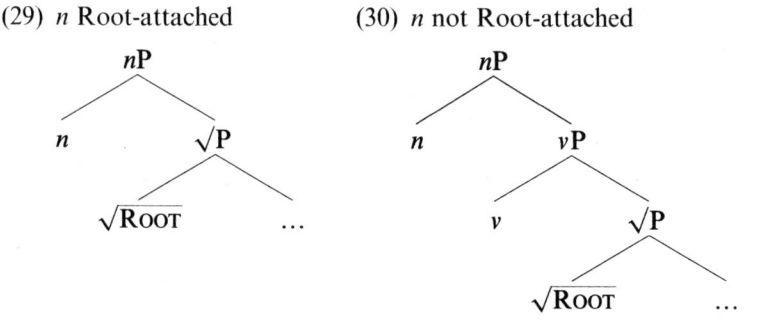

In the inner domain schematized in (29), the *n* head has a large number of allomorphs: *-al*, *-ity*, *-age*, *-(t)ion*, *-Ø*, and others. In the outer domain schematized in (30), on the other hand, the phonological form of n is only -*ing*:[12]

(31) Nominals and allomorphy

Derived/Simple	*Gerund*
refus-al	refus-ing
marri-age	marry-ing
destruct-ion	destroy-ing
break-Ø	break-ing

Corresponding to this, the interpretations of the Root-attached cases are potentially idiosyncratic in ways that have been detailed amply in the literature, whereas the gerundive nominals do not have this property. The asymmetry in both interpretation and allomorphy seen in derived nominals versus gerunds constitutes the ideal state of affairs from the point of view of the kind of cyclic theory that is behind (27).

A provisional analysis of these effects can be framed in terms of the inner/outer domain distinction discussed above. In the inner domain, where access to the Root is allowed, there is Root-determined allomorphy. In the outer domain, on the other hand, there is only one VI that applies; this is shown in (32), where the LISTs contain the Roots that select the exponents in question:

(32) a. Inner domain

$n \leftrightarrow$ -al/   LIST1__
$n \leftrightarrow$ -age/ LIST2__
$n \leftrightarrow$ -tion/ LIST3__
   ⋮

b. Outer domain

$n \leftrightarrow$ -ing

The intuition behind (32) is that in the inner domain, the Root is in a "visible" relationship with the functional head n. By hypothesis, this relationship is the one defined by being in the same initial cycle as n—that is, where n is the head that categorizes the Root. I put aside more discussion of how patterns like the one in (32) could be accounted for formally until additional sets of data have been considered.

2.2.2 A $\mathbb{C}_0$ Theory

A theory based on (27) that takes x to range over all types of heads holds that it is only in the inner domain that Root-specific allomorphy can be found. I refer to this as the $\mathbb{C}_0$ *theory*, since allomorphic relations are restricted to the cyclically closest (Root-attached) environment:[13]

(33) $\mathbb{C}_0$ theory

Head x can be allomorphically sensitive to a head Y only if x is in the inner domain of Y (typical case: x is attached to a Root Y).

An important empirical discovery is that the $\mathbb{C}_0$ theory is too restrictive. There are well-known cases of allomorphy that could not be derived if this theory were correct (see Embick 2003, 2004a on English participial formations; Embick and Marantz 2008 on past tense). Consider, for example, the English past tense. The first two VIs in (34) contain exponents that are inserted in the context of certain Roots:

(34) Vocabulary items for Tense

T[past] $\leftrightarrow$ -t/__ {$\sqrt{\text{LEAVE}}$, $\sqrt{\text{BEND}}$, . . . }
T[past] $\leftrightarrow$ -Ø/__ {$\sqrt{\text{HIT}}$, $\sqrt{\text{SING}}$, . . . }
T[past] $\leftrightarrow$ -d

The structures in which T[past] is spelled out have a v and the T[past] node, as in (35):

(35) Past tense verb

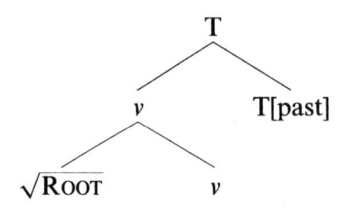

The $\mathbb{C}_0$ theory holds that T[past] cannot be sensitive to the Root, because T[past] is not in the inner cycle. According to this theory, there should be no Root-specific allomorphy at T[past], but this is clearly incorrect.

The T[past] node and the Root interact in another way that suggests a similar conclusion. This interaction does not involve suppletive allomorphy; instead, it involves the stem allomorphy found in certain irregular verbs. Specifically, the node T[past] triggers *readjustment rules* on certain Roots, and not others. For example, the Root $\sqrt{\text{SING}}$ undergoes such a rule to yield *sang*; the Root $\sqrt{\text{BREAK}}$ undergoes another such rule to yield *broke*; and so on. This means again that the Root must be visible qua Root when T[past] is processed at PF, something that the strict $\mathbb{C}_0$ theory rules out.[14]

In sum, the $\mathbb{C}_0$ theory is too strict, and an alternative must be developed. The following sections are devoted to this task.

2.2.3 Generalizations about Allomorphic Locality

With a few exceptions, there is very little work describing the limits of allomorphic interaction. For the purposes of developing a theory of allomorphy, this means that there is no clear consensus in the literature about what kinds of locality conditions regulate allomorphic closeness. Seminal works like Carstairs 1987 discuss this question, but overall a clear descriptive statement of what kinds of patterns are found (and what kinds are not) has not been forthcoming.[15]

Given what has been described in the literature, and what is to be described below, the following generalizations appear to hold:

(G1) Root-attached cyclic x can see the Root. This is clear from many of the examples above and is, in a sense, unsurprising. For example, the wide range of nominalizing (n) exponents in English is found when n is Root-attached. This was illustrated in section 2.2.1.

(G2) A noncyclic (i.e., non-category-defining) head X can see a Root in spite of intervening cyclic x, but this seems to happen only when x is nonovert. This is the situation in the English past tense, where the phonologically null v head does not prevent the T[past] head from having its allomorphy conditioned by the Root.

(G3) When there are two cyclic heads x and y in a structure like $[[\sqrt{\text{ROOT}}\ x]\ y]$, it seems that y cannot see the Root, even if x is not overt. That is, outer or "category-changing" cyclic heads do not seem to be sensitive to the Root.

Although (G1)–(G3) speak of functional heads seeing Roots, this is a simplification. The generalizations here apply as well to other heads that could be inside a cyclic domain defined by x. For example, (G2) should be read as saying that X can see W in $\ldots\ W]\ y]\ X]$, as long as cyclic y is not overt; it does not matter whether W is a Root or a noncyclic functional head. The same extension applies to (G3); y cannot see the Root or any functional heads that are in the complement of x.

There are many cases in which a functional head shows allomorphic sensitivity to another functional head. One is found with the adjectival a head that has the exponent -*able*, which *potentiates* (makes fully productive) the -*ity* exponent of *n*. Any -*able*-affixed word in English, such as *break-able* from *break*, can be nominalized with an *n* that is pronounced -*ity*, such as *break-abil-ity*.[16] The VI with -*ity* as exponent is specified for a set of Roots including $\sqrt{\text{CURIOUS}}$ and $\sqrt{\text{ATROC}}$, which have nominal forms *curios-ity* and *atroc-ity*; along with these and other -*ity*-taking Roots, the *a* head that takes -*able* also appears on this list:[17]

(36) $n \leftrightarrow$ -ity/X__
     X = Roots ($\sqrt{\text{ATROC}}$, $\sqrt{\text{CURIOUS}}$, ...); [*a*, -able]

In structures with this *n* attached outside of the *a* with -*able*, Vocabulary Insertion inserts the -*ity* exponent at *n* (the structure here ignores material that might appear between the Root and the *a* head):

(37) a. Structure: [[$\sqrt{\text{ROOT}}$ *a*] *n*]
     b. Vocabulary Insertion: [[$\sqrt{\text{ROOT}}$ [*a*, -able]] [*n*, -ity]]

In this type of case, a functional head (in this example, *n*) has its allomorphy determined by an adjacent functional head (in this example, *a*).

2.3   Implementation of the Localist Theory

Above, it was shown that the $\mathbb{C}_0$ theory is too restrictive: it rules out allomorphic interactions that are attested, such as Root-sensitive allomorphy of T[past] in English. At the same time, it appears that cyclic structure is still relevant for allomorphy, in the form of the generalization (G3). That is, to the extent that there are no cases of Root-sensitive allomorphy for cyclic *y* in structures like [[$\sqrt{\text{ROOT}}$ *x*] *y*], cyclic structure plays an important role in constraining which nodes can interact with each other.

The theory of allomorphy presented in this section is "hybrid" in the sense that it employs both linear and cyclic notions of locality. Representationally, the theory is highly restricted: it hypothesizes that contextual allomorphy is restricted to a node that sees another node by virtue of being concatenated with it:

(H1) Contextual allomorphy is possible only with elements that are
       concatenated by ⌢.

This aspect of the theory is somewhat restrained in comparison with (e.g.) early formulations of contextual visibility, such as Halle and Marantz 1993, where the structural notion of *government* is mentioned as a factor in allomorphic locality. At the same time, it is less restrictive than the $\mathbb{C}_0$ theory, in that it allows allomorphic interaction across a cyclic domain boundary, as long as the interacting elements are concatenated (and as long as intervening elements have zero phonetic exponents; see below). The linear aspect of the theory allows for "mismatches" between linear and hierarchical structure (i.e., different "bracketings"); in principle, linear relations like concatenation can ignore any number of intervening syntactic brackets.

The idea that linear relations are important for allomorphy has been advanced in the literature. A proposal along the lines of (H1) is also advanced in Adger, Béjar, and Harbour 2001, where a theory of allomorphy is proposed in which (with some additional conditions relating to syntactic Agree) linear adjacency plays a defining role. See also the discussion in Bobaljik 1999, 2000, and related work, and the analysis of participial allomorphy in Embick 2003, which requires linear relations as well.

Beyond the restrictions imposed by (H1), the theory of cyclic domains constrains allomorphic interactions as well, by placing precise restrictions on which elements can conceivably interact in a given PF cycle. To a first approximation, some "outer" material cannot play a role in certain derivations, because it is not present when allomorph selection at inner nodes takes place. Similarly, some "inner" material is not present when the outer morphemes undergo Vocabulary Insertion, because this inner material is derivationally closed off. These cyclic hypotheses are summarized in (H2):

(H2) Cyclic Spell-Out domains define which nodes are present in a given cycle of PF computation and thus are potentially "active" (capable of being referred to) for the purposes of contextual allomorphy. Some outer nodes are not present when inner nodes are sent to PF. In addition, superficially adjacent nodes sometimes cannot influence each other allomorphically because in terms of cyclic Spell-Out, they are not active in the same PF cycle.

Together, hypotheses (H1) and (H2) are formalized and elaborated in the rest of this chapter. Before going into the details of (H1) and (H2), I should stress that these hypotheses are independent of one another. That is, it does not follow from anything that both should be relevant to allomorphy; nor does the falsity of one entail the falsity of the other. It is a hypothesis of this book that (H1) and (H2) work together to restrict possible patterns of allomorphy in natural language.

2.3.1 Cyclic Spell-Out: The $\mathbb{C}_1$-LIN Theory

The theory centered on (H1) and (H2) is implemented in terms of a set of assumptions about syntactic derivations and how they are spelled out. Following some assumptions reviewed above, I take the category-defining heads *n*, *v*, *a*, and so on, to be *cyclic*:

(38) Category-defining heads *n*, *v*, *a*, and so on, are *cyclic* heads: such heads define the *phases* that trigger Spell-Out.

The crucial theoretical question is how phase-based Spell-Out functions. Additional notions that advance toward this point are illustrated in (39), where *x* is a cyclic head, and *W*, *Z* are noncyclic; other material (e.g., specifiers, and material adjoined to any of these projections) is omitted for ease of exposition:

(39) Sample structure

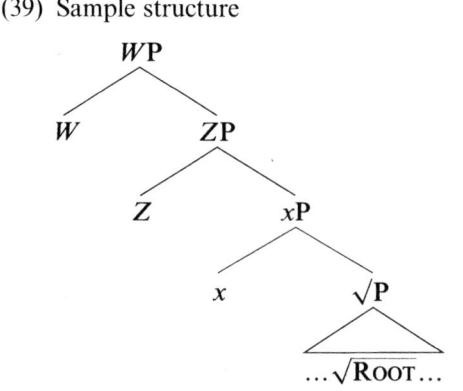

The head *x* is a phase head. The *complement* (or *domain*) of this head is the material in $\sqrt{}$P. The phase head *x* is an *edge* element in the phase *x*P; material adjoined to *x*P—or specifiers of *x*P—is also defined as edge material (cf. Chomsky 2001). The noncyclic heads *W* and *Z*, which are merged higher than *x*P, do not have a special status in standard definitions of the phase. It appears that these heads are treated phonologically in the same cycle as the phase head *x*. For this reason, I refer to "interphasal" elements like *W* and *Z* with the cover term *edge*$^+$.

Cyclic heads define phases and trigger the Spell-Out of material to the interfaces. The assumption (SO1) specifies the manner in which such heads trigger Spell-Out:

(SO1) When cyclic head *x* is merged, cyclic domains in the complement of *x* are spelled out.

For concreteness, take (40), which extends (39); as before, x and y are cyclic, whereas W and Z are not. (41) shows the complex head created in (40):

(40) Sample structure

```
        yP
       /  \
      y    WP
          /  \
         W    ZP
             /  \
            Z    xP
                /  \
               x    √P
                   /____\
                  ...√ROOT...
```

(41) Complex head

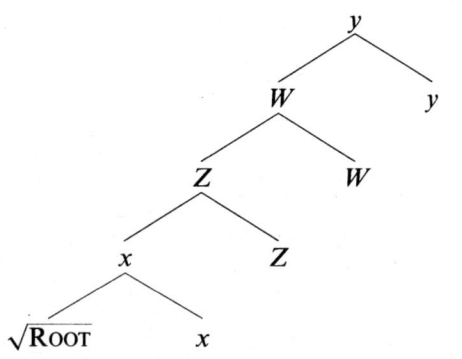

Although presented as a whole, these structures are built in a sequential derivation. First the syntax derives the √P; then it merges x with this. Since x is a cyclic node, Spell-Out is triggered. This means that cyclic domains in the complement of x are spelled out; in (40), the result is that any cyclic domains in the √P are subject to Vocabulary Insertion and phonological processing.

Subsequent syntactic derivation merges noncyclic W and Z with the xP; to this object, cyclic y is then merged, and Spell-Out is triggered at this point because y is cyclic. By (SO1), merging cyclic y triggers Spell-Out of cyclic domains in y's complement. A further assumption is required to specify what material is spelled out in this way. The general principle at play in defining which material is spelled out is (SO2):

(SO2) Merge of cyclic y triggers Spell-Out of cyclic domains in the complement of y, by (SO1). For a cyclic domain headed by cyclic x in the complement of y, this means that the complement of x, the head x itself, and any edge$^+$ material attached to x's domain undergoes Vocabulary Insertion.

While (SO1) specifies which nodes trigger Spell-Out, (SO2) specifies what piece of structure is operated on. With reference to (40), the cyclic domain headed by x is sent to PF when y is merged. This cycle of computation operates on the Root, the head x, and the edge$^+$ heads W and Z. In this PF cycle, the head x undergoes Vocabulary Insertion, as do W and Z. Roots are not (by hypothesis) subject to Vocabulary Insertion, but in this cycle, the Root undergoes phonological processing (the exponents inserted at the functional nodes might be processed phonologically as well).

The main idea behind (SO2) is that material in the complement of a phase head is spelled out. There are other conceivable formulations that achieve this effect. One possibility—(SO2′)—would be to hold that when a phase head y is merged, the complement of y is spelled out, as long as there is a phase-defining head x in the complement of y. This (SO2′) does much of what (SO2) does, by spelling out material in the complement of the phase head, but there are some important differences as well. In particular, consider (42), where the phase head x takes a complement consisting of a Root with a DP complement:

(42) Root with DP complement

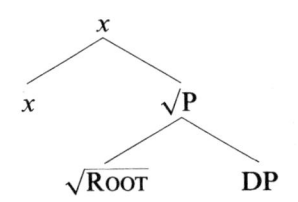

If DP is a phase (cyclic domain), then (SO2) and (SO2′) differ with respect to how this object is processed. By (SO2), the $\sqrt{\text{Root}}$ is not spelled out until a higher cycle when another cyclic head y is merged. By (SO2′), on the other hand, the presence of a phase (i.e., the DP) in the complement of x would cause the complement of x to be spelled out at the stage shown in (42). This might make it impossible for the Root to affect allomorphy of nodes outside of x, as is required in the case of the English past tense; see below. There are other formulations of (SO2) (or (SO2′)) that could address this point (e.g., (SO2′) could be modified so that y's complement is spelled out when it contains a phase in some particular configuration with respect to y). As long as these formulations spell out the complement of the phase head under conditions like those found in (SO2)/(SO2′), they are appropriate for the purposes at hand, although of course such alternatives might produce a number of distinct predictions in other domains.

As far as allomorphy is concerned, the essential empirical questions addressed by (SO2) concern when the heads that occur between phase heads like y and x are spelled out; these are heads like W and Z in (40)–(41). A consequence of (SO1) and (SO2) is that noncyclic heads like W and Z that are attached to a cyclic head x can show allomorphic sensitivity to x or elements like the Root in the complement of x, because all of these nodes are present and subjected to Vocabulary Insertion in the same cycle. The assumption that the edge$^+$ material attached to phase head x is spelled out in the same cycle as x is motivated empirically; it is an assumption that does not follow from other aspects of the system. In particular, spelling out edge$^+$ material in a cycle in which the complement of the cyclic head is still active allows for (e.g.) the Root-determined allomorphy of English past tense nodes (the derivation of the past tense is presented step by step in section 2.3.3).

What remains to be defined is the manner in which substructures that have been spelled out come to be "closed off" for later cycles of computation. The definition in (SO3) specifies this part of the theory:[18]

(SO3) Material in the complement of a phase head that has been spelled out is not active in subsequent PF cycles. That is, the complement of a cyclic head x is not present in the PF cycle in which the next higher cyclic head y is spelled out.

With reference to (40), the effects of (SO3) are as follows. When y is merged, the cyclic domain defined by x is spelled out. By (SO2), then, x, the complement of x, and edge$^+$ heads attached to x undergo Vocabulary Insertion. In a subsequent stage of the syntactic derivation, when some cyclic head above y is merged, the cyclic domain centered on y is spelled out. In this cycle, (SO2) specifies that y, its complement, and edge$^+$ material are present. The head x and its edge$^+$ material—W and Z in (40)—are also present in this cycle of Spell-Out. These heads are already instantiated phonologically, however, since they are subjected to Vocabulary Insertion in the cycle triggered by Merge of y. No other material is present when y is spelled out; in particular, (SO3) says that material in the complement of x is not present in this cycle.

The effect of (SO3) is to remove certain nodes from the computation past a certain cyclic boundary. The way that (SO3) is defined, an outer cyclic head has its phonological form computed in a cycle in which the complement of an inner cyclic head is not present. This aspect of the theory accounts for (G3) (i.e., the absence of Root-specific allomorphy for outer cyclic heads), and its effects are seen in other domains as well.

Taken together, the effects of (SO1)–(SO3) are shown schematically in (43), where the subscript on each bracket indicates the node that triggers Spell-Out, and the nodes contained within the bracket are the nodes present in that PF cycle. Because there are no cyclic domains in the complement of x in the hypothetical structure that is being considered, (43) begins with the cycle triggered by y, in which the bracketed material in (43a) is present. In the cycle determined by z, the bracketed material in (43b) is present:

(43) a. $[[[[\sqrt{\text{Root}}\ x]\ W]\ Z]\ y]$
          $\underbrace{}_{y}$

    Cyclic y triggers Spell-Out of cyclic domains in its complement. The head x undergoes Vocabulary Insertion, as do the edge$^+$ heads W and Z. The Root is processed phonologically.

      b. $[[[[\sqrt{\text{Root}}\ x^*]\ W^*]\ Z^*]\ y] \ldots z]$
          $\underbrace{}_{z}$

    Merge of higher cyclic z triggers Spell-Out of cyclic domains in its complement. The head y defines a cyclic domain and is subjected to Vocabulary Insertion (along with any edge$^+$ heads it might have). The heads marked with *—x, W, Z—are present when y undergoes Vocabulary Insertion, but have undergone Vocabulary Insertion in the earlier cycle.

From (SO1)–(SO3), two important corollaries follow. It is convenient to refer to these by name, since they are central to explaining the empirical generalizations (G1)–(G3), along lines sketched above.

The first corollary, which follows from (SO1), is that a cyclic head is not present in the cycle of Spell-Out that it induces. This is the *Domain Corollary*:

(44) Domain Corollary

Cyclic head x is not present in the PF cycle of computation that is triggered by Merge of x. Thus, x is *not* subjected to Vocabulary Insertion (and thus cannot undergo any phonological processing) until the next cycle of Spell-Out, when it is in the *domain* of another cyclic head.

A second corollary, which is derived from (SO2) and (SO3), concerns which nodes are present in a cycle of PF computation. These nodes could potentially interact for allomorphic or other purposes. Another way of stating this is that the nodes that are co-present in a given cycle are potentially *active* with respect to one another. The most important work done by this aspect of the theory is in structures with more than one cyclic head. The *Activity Corollary* is tailored to this type of case:[19]

(45) Activity Corollary

In $[[\ldots x] \, y]$, x, y both cyclic, material in the complement of x is not *active* in the PF cycle in which y is spelled out.

It is useful to refer to the Domain Corollary and the Activity Corollary in discussing how particular empirical results are derived. It must be emphasized, however, that these are not separate hypotheses beyond (SO1)–(SO3); as their names imply, they are corollaries of that general set of assumptions about how cyclic Spell-Out works.

I refer to the theory based on (SO1)–(SO3) as a $\mathbb{C}_1$ *cyclic theory*. Unlike the $\mathbb{C}_0$ theory discussed above, it allows allomorphic interaction beyond the Root-attached domain. At the same time, while allomorphic visibility is possible when *one* cyclic head is present, elements in the domain of a cyclic head are inactive in the cycle in which an outer cyclic head is spelled out.

The linear condition of (H1) operates in addition to the $\mathbb{C}_1$ cyclic theory of (H2). I call their combination the $\mathbb{C}_1$-*LIN theory*.

2.3.2 Application to Cyclic Heads

The $\mathbb{C}_1$-LIN theory can be illustrated with some initial examples, centering on the key contrast between the behavior of inner cyclic heads and that of outer cyclic heads: (G1) and (G3) above. Recall that the important comparisons used for exposition in section 2.2.1 center on derived/simple nominals versus gerunds.

Beginning with the former, a simple noun like *marriage* has the structure in (46). Here and below, I employ structures that are complex heads:

(46) Merge of *n*

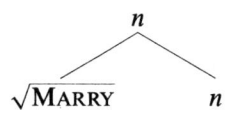

The cyclic *n* morpheme triggers Spell-Out, such that any phases in the complement of *n* are spelled out at this stage. In (46), there are no phases in *n*'s complement. During the next cycle of Spell-Out, triggered by a higher cyclic head, the cyclic domain centered on *n* in (46) is spelled out. In this cycle, the Root √MARRY and the *n* are linearized, and the VI with *-age* as exponent applies to *n*. The steps in the derivation of *marriage* are summarized in (47):

(47) Syntax: Higher cyclic head triggers Spell-Out of *n*
     a. PF: Linearization: √MARRY⌢*n*
     b. PF: Vocabulary Insertion at *n*: √MARRY⌢[*n*, -age]

The derivation of the "category-changing" deverbal nominal *marry-ing*, in which *n* is attached outside of *v*, involves some additional steps. To begin with, the Root and *v* are merged:

(48) Merge of *v*

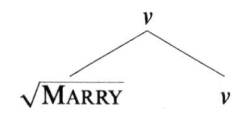

The *v* head triggers Spell-Out as described above. A subsequent stage of the syntactic derivation merges *n* with (48):[20]

(49) Merge of *n* over *v*

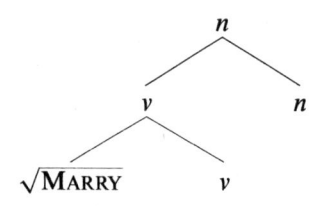

The *n* head triggers Spell-Out of material in its domain. In the PF cycle defined by *n*, the *v* head undergoes Vocabulary Insertion, which inserts *-Ø*. In a subsequent cycle, the *n* head is subject to Vocabulary Insertion, which inserts the *-ing* exponent. These steps are summarized in (50), which begins with Merge of *n*:

(50) a. Merge of n triggers Spell-Out of v-headed phase
     i. PF: Linearization: $\sqrt{\text{MARRY}}{}^\frown v$
     ii. PF: Vocabulary Insertion at v: $\sqrt{\text{MARRY}}{}^\frown [v, \text{-}\emptyset]$
   b. Syntax: Later cycle triggers Spell-Out of n-headed phase
     i. PF: Linearization: $[v, \text{-}\emptyset]{}^\frown n$
     ii. PF: Vocabulary Insertion at n: $[v, \text{-}\emptyset]{}^\frown [n, \text{-ing}]$

In the derivation of *marry-ing*, the n head cannot see the Root for contextual allomorphy, even though the n and the Root $\sqrt{\text{MARRY}}$ are superficially adjacent (i.e., there are no overt morphemes intervening between them). As shown in (50bii), when n is subjected to Vocabulary Insertion, the Root is not present in that cycle. Thus, n could never show allomorphy conditioned by the Root in this type of formation. The insensitivity of outer cyclic nodes to elements in the complement of an inner cyclic node is a manifestation of the Activity Corollary.

2.3.3 Transparency and Pruning

While outer cyclic nodes cannot see across inner cyclic nodes, noncyclic nodes outside of a cyclic head are able to see into the inner domain; recall that, as stated in (G2), in structures like (51) noncyclic Z can show Root-specific allomorphy across cyclic x:

(51) $\dots \sqrt{\text{ROOT}}] \, x] \, Z]$

This is the kind of structure found in the English past tense, where x is v, and Z is the tense node T[past]. The latter head can show Root-determined allomorphy.

The importance of this type of example for cyclic structure was stressed above, where it was shown that cases like (51) require something more than the $\mathbb{C}_0$ theory of cyclicity. Another important point about (51) can be seen with reference to (H1), the concatenation requirement on contextual allomorphy. The linearization procedure employed above derives the linearization statements in (52) from (51):

(52) $\sqrt{\text{ROOT}}{}^\frown x, \, x^\frown Z$

In these statements, Z is not concatenated with the Root, yet it potentially shows Root-determined allomorphy. The hypothesis (H1) that contextual allomorphy is restricted to concatenated elements narrows the range of options for treating the type of case in (51). If this hypothesis is correct, it must be the case that the Root and Z are concatenated when Vocabulary Insertion occurs at Z.

This type of question is addressed in Embick 2003, where it is proposed that some nodes with null (-Ø) exponents are transparent for certain linear relations. This can be made precise by positing a type of *pruning* rule that eliminate nodes from concatenation statements. As a working hypothesis, I assume that this kind of rule has the properties specified in (53):

(53) Pruning schema

$$\sqrt{\text{Root}}\frown[x, \text{-Ø}], [x, \text{-Ø}]\frown Y \rightarrow \sqrt{\text{Root}}\frown Y$$

The rule eliminates pieces with null exponents. Pruning rules are, evidently, not obligatory for all nodes with zero exponents. There might be some cases in which it appears that a head with a null exponent is present in concatenation statements. Whether or not there are significant generalizations about which zeroes are pruned and which are not remains to be investigated. In the discussion below, I will posit pruning rules where required.

The effects of Pruning can be illustrated with reference to the English past tense. Past tense verbs have the structure in (54). The v node intervenes between the Root and T[past], as shown in (55a). Pruning eliminates the $[v, \text{-Ø}]$ node from the concatenation statements, as shown in (55b). When Vocabulary Insertion at T[past] takes place, the concatenation statement in (55b) is present:

(54) Structure

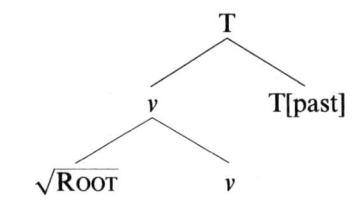

(55) a. $\sqrt{\text{Root}}\frown v, v\frown\text{T[past]}$
     b. $\sqrt{\text{Root}}\frown\text{T[past]}$

The steps in the derivation of a past tense form are shown in (56):

(56) a. Syntax: v and the Root are merged
        i. PF: Spell-Out of phases in the domain of v
     b. Syntax: T head merged with vP
     c. Syntax: Higher cyclic head triggers Spell-Out of v-headed phase
        i. (T lowers to v to create complex head $[[\sqrt{\text{Root}}\ v]\ \text{T[past]}])$
        ii. Linearization: $\sqrt{\text{Root}}\frown v, v\frown\text{T[past]}$

    iii. Vocabulary Insertion at v: $\sqrt{\text{ROOT}}^\frown[v, \text{-}\varnothing], [v, \text{-}\varnothing]^\frown\text{T[past]}$
    iv. Pruning: $\sqrt{\text{ROOT}}^\frown[v, \text{-}\varnothing], [v, \text{-}\varnothing]^\frown\text{T[past]} \rightarrow$
        $\sqrt{\text{ROOT}}^\frown\text{T[past]}$
    v. Vocabulary Insertion at T[past]

In the last step, Vocabulary Insertion at T[past] takes place when T[past] is concatenated with the Root, making Root-determined allomorphy possible.

2.3.4 Synopsis

The generalizations (G1)–(G3) above were framed against the predictions of the $\mathbb{C}_0$ theory of allomorphy, which holds that contextual allomorphy is possible only for morphemes in inner cyclic domains. The fact that outer, noncyclic morphemes do in fact show Root-determined allomorphy, as seen in the English past tense and summarized in (G2), shows that the $\mathbb{C}_0$ theory is too restrictive. The empirical contrast that must be accounted for is that between outer noncyclic nodes covered by (G2), and outer cyclic nodes. By (G3), the latter do not see elements in the complement of an inner cyclic head.

    The defining hypotheses advanced above are (H1) (contextual allomorphy is restricted to the relation of concatenation) and (H2) (a node must be *active* in the cyclic sense in order to be visible to another node). How insertion interacts with cyclic Spell-Out is defined by assumptions (SO1)–(SO3). Finally, the concatenation-based theory requires the further assumption that Pruning takes place with some nodes that have zero exponents. As a whole, this approach is referred to as the $\mathbb{C}_1$-LIN theory, and it accounts for (G1)–(G3) in the manner outlined above.

2.4 Vocabulary Items

While cyclic structure plays a crucial role in the $\mathbb{C}_1$-LIN theory, the theory also makes claims about the forms that a VI can take. This section outlines further aspects of this component of the theory.

2.4.1 Specification

According to (H1), the only type of information that may appear in the contextual conditions of a VI is the relation of concatenation. Schematically, then, this means that the theory allows VIs of the types shown in (57):

(57) a. $[X] \leftrightarrow /y/ \ / \ [Y]^\frown \_\_$

 b. $[X] \leftrightarrow /y/ \ / \ \_\_^\frown [Y]$

To this point, I have employed binary concatenation statements. One additional question concerning the specification of VIs is whether there are cases in which a node shows contextual allomorphy that is determined by elements both to its right and to its left—that is, (58), which could be seen as abbreviating two binary statements (an alternative would be to redefine the relevant linear operator so that it is not binary):

(58) $[X] \leftrightarrow /y/ \ / \ [Y]^\frown\_\_^\frown[Z]$

One potential example of this type is found in the first person singular subject agreement morpheme in the Athabascan language Hupa (Golla 1970, 69ff.). This prefix typically appears as *W*-, as in (59a). However, when this morpheme is preceded by a perfective prefix, it surfaces as *e*-. This contextual allomorphy of 1sg is found only with active (i.e., eventive) verbs (59b). In statives, the default *W*-allomorph appears (59c):

(59) a. no:xoWtiW

   no-   x^{w}i- **W**-   ł-   tiW

   ADV OBJ 1SG.SUBJ TRANS put

   'I put him down.'

 b. na:se:ya?

   na- si-   e-   ya?

   ADV PERF 1SG go

   'I have gone about.'

 c. siWda

   si-   **W**- da

   PERF 1SG sit

   'I am sitting.'

On the assumption that eventivity or stativity is encoded in *v*, the distribution of the *e*- allomorph of 1sg requires reference to a preceding perfective morpheme and a following eventive *v*:

(60) $[1sg] \leftrightarrow$ e-/[perf]$^\frown\_\_^\frown v$[eventive]

 $[1sg] \leftrightarrow$ W-

Rules with conditioning factors to the left and the right of the element undergoing the change are seen elsewhere in PF; certain phonological rules have this property, for example. If more detailed investigations reveal that examples like the Hupa one are possible, then some formal modifications might be required for the operator that defines locality relevant for allomorphy. Alternatively, it could simply be the case that conjoined concatenation statements are visible for the purposes of Vocabulary Insertion.

Another question to consider is what kinds of information can appear in the contextual conditions for a single VI. In particular, it can be asked whether a single VI could be specified so that it is inserted to the left of certain objects but to the right of other objects, as shown in (61):

(61) $[X] \leftrightarrow /x/ \mathbin{/} [Y]^\frown\_\_, \_\_^\frown[Z]$

This hypothetical VI is employed to the right of Y elements and to the left of Z elements. As far as can be determined at this point, this type of representation is consistent with the restrictions on Vocabulary Insertion hypothesized here, although I am not aware of any clear cases of this type.

2.4.2   Outward Sensitivity

Many of the above examples of allomorphy show what has been called *inward sensitivity*: an outer morpheme has its allomorphy determined by the properties of a morpheme that is structurally inside of it.[21] Morphemes may also show *outward-sensitive* contextual allomorphy, in which the properties of a structurally outer morpheme determine allomorph selection at an inner node.

As an illustration of this effect, consider the outward sensitivity of the Hungarian plural. The plural morpheme surfaces as *-(V)k* in unpossessed forms, but as *-((j)a)i-* when there is a following possessive morpheme:

(62) Hungarian plural possessive (Carstairs 1987, 165)

	Singular–1sg		Plural–1sg	
	Poss		*Poss*	
Singular		*Plural*		*Gloss*
ruha	ruhá-m	ruhá-k	ruha-ái-m	'dress'
kalap	kalap-om	kalap-ok	kalap-jai-m	'hat'
ház	ház-am	ház-ak	ház-ai-m	'house'

It is assumed that these nouns have the structure in (63):

(63) Structure

  $[[[_n \sqrt{\text{ROOT}} \; n] \; \text{pl}] \; \text{poss}]$

In the PF cycle in which the phonological forms of [pl] and [poss] are determined, the linearization procedure derives statements that concatenate these nodes prior to Vocabulary Insertion. If the Vocabulary of

Hungarian contains the following VIs, the correct results are derived (ignoring the conditions on the parenthesized components):

(64) [pl] ↔ -((j)a)i-/__⌢[poss]
     [pl] ↔ -(V)k

Different discussions of allomorphy have had different things to say about potential asymmetries between these types of sensitivities, beginning with the discussion by Carstairs (1987). Within the context of the "inside-out" type of Vocabulary Insertion that has been assumed in Distributed Morphology and some theories that precede it, certain predicted asymmetries are clear. For example, in such a theory an "inner" morpheme cannot have its allomorphy determined by *phonological* properties of an outer morpheme, since, by hypothesis, this outer morpheme has not yet undergone Vocabulary Insertion (see Bobaljik 2000 for additional discussion). Carstairs-McCarthy (2001, 2003) discusses some other possible differences.[22]

Cyclic derivation places further constraints on when outward sensitivity can occur. These predictions are outlined in section 2.6. The limited outward sensitivity allowed in the $\mathbb{C}_1$-LIN theory is particularly important in the light of globalist alternatives, which are examined in chapter 6.

2.5 Potential "Long-Distance" Effects

If the theory presented above is correct, contextual allomorphy is highly restricted in scope. Apparent cases of allomorphy that do not take place under linear adjacency in a cyclic domain must result from other phenomena. At least two different types of effects that can result in prima facie less local interactions must be considered.[23]

2.5.1 Contextual Allomorphy versus Impoverishment

The linear component of the $\mathbb{C}_1$-LIN theory is centered on concatenation. The concatenation operator plays a role in other domains as well; for example, it seems that many cases of postsyntactic affixation ("affixation under adjacency") can be treated in these terms (see Embick 2007b, following much earlier literature cited there). Other operations during the PF derivation are defined in terms of other relations of locality. In particular, it appears that *impoverishment* rules must be defined over larger structures, in terms of nonlinear conditions of locality.

An impoverishment rule is a rule that deletes the features on a node in a particular context. The result of this deletion in a theory in which

competition for insertion is determined by specificity is clear: a less specified (or default) VI applies to the impoverished node. This type of effect
has been discussed extensively since early research in the Distributed
Morphology framework (see Bonet 1991; Noyer 1997). A familiar example is the "spurious *se*" rule in Spanish: instead of the expected dative
clitic *le*, the "default" clitic *se* is inserted in the context of an accusative
clitic. This effect can be analyzed in terms of two steps: first, the features
otherwise responsible for the insertion of *l(e)* are deleted in the relevant
context; and, second, the language contains *s(e)* as a default for the clitic
node (see the works cited above and Halle and Marantz 1994 for some
discussion and illustration).

In a sense, the effects of impoverishment could look like allomorphy.
Impoverishment rules are employed when an "expected" exponent does
not surface in a particular context, and another exponent is found instead. Consider the Spanish example again. Rather than the otherwise
expected *l(e)* allomorph, the *s(e)* allomorph appears in a particular context. At this level of description, this is similar to contextual allomorphy,
where an expected exponent fails to occur as well. Here, however, the
similarities end. In impoverishment, the point is that a less specified VI
that already exists in the system is employed in a context in which a
more specified VI is expected. In contextual allomorphy, the situation is
reversed: a VI with contextual conditions on insertion is posited to block
the insertion of the expected or default VI for a certain environment.
Since contextual allomorphy and impoverishment differ in terms of
whether a more specified or less specified VI applies, it is to be expected
that, in the normal case, it will be clear whether one is dealing with the
contextual effects of impoverishment or the contextual effects associated
with allomorphy (special VIs).

In addition to these differences in terms of feature specification, there
appear to be locality differences between impoverishment and contextual
allomorphy as well. Investigation of impoverishment rules in Halle and
Marantz 1993 and subsequent work involves application of these rules in
cases that involve nonadjacent morphemes. One working hypothesis,
which relates directly to the main point of this section, is that impoverishment could give the effect of action at a distance for insertion by operating on nodes that occur within a cyclic domain (phase), whether or not
these nodes are concatenated; this position has been discussed by Alec
Marantz in unpublished work, with examples from Nimboran (see Inkelas 1993; Noyer 1998) and some other languages.

It is possible, then, that certain prima facie counterexamples to the adjacency-based theory of allomorphy do not in fact involve contextual allomorphy, but instead are cases of impoverishment.

2.5.2 Syntax: Features from Agree

An additional source of superficially long-distance interactions derives from certain assumptions about syntactic relations. Specifically, if it is assumed that the operation Agree (Chomsky 2000) applies between elements like v and T and other phrases in the clause (i.e., DPs), then the features of these phrases might be visible in a complex head in positions that are not necessarily where agreement morphemes (i.e., "Agr nodes") are found.

More concretely, it is standardly assumed that the head v in a transitive vP enters the relation of Agree with the object, while T enters into this relation with the external argument. In a typical "verb" for a hypothetical language, then, the complex head that is spelled out as the verb might, all other things being equal, have features of the object and the subject in v and T, respectively (the structure in (65) shows an Agr node adjoined to T for expository purposes as well):

(65) Verb: Features from Agree

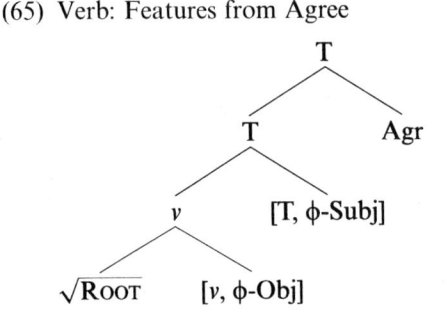

Without the ϕ-features from Agree on v and T as in (65), the predictions about allomorphy in a verb with the structure $\sqrt{\text{ROOT}}$-v-T-Agr are clear. The v head, for example, could not be affected by the person/number features of the subject associated with Agr.

On the other hand, if the features are placed (or valued) by Agree in the manner shown in (65), then some additional interactions are possible; this point is discussed in Adger, Béjar, and Harbour 2001, where it is proposed that at least some long-distance effects are the result of Agree (cf. also Bobaljik and Wurmbrand 2002). Importantly, these interactions are of a type that appears problematic for an adjacency-based theory, as discussed in detail by Bobaljik (2000).

More precisely, it would be possible for the v head to see features of the subject, by hypothesis valued on T; similarly, the T head might see the features of the object on v. This is clearly less restrictive than the theory without features distributed by Agree in this manner, and whether this range of interactions is found must be determined empirically (see chapter 3 for additional discussion).

2.6   Core Predictions of the $\mathbb{C}_1$-LIN Theory

Many of the key predictions of the $\mathbb{C}_1$-LIN theory were outlined in section 2.3. In a slightly expanded form that takes more subcases into consideration, these predictions are reiterated in this section. The predictions are organized according to inward versus outward sensitivity, and, within these categories, whether the node being spelled out is noncyclic or cyclic.

Beginning with inward sensitivity, the predictions for noncyclic heads are as follows:

(66) Noncyclic heads

   a. Noncyclic Y may show allomorphy determined by Root or noncyclic head α in cyclic x's complement in

   $\ldots \alpha]\, x]\, Y]$

   provided that α and Y are concatenated when Vocabulary Insertion occurs.

   b. Noncyclic Y may also have its allomorphy determined by x, or by another noncyclic W between x and Y in

   $\ldots x]\, Y]$ or

   $\ldots x]\, W]\, Y]$

   provided that Y and the element conditioning its allomorphy are concatenated when Vocabulary Insertion occurs.

   c. Noncyclic Y that is part of the edge$^+$ of cyclic y cannot have its allomorphy determined by (cyclic or noncyclic) α that is in the complement of inner cyclic x in

   $\ldots \alpha]\, x]\ldots y]\, Y]$

   under any circumstances.

For cyclic heads and inward sensitivity, the $\mathbb{C}_1$-LIN theory predicts the following:

(67) Cyclic heads

    a. Cyclic x may show allomorphy determined by Root or noncyclic
       α in its complement:

       $\ldots \alpha] \ldots x]$

       provided that α and x are concatenated when Vocabulary
       Insertion occurs.

    b. Cyclic y may not have its allomorphy determined by α in the
       complement of cyclic x in

       $\ldots \alpha] \, x] \, y]$

       under any circumstances.

    c. Cyclic y may have its allomorphy determined by cyclic x or by
       noncyclic W in

       $\ldots] \, x] \, W] \, y]$

       provided that y and the conditioning element are concatenated
       when Vocabulary Insertion occurs.

Turning to outward sensitivity, the predictions of the $\mathbb{C}_1$-LIN theory
are as follows, beginning with noncyclic heads:

(68) Noncyclic heads

    a. Noncyclic Z that is part of the edge$^+$ of cyclic x may have its
       allomorphy conditioned by noncyclic W in

       $\ldots x] \, Z] \, W]$

       provided that Z and W are concatenated when Vocabulary
       Insertion occurs.

    b. Noncyclic Z that is part of the edge$^+$ of cyclic x may not have
       its allomorphy conditioned by outer cyclic y in

       $\ldots x] \, Z] \, y]$

       under any circumstances.

The first prediction follows straightforwardly from the fact that noncyclic heads like Z and W are spelled out in the same cycle. The second
prediction follows from the assumption in (SO2) that when a cyclic domain headed by x is spelled out, the edge$^+$ material attached to x is
spelled out as well. In this cycle, y is not present and thus cannot condition the allomorphy of x's edge$^+$ heads.

For cyclic heads looking outward, the predictions are as follows:

(69) Cyclic heads

    a. Cyclic x may have its allomorphy determined by noncyclic Z in its edge^{+} in

       $\ldots x] Z]$

      provided that x and Z are concatenated when Vocabulary Insertion occurs.

    b. Cyclic x may not have its allomorphy determined by cyclic y in

       $\ldots x] \ldots y]$

      under any circumstances.

The predictions outlined in this section are examined and illustrated in many further examples in chapter 3. They are *core* predictions in the sense that they cover a number of the cases that appear to be empirically significant. Other predictions can be derived from the C_1-LIN theory, and some of these are identified as the discussion proceeds.

3 Applications and Implications

This chapter presents some case studies that are either motivations for or consequences of the $\mathbb{C}_1$-LIN theory. The initial discussion concentrates on the predictions that this theory makes concerning (linear) *intervention effects* and certain kinds of *domain effects*. These derive from the linear and the cyclic parts of the theory, respectively.

With respect to linear intervention, the theory predicts that if a node X is conditioned allomorphically by another node Y, a linearly intervening element W will cause X to default to an "unconditioned" alternant (or one conditioned by W), since Y is not visible to X. Some cases of this type are examined in section 3.1.

The predictions concerning domains take different forms. In the $\mathbb{C}_1$-LIN theory, a cyclic head triggers Spell-Out of a phase in its complement. This means that a cyclic head x and its attendant material undergo Vocabulary Insertion in the domain of another cyclic head, y, which is not itself spelled out in the cycle that it triggers. This aspect of the theory is shown to have implications in numerous domains in section 3.2. First, it follows from this theory that two cyclic heads cannot undergo Vocabulary Insertion in the same cycle. This rules out *fusion* of derivational morphemes of a particular type, as shown in section 3.2.1. Second, it is predicted that inner cyclic heads cannot see outer cyclic heads at the point where Vocabulary Insertion occurs. Some important case studies for this prediction are examined in section 3.2.2. Finally, it is predicted that while cyclic heads cannot see outer cyclic material, there could be allomorphy triggered by outer *non*cyclic material for such nodes. The latter set of predictions is illustrated with reference to *stem suppletion* in section 3.2.2.

Another set of questions is addressed in section 3.3, which examines complex systems of affixation where the same type of functional head is found in both inner (Root-attached) and outer (outside of other cyclic head) domains. This type of distribution was also seen in chapter 2, where it was shown that English nominals have a number of different Root-determined *n* allomorphs in the Root-attached domain, but take *-ing* across the board in gerunds. Further patterns of allomorphy in which the same type of head is attached in both inner and outer domains illustrate the cyclic aspect of the theory and raise many additional questions about allomorphy as well. For example, while *-ing* appears as the exponent of outer *n* in gerunds, there are also instances in which Root-attached *n* shows this allomorph. This raises the question of how such instances of identity across domains are represented in the Vocabulary.

A final set of questions, addressed in section 3.4, centers on some of the ways in which the C_1-LIN theory interacts with the phonological component of the grammar, paving the way for part II of this book. A preliminary part of this discussion shows what types of phonologically conditioned allomorphy are expected under the C_1-LIN theory. Further questions are addressed as well, concerning (i) the locality constraints on readjustment rules and (ii) how the phonology may "obscure" a local allomorphic relationship.

3.1 Illustrations I: Visibility and Linear Intervention

If contextual allomorphy is restricted to concatenation, then it should be possible to detect *linear* intervention effects: cases in which a head shows a special allomorph or allomorphs when it is adjacent to some conditioning head, but is realized a different way when another piece intervenes.

In the abstract, cases like this are important for two reasons. The first is that intervention of any sort promises to reveal much about locality, a point that is clear in many domains, both in syntax and in phonology. The second concerns the specific types of relations that are implicated for locality. To the extent that the intervention effects in contextual allomorphy are linear (as opposed to hierarchical) and do not involve changes in cyclic structure, they provide evidence for a theory in which linear relations play a defining role.

3.1.1 Adjacent Heads in Latin Perfects
The Latin perfect indicative shows unique agreement affixes for certain person/number combinations. These special agreement morphemes are not seen in any other part of the verbal system. Significantly, these endings are found only when the agreement morpheme is linearly adjacent to the Aspectual head associated with the perfect meaning.

The Latin tense/mood/aspect system includes both imperfect and perfect forms, which may be further specified for tense (present, past, future) and mood (indicative, subjunctive). The examples that I analyze here are all part of the perfect system. I assume that these are based on the structure in (1), a complex head that contains the head Asp[perf] and a T(ense) head (see Embick 2000 for some discussion; I put aside Voice and Mood (subjunctive) in this structure for simplicity):

(1) Structure

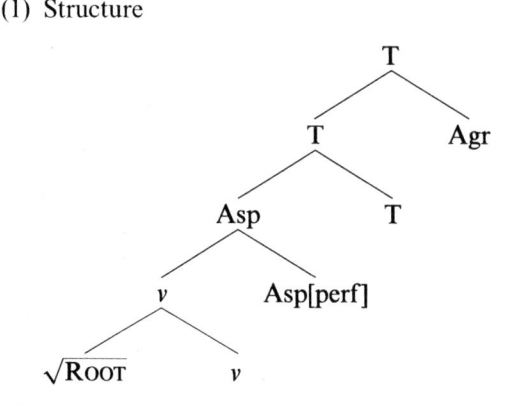

(2) Features of T

[pres] = present perfect
[past] = pluperfect
[fut] = future perfect

The features in (2) appear in the structure in (1) to create present perfects, pluperfects, and future perfects, respectively.

The allomorphy of interest is found in the person/number endings, which realize Agr in (1). As noted above, the perfect indicative shows unique endings not seen elsewhere in the verbal system; these are in the "Perfect indicative" column of (3), where the boldfaced agreement morphemes are different from those found in the other columns:

(3) Perfect forms of *amō* 'love'

P/N	Perfect indicative	Pluperfect indicative	Perfect subjunctive	Pluperfect subjunctive	Future perfect
1sg	amā-v-**ī**	amā-ve-ra-m	amā-ve-ri-m	amā-vi-s-se-m	amā-ve-r-ō
2sg	amā-v-**istī**	amā-ve-rā-s	amā-ve-rĭ-s	amā-vi-s-sē-s	amā-ve-rĭ-s
3sg	amā-vi-t	amā-ve-ra-t	amā-ve-ri-t	amā-vi-s-se-t	amā-ve-ri-t
1pl	amā-vi-mus	amā-ve-rā-mus	amā-ve-rĭ-mus	amā-vi-s-sē-mus	amā-ve-rĭ-mus
2pl	amā-v-**istis**	amā-ve-rā-tis	amā-ve-rĭ-tis	amā-vi-s-sē-tis	amā-ve-rĭ-tis
3pl	amā-v-**ērunt**	amā-ve-ra-nt	amā-ve-ri-nt	amā-vi-s-se-nt	amā-ve-ri-nt

Some additional comments are in order concerning the forms in (3), with respect to the assumed segmentation and the operation of phonological rules.

The segmentation shown in (3) assumes that the Asp[perf] morpheme has the phonological exponent -*vi*. This -*vi* exponent is the default for this head, which also shows other Root-determined allomorphs. In particular, the perfects of other verbs show -*si* and -*i* allomorphs of Asp[perf], as shown in (4) (first person plural forms are used for clarity):

(4) Asp[perf] exponents

    a. -*si* in (e.g.) *scrip-si-mus* 'we wrote'

    b. -*i* in (e.g.) *vēn-i-mus* 'we came'

Some important patterns that center on the allomorphy of the Asp[perf] head are discussed in chapter 6.

Linearly following the Asp[perf] morpheme in many of the forms in (3) are morphemes associated with tense, or tense and mood in the case of subjunctives. These morphemes intervene linearly between the Asp[perf] piece and the final morpheme of the word, which is the Agreement (Agr) morpheme. So, for example, the pluperfect indicative is broken down as follows (*TH = theme vowel*):

(5) am -ā -ve   -rā -mus
    love TH Asp[perf] T   AGR
    'we had loved'

The appearance of Tense morphemes between Asp[perf] and Agr occurs in almost all of the tenses shown in (3). In the present indicative, however, there is no Tense morpheme between Asp[perf] and Agr; see below.[1]

The effects of a number of phonological rules can be seen throughout the forms in (3). Full discussion and justification of these rules can be found in Embick and Halle, in preparation; for present purposes, I will merely outline the relevant processes.

One rule whose effects are seen in many of the forms in (3) affects the vocalic component of -*vi*. Specifically, the /i/ component of Asp[perf] -*vi* is deleted when it precedes a vowel. This rule produces, for example, surface *amā-v-ī* from underlying *amā-vi-ī*.

In addition, underlyingly long vowels are shortened in syllables that are closed by certain consonants. For example, the underlying -*rā* morpheme of the pluperfect surfaces as -*ra* in the 1sg and 3sg forms, where it appears in syllables closed by /m/ and /t/, respectively.

There is also an alternation between /i/ and /e/ in the Asp[perf] morpheme. This is the effect of a *Lowering* rule, which is formulated as follows:[2]

(6) Lowering

$$/i/ \rightarrow /e/ \, /\text{\_\_}/r/$$

This rule accounts for the fact that the Asp[perf] head surfaces as -*vi* in the pluperfect subjunctive, for example, but as -*ve* in the pluperfect indicative, where the /i/ immediately precedes the /r/ of the Tense exponent.

When the system of Latin verbal morphology is considered beyond the perfect, there is motivation for other morphophonological rules beyond those just mentioned. An important one is *Rhotacism*, which changes /s/ to /r/ intervocalically:

(7) Rhotacism

$$/s/ \rightarrow /r/ \, /V\text{\_\_}V$$

This rule accounts for a number of alternations between /s/ and /r/ found in Latin verbs. For example, the infinitival suffix surfaces as -*se* with the athematic verb *es-se*, but as -*re* with other verbs like *amā-re*. With the Rhotacism rule (7), it is possible to derive these two surface realizations from a single -*se* infinitival exponent.

With Rhotacism, the Tense exponents in (3) can be treated as in (8):

(8) Pluperfect indicative: -*sā*
    Perfect subjunctive: -*sī*
    Pluperfect subjunctive: -*s*, -*sē*
    Future perfect: -*si*

The effects of Rhotacism and the general set of assumptions just outlined are seen in various examples from Latin presented throughout this book. See also Embick and Halle, in preparation, for extensive discussion of this point and related ones.

In short, the structure presented in (1) underlies the different forms in (3), which are subjected to the morphological and phonological processes outlined immediately above.

Returning to the question of agreement allomorphy, it can be seen in (3) that the perfect indicative shows more than one "special" agreement allomorph. For example, 1sg agreement is typically -*ō* or -*m* in Latin, but in the perfect indicative it is -*ī*; 2sg agreement is typically -*s*, but in the perfect indicative it is -*istī*; and similar considerations extend to 2pl and 3pl agreement. The agreement endings seen with the other perfect forms in (3) are not unique to perfects; they are found in other parts of the verbal system, as in the presents and imperfects in (9):

(9) Present and imperfect indicative of *amō*

P/N	Present	Imperfect
1sg	am-ō	amā-ba-m
2sg	amā-s	amā-bā-s
3sg	ama-t	amā-ba-t
1pl	amā-mus	amā-bā-mus
2pl	amā-tis	amā-bā-tis
3pl	ama-nt	amā-ba-nt

In the perfects in (3), it is clear that the special allomorphs appear when the Agr node is linearly adjacent to the perfect morpheme (see also Carstairs 1987; Carstairs-McCarthy 2001, 2003; Adger, Béjar, and Harbour 2003; Lieber (1992) discusses this same point, with reference to (the absence of) percolation in perfect forms). A glossed segmentation showing this is provided in (10), for the first person singular perfect indicative and pluperfect; the underlying form of the exponents is shown prior to the application of the phonological rules discussed above:

(10) a. amāvī
        am -ā -vi -Ø -ī
        love TH ASP T AGR
        'I loved'
    b. amāverām
        am -ā -ve -sā -m
        love TH ASP T AGR
        'I had loved'

The Tense node in the perfect indicative is always null. Whenever an overt Tense morpheme (or overt Tense and Mood morphemes) intervenes between Agr and Asp[perf], the "normal" exponents of Agr—those that surface in (9)—are found.

The linear nature of this effect is important in comparison with exclusively cyclic and hierarchical theories of allomorphic locality. Beginning with the former, there is no reason to think that the perfect indicative differs from the other perfects in terms of its cyclic structure. According to standard definitions of cyclic domains, Agr is in the same cycle as Asp[perf] in both the perfect indicative and, for example, the pluperfect indicative. Even if T were assumed (against many current working hypotheses) to be a phase-defining head, the relevant differences could not be stated. Each type of perfect listed here has a T head, as far as the syntax goes. Thus, if the realization of the Agr nodes for the perfect had a cyclic conditioning environment, we should find identical agreement endings -ī, -istī, and so on, in all of the different types of perfects in (3), contrary to fact.

Similarly, it is difficult to see how, under a hierarchical notion of "command," Agr would be in a local environment with the Asp[perf] head only in the perfect indicative. It might be possible to stipulate a condition on intervening nodes, but this only recapitulates the intuition that the effect is linear; it makes no novel predictions that can be tested.

To account for the special allomorphs of Agr, I propose that in the perfect indicative, the head T[pres] has a zero exponent and that it is pruned.[3] The VIs inserting the special agreement forms may then be specified for a contextual condition where Asp[perf] is concatenated with Agr, as illustrated with the following VIs:[4]

(11) Vocabulary items: A fragment of agreement in Latin

    1sg ↔ -ī   /Asp[perf]⁀__
    2sg ↔ -istī   /Asp[perf]⁀__
    2pl ↔ -istis /Asp[perf]⁀__
    3pl ↔ -ērunt /Asp[perf]⁀__
    1sg ↔ -ō
    2sg ↔ -s
    2pl ↔ -tis
    3pl ↔ -nt

In the perfect indicative, the Agr node is concatenated with Asp[perf], so that the "special" VIs in (11) win over their counterparts that are not specified contextually in this way. In all of the other parts of the perfect system, there are overt exponents for T. These nodes are not pruned in the way that T[pres] is. Thus, the local relationship with Asp[perf] is not found, and Agr defaults to the VIs employed elsewhere in the system.[5]

3.1.2   Some Latin Themes

Another type of effect that implicates linear adjacency is seen in Latin *theme vowels*. I assume that Theme morphemes are, in general, "ornamental" pieces of morphology, items that are apparently relevant for morphological well-formedness, but not part of syntax; these are *dissociated* morphemes in the terminology of Embick 1997. Latin verbs show the different theme vowels in (12):

(12) Conjugations and theme vowels

Conjugation	Example	Theme vowel
I	laud-ā-mus	-ā-
II	mon-ē-mus	-ē-
III	dūc-i-mus	-i-
III(i)	cap-i-mus	-i-
IV	aud-ī-mus	-ī-

Except for the -i- theme posited with conjugation III verbs like *dūcō*, this is a relatively uncontroversial view of the theme system. It suffices for the purposes of this discussion that the theme of verbs like *dūcō* be a short -i- that is different from that found with III(i) "-io" verbs like *capiō*.

The fact that a particular Root belongs to a particular conjugation class—for example, that *aud-ī-re* 'hear' belongs to conjugation IV with theme vowel -ī- as opposed to some other conjugation—is not predictable. A natural assumption about diacritic declension or conjugation class features with this property is that they are specified as properties of individual Roots, as shown in (13):

(13) $\sqrt{\text{AUD}}_{[IV]}$

The feature [IV] is neither a semantically interpretable feature nor an uninterpretable feature in the sense familiar from syntactic theory. Rather, it is a diacritic with effects that are seen in the PF derivation, where it determines the Spell-Out of the theme vowel.

I assume with Oltra-Massuet (1999) that the theme vowels are realizations of a Th(eme) position that is added to *v*, as in (14b):[6]

(14) a. Input   b. Th added

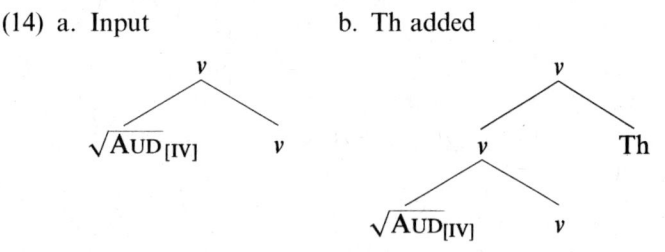

When the object in (14b) is linearized prior to Vocabulary Insertion, the Th node and the Root are concatenated, after the (null) *v* is pruned. The Th node is in the context of an element with the feature [IV] and is spelled out with the following VI:[7]

(15) Th ↔ -ī-/[IV]⌢__

The cases in which locality considerations play a role in the theme system involve derivations where *v* has an overt exponent. For example, the conjugation III(i) Root *cap-i-ō* 'take, seize', which takes the short *-i-*theme vowel, appears in a "desiderative" form *capessō* 'take/seize eagerly', where the Root is suffixed with the desiderative exponent *-ess*. This exponent can be treated as a realization of a type of *v*, *v*[des]. Notably, a verb with the exponent *-ess* is always inflected as a verb of conjugation III: 1sg *cap-ess-ō*, 1pl *cap-ess-i-mus*, and so on. This suggests that this exponent is itself inherently specified for the class feature [III]:

(16) ess[III]

When the Root √CAP appears with other types of *v*, whose exponent is -Ø, the feature visible to the Th node is a feature of the Root itself, as in (17). However, this is not the case when *-ess* appears as the exponent of *v*[des], as shown in (18):

(17) Lower structure for *capimus*

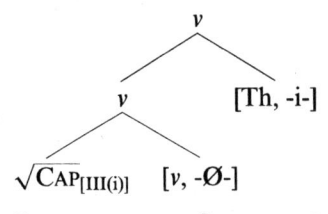

(18) Lower structure for *capessō*

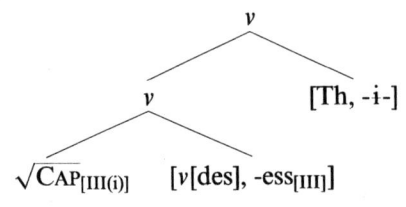

That is, the fact that the Th position attached to *v* sees the [III] feature of the exponent *-ess* in (18) and not the [III(i)] feature of √CAP is a matter of locality: the Th head sees the feature of the terminal that it is concatenated with, which in (18) is the [III] feature of *-ess*[III] and not the [III(i)] feature of √CAP[III(i)]. This is a further illustration of linear intervention.

3.2   Illustrations II: Cyclicity and Domain Effects

The general principle (SO1) of cyclic Spell-Out employed in the theory of chapter 2 holds that a cyclic head triggers Spell-Out of cyclic domains in its complement. One consequence of this theory is the Domain Corollary, repeated in (19):

(19) Domain Corollary

Cyclic head x is not present in the PF cycle of computation that is triggered by Merge of x. Thus, x is *not* subjected to Vocabulary Insertion (and thus cannot undergo any phonological processing) until the next cycle of Spell-Out, when it is in the *domain* of another cyclic head.

Two important sets of empirical predictions stem from the Domain Corollary. First, cyclic x cannot *fuse* with outer, cyclic y. Second, cyclic x cannot be sensitive to outer, cyclic y for purposes of Vocabulary Insertion; however, x can show allomorphy determined by outer, noncyclic heads in its domain. These predictions are examined in turn in the following sections.

3.2.1 No Fusion in "Derivational" Morphology

It is assumed above that category-defining heads are cyclic. These heads are typical derivational morphemes, in the sense that they categorize what they attach to. The Domain Corollary (19) holds that cyclic heads are always subjected to Vocabulary Insertion in different cycles. In this way, the theory accounts for the observation that there are no *portmanteaux* or *fused* affixes in derivational morphology (e.g., Anderson 1992, 76, citing David Perlmutter, pers. comm.).[8] While cases of fusion are widely attested in other domains (e.g., case/number morphemes, fusion of agreement and tense), the behavior of category-defining heads seems to be strikingly different, and, importantly, this difference follows from a theory with cyclic Spell-Out.

An operation of *Fusion* that combines two pieces into one prior to Vocabulary Insertion is argued for in Halle and Marantz 1993. Fusion of morphemes occurs when the basic morphosyntactic structure involves two separate nodes X and Y. Under particular circumstances—that is, when X and Y contain particular features—these nodes can be fused into one object. A Fusion rule is schematized in (20), where α and β are features of X and Y:

(20) Fusion

$$[_X\ \alpha]\frown[_Y\ \beta] \to [_{X/Y}\ \alpha,\beta]$$

Rules of this type must precede Vocabulary Insertion. The output of Fusion yields one piece, so that Vocabulary Insertion inserts only one exponent.

In the $\mathbb{C}_1$-LIN theory (more generally, in any theory with (SO1)), the absence of fusion with cyclic heads is a consequence of how Spell-Out works. To see this, consider the structure in (21), which consists of a Root and two category-defining heads x and y:

(21) Structure

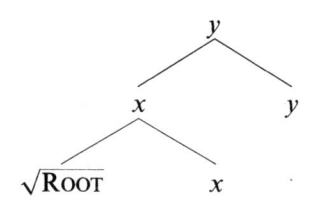

When x is merged syntactically, it triggers Spell-Out of phases in its domain. In the cycle of Spell-Out that is triggered when y is merged, the same principle causes Spell-Out of the phase head x and attendant material in the domain of y. Thus, when x undergoes Vocabulary Insertion in this cycle, y is not present. Only later, in a cycle triggered by other (i.e., outer) material, is the head y spelled out. Since x must undergo Vocabulary Insertion in a PF cycle in which y is not present, the theory makes fusion of cyclic heads with each other impossible.[9]

3.2.2 Interactions with Multiple Cyclic Heads

Another set of predictions of the $\mathbb{C}_1$-LIN theory is seen in structures that contain more than one cyclic head: $[[\sqrt{\text{ROOT}}\ x]\ y]$. Chapter 2 shows in detail how x, but not y, can show allomorphy conditioned by the Root, or material in the complement of x, in this kind of configuration.

In the type of case just mentioned, the allomorphic sensitivity goes in the "inward" direction. As also discussed in chapter 2, the theory makes further predictions concerning "outward" sensitivity of heads. In particular, while y may show allomorphy determined by x, in $[[\sqrt{\text{ROOT}}\ x]\ y]$ the reverse is not true: an inner cyclic head like x may not have its allomorphy conditioned by an outer cyclic head. This prediction derives from the assumption that it is cyclic domains in the complement of cyclic heads that are spelled out. In $[[\sqrt{\text{ROOT}}\ x]\ y]$, the elements that are spelled out when y is merged are in the cyclic domain headed by x, or the nodes attached to it (any edge$^+$ material that might be present). In this cycle, the head x is subjected to Vocabulary Insertion. Crucially, because y is not present in this cycle, the head x cannot show outward sensitive contextual allomorphy to y.

It is possible to find prima facie counterexamples to this prediction. Section 3.2.2.1 looks at an example from Hindi in which a "causative" morpheme appears to show outward sensitivity to another causative head. If these heads were both cyclic (i.e., both v), this would be contrary to the predictions just reviewed. However, there is an alternative analysis in which no outward sensitivity of this type is required.

While outward sensitivity of a cyclic head to another cyclic head is not possible, it is possible for a cyclic head x to have its allomorphy conditioned by an outer, noncyclic head that is attached to x's cyclic domain. This phenomenon is illustrated in section 3.2.2.2 with reference to *suppletion*.

3.2.2.1 Hindi Causatives Certain patterns of allomorphy in Hindi causative constructions look like a case in which an inner cyclic head sees an outer cyclic head for purposes of allomorphy. In particular, a head that shows Root-determined allomorphy between -*aa* and -*Ø* in transitives invariably shows the -*aa* allomorph in a type of causative construction. If this head were a cyclic head—that is, v—then this would look like a case in which a v head has its allomorphy determined by an outer ("causative") v head. However, I argue below that the head showing -*aa* and -*Ø* is not in fact cyclic v; it is a noncyclic Voice head.

The discussion of Hindi here draws on unpublished work by Bhatt and Embick (2003). The head that shows the relevant allomorphic pattern appears in different verbal structures. One is a transitivity alternation of the causative/inchoative type. From a morphological point of view, Hindi has two types of transitivity alternation, shown in (22):

(22) Intransitive/Transitive alternations

	Intransitive	Transitive	Gloss
a.	bãṭ-naa	bããṭ-naa	'be divided/divide'
	chhil-naa	chhiil-naa	'be peeled/peel'
	ḍhal-naa	ḍhaal-naa	'shape/sculpt'
	ghir-naa	gher-naa	'be surrounded/surround'
b.	bach-naa	bach-aa-naa	'be saved/save'
	chamak-naa	chamk-aa-naa	'shine'
	chhip-naa	chhip-aa-naa	'hide'
	gal-naa	gal-aa-naa	'melt'

In the intransitive, neither the (22a) type nor the (22b) type has an overt exponent.[10] In the transitive, the two classes are different: in the (22a) cases, there is a head that is pronounced -Ø, whereas in the (22b) cases, this head is pronounced -aa. An important question is what type of head shows the -aa/-Ø alternation. The analysis I present takes it to be a *Voice* head associated with agentivity (see Kratzer 1994, 1996; Pylkkänen 2002). The Voice head is a noncyclic head that appears outside of the *v* head that verbalizes these Roots. The structure for transitives is thus as in (23), where Voice[ag] is the head that introduces agentive semantics:

(23) Transitive structure

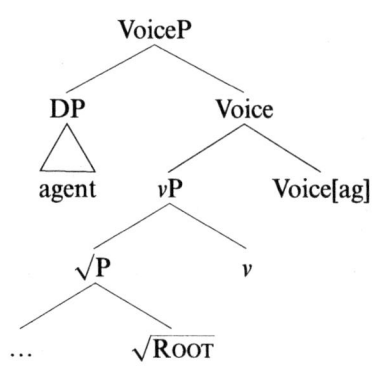

Each of the classes in (22) contains a number of verbs, and membership in one class or the other seems to be idiosyncratic, although there are some tendencies in terms of the semantics of the Roots in each class. Part of the analysis of Voice allomorphy must therefore take this Root-specific contextual factor into account, by having the Voice[ag] head spelled out as either -aa or -Ø depending on the Root it is attached to.

Another component of Voice allomorphy is seen in what can be called the *indirect causative*. This is a structure that, to a first approximation, is a type of sentential causative:

(24) zamiindaar-ne (ḍakaitõ-se)   makaan   jal-**vaa**
     landlord-ERG bandits-INST house.MASC burn-CAUS
     diy-aa.
     give-PERF.MASC
     'The landlord had the house burned (by the bandits).'

Syntactico-semantically, this kind of causative has a causative *v* (with its own Voice head) that takes a passive VoiceP as its complement. Morphologically, the indirect causative shows the -*vaa* component that is boldfaced in (24).

The *-aa* and *-Ø* class verbs show an interesting behavior in the indirect causative, which is seen in comparison with the transitive. These verbs uniformly take *-vaa* in the indirect causative, not *-aa-vaa*—even the ones that take *-aa* in the transitive (i.e., the verbs in (25b)):

(25) Forms of *-vaa* causatives

	Intransitive	*Transitive*	*Indirect causative*
a.	bãṭ-naa	bããṭ-naa	bãṭ-vaa-naa
	chhil-naa	chhiil-naa	chhil-vaa-naa
	ḍhal-naa	ḍhaal-naa	ḍhal-vaa-naa
	gir-naa	ger-naa	gir-vaa-naa
b	bach-naa	bach-aa-naa	bach-vaa-naa
	chamak-naa	chamk-aa-naa	chamɔk-vaa-naa
	chhip-naa	chhip-aa-naa	chhip-vaa-naa
	gal-naa	gal-aa-naa	gal-vaa-naa

The realization of *-vaa* across the board is somewhat unexpected, in the sense that the lower Voice[ag] head that is realized as *-aa* with the transitive forms in (25b) does not appear when this agentive is embedded under the causative structure. That is, if the indirect causative is formed by simply adding to the transitive a *v* head (or a *v* head and a Voice head) that is pronounced *-vaa*, then we expect to find **bach-aa-vaa-naa* and the like, but this never happens.

The alternation between *-aa* and *-Ø* in transitives and indirect causatives highlights the question of "outward sensitivity" raised at the beginning of this section. This might appear to be a case of outward sensitivity of cyclic heads, such that a *v* head that is pronounced *-aa* in transitives is pronounced *-Ø* when it is in the complement of another *v* head. However, if *-aa* realizes a Voice[ag] head in transitives, as suggested above with reference to (23), the interaction is not between two cyclic heads. Rather, *-aa* does not appear in indirect causatives because the VoiceP in these constructions is passive, not active. This passive head—Voice[ag]†—licenses agentive semantics but not an external argument (see Embick 2004b); crucially, it has its own allomorph that beats both *-aa* and *-Ø*.

Additional details of this analysis involve a closer look at the *-vaa* that appears in indirect causatives. According to the analysis outlined in Bhatt and Embick 2003, *-aa* does not surface in the (25b) cases because the *-vaa* morpheme is actually two morphemes: a *-v* Spell-Out of the lower "passive" Voice head, Voice[ag]†, along with the *-aa* exponent seen elsewhere in the system for the higher Voice[ag] of the indirect causative. This analysis is shown in (26):[11]

(26) Indirect causative

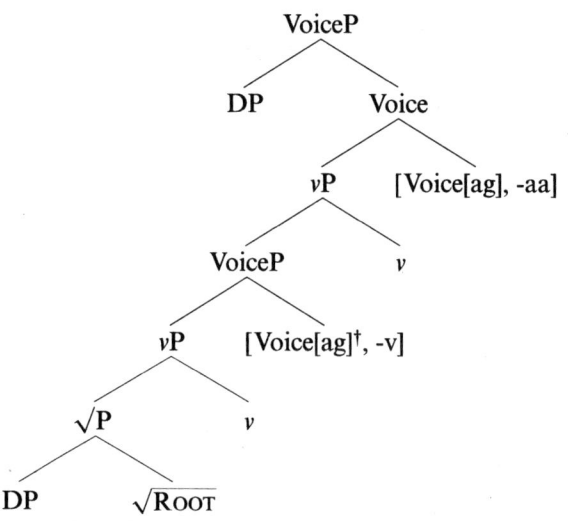

In the derivation of the indirect causative (26), a first cyclic domain is created when the lower v is merged with the Root. This v head has the passive Voice[ag]† merged with it. When the second v is merged, it triggers Spell-Out of cyclic domains in its complement. In this cycle of PF, the lower v is realized with a null exponent, and the head Voice[ag]† has -v inserted.

In the subsequent PF cycle in which the outer v and its Voice head undergo Vocabulary Insertion, -Ø is inserted at v, and -aa for Voice[ag]. The fact that -aa is inserted invariably in this context follows from locality: there is no possibility for Root-determined allomorphy at this head, because the Root is cyclically inaccessible. Thus, the default -aa appears.

With the following VIs, then, the distributions described above are accounted for:[12]

(27) Spell-Out of Voice heads in Hindi

Voice[ag]† ↔ -v
Voice[ag] ↔ -Ø /LIST1⌒__ (LIST1 = Roots in the null class)
Voice[ag] ↔ -aa

In short, there are two components to the analysis. First, the analysis of causativization involves two heads, v and Voice; the overt morphemes seen in Hindi are realizations of the latter. Second, the VI with -v beats the VIs with -aa and -Ø in the indirect causative context, because the head that is being spelled out is passive.[13]

3.2.2.2 Domain Effects in Stem Suppletion   The $\mathbb{C}_1$-LIN theory allows certain types of outward sensitivity but disallows others. This aspect of the theory is important in cases of *stem suppletion* of the type often associated with extremely common verbs like *be* and *go*. Suppletion is, of course, highly irregular, and it is moreover not necessarily a uniform concept. Any systematic investigation of suppletion would have to address a number of issues far beyond the scope of this discussion.[14] However, it appears that in a core set of cases, a number of strong predictions can be made about the factors that could trigger stem suppletion.

Many instances of suppletion are found with elements that could plausibly be the types of morphemes that show contextual allomorphy. Canonical cases such as *be* and *go* are *light verbs*: members of the functional vocabulary. Marantz (1995) and others have emphasized that in a theory with some late insertion, restricting suppletion to the functional vocabulary is an important desideratum.[15] In this type of theory, suppletion is simply contextual allomorphy, but with "freestanding" verbs and the like rather than with affixed morphemes. Thus, the fact that the element being realized is a verb—a kind of *v*—makes it more noticeable than other types of allomorphy, but the mechanisms for handling these effects, involving competing VIs, are the same whether the object in question is an affix or a "stem."

In the present context, it is of course expected that suppletion in this sense, as the result of contextual allomorphy, should be subject to the locality conditions expressed in the $\mathbb{C}_1$-LIN theory. One illustration of this point, which implicates the Domain Corollary (19) as well, is seen with the suppletion of the light verb *go*, which is the realization of a functional head that I abbreviate as v_{go}. The VIs that apply to this morpheme are given in (28), where, crucially, the first makes reference to the T[past] morpheme:

(28) $v_{go} \leftrightarrow$ went$/$__^T[past]
       $v_{go} \leftrightarrow$ go

With respect to the Domain Corollary, the important point is that v_{go}, a cyclic head, cannot be spelled out phonologically in the cycle that it induces. This is clear from the fact that if Vocabulary Insertion applied to v_{go} itself in the cycle determined by that head, then v_{go} would be spelled out before being merged with T, and suppletion of *v* conditioned by T would be impossible. If, on the other hand, v_{go} is not itself subjected to Vocabulary Insertion until a later cycle, this type of pattern can be handled straightforwardly.

The general prediction of the C_1-LIN theory is that a functional head can have its allomorphy determined by linearly adjacent outer material up to the next cyclic domain. The schema in (29) illustrates this point and some others:

(29) $\ldots x]\ W]\ y]$

A cyclic head x showing suppletion could be sensitive to the presence of W. However, x could not be sensitive to phonological properties of W, on the assumption that Vocabulary Insertion proceeds from the inside out. Beyond W, x could show no sensitivity to outer cyclic y at all; y is not present when x undergoes insertion. In well-studied cases of suppletion, the first part of this prediction appears to be correct. That is, the factors that condition stem suppletion of light verbs like English *go* and *be* are morphosyntactic: either tense features, person/number features, or a combination of tense and person/number features condition the allomorphy of these v heads.

In more complicated cases, additional questions arise. For example, according to the formulation in chapter 2, the Pruning rule that eliminates nodes with -∅ exponents follows Vocabulary Insertion. For Vocabulary Insertion at a light verb v in a syntactic structure [[v T] Agr], it should therefore be expected that v can supplete only on the basis of T's features, and not those of Agr.

Questions along these lines arise with the behavior of Latin *esse* 'be'. In the present indicative, (30a), there is an alternation between *es-* and *su-* depending on the person and number of the subject. In other tenses, suppletion of *esse* is not affected by person and number features. In the past and future tenses, (30b,c), the stem *es-* appears (with the /s/ rhotacized intervocalically to yield surface /r/); and in the perfect tenses, (30d–f), the stem is *fu-*:

(30) Indicative: *esse*

	a.	b.	c.	d.	e.	f.
						Future
	Present	*Imperfect*	*Future*	*Perfect*	*Pluperfect*	*perfect*
1sg	su-m	er-a-m	er-ō	fu-ī	fu-e-ra-m	fu-e-r-ō
2sg	es	er-ā-s	er-i-s	fu-istī	fu-e-rās	fu-e-ri-s
3sg	es-t	er-a-t	er-i-t	fu-i-t	fu-e-ra-t	fu-e-ri-t
1pl	su-mus	er-ā-mus	er-i-mus	fu-i-mus	fu-e-rā-mus	fu-e-ri-mus
2pl	es-tis	er-ā-tis	er-i-tis	fu-istis	fu-e-rā-tis	fu-e-ri-tis
3pl	su-nt	er-a-nt	er-unt	fu-ē-r-unt	fu-e-ra-nt	fu-e-ri-nt

Some aspects of (30) are straightforward. As discussed in section 3.1, the perfect tenses in Latin contain a head Asp[perf] between v and Tense. Clearly, then, the *fu*- allomorph is inserted in the context of this perfect head. Moreover, it appears that the *es*- stem is the default:

(31) $v_{be} \leftrightarrow fu/\_\frown Asp[perf]$

$\quad\;\; v_{be} \leftrightarrow es$

This leaves the *su*- forms, which appear to be conditioned by person and number features. The question is this: if the structure of these forms is $[[v_{be}\ T]\ Agr]$, and the Tense node cannot be pruned until it undergoes Vocabulary Insertion, how can v_{be} be sensitive to person/number features?

Two kinds of answer can be given to this question. One possibility was outlined at the end of chapter 2. It was noted there that in a theory with Agree, person and number features of the subject are present on the Tense node. Possibly, then, what v_{be} is sensitive to is valued ϕ-features on T, and not features on the Agr node per se. In this particular case, the Spell-Out of v_{be} would have to be made sensitive to certain ϕ-features, and moreover, only on present tense T[pres]. The restriction to this particular head is forced by the fact that the past and future tenses do not show any variation in v_{be}'s shape (30b,c) driven by person and number.

A variant of this solution is that v_{be} and T[pres] undergo Fusion when T[pres] has certain ϕ-feature values (i.e., in those cases where the stem is *su*-). Then the VIs for v_{be} would be as follows:

(32) $[v_{be},\ T] \leftrightarrow su$

$\quad\;\; [v_{be}] \leftrightarrow fu/\_\frown Asp[perf]$

$\quad\;\; [v_{be}] \leftrightarrow es$

If Fusion combines v_{be} only with T[pres] with 1sg, 1pl, and 3pl features, then *su*- is inserted into the correct environments by the first VI in (32). Overall, though, this type of account deals with person/number-driven suppletion without ordering problems related to Pruning.[16]

A second type of analysis is based on the general idea that present indicative tense (T[pres]) plays no role in Latin morphology. As discussed in Embick and Halle, in preparation, this might be the result of a general "radical" Pruning rule that applies early in PF derivations involving T[pres], eliminating this node from the representation. According to this account, v_{be} would be adjacent to Agr in the present indicative, and the *su*- allomorph would be sensitive to the person/number features on the Agr node.

Determining the viability of these options in the case of Latin *esse* and similar examples raises significant questions that could be addressed in a more sustained study of suppletion. For present purposes, the important point is that the C_1-LIN theory narrows down considerably the kinds of information that are available for outward-sensitive allomorphy. While there are many cases in which suppletion is conditioned by outer morphemes (and perhaps their features), there are no cases in which the phonology of outer morphemes, or the output phonology of a particular form, plays a role in conditioning suppletion. This behavior is expected on a localist theory like the one presented here, which restricts the number of factors that can play a role in allomorphy. Some important consequences of this view are examined in greater detail in chapter 6, where further aspects of suppletion are considered with reference to the predictions of globalist theories.

3.2.3 French Prepositions and Determiners: A Question about Cyclic Heads

On the general theme of how different types of heads interact with each other, one question for a cyclic theory is how category-defining cyclic heads like *n* and *v* relate to other domains that are hypothesized to be cyclic on syntactic grounds, such as CP and DP. That is, if Spell-Out targets phases headed by category-defining heads, does it also target DPs and PPs? The general set of questions that is at play here can be seen in the interaction of prepositions and determiners in French, where different assumptions about which heads define Spell-Out domains force different types of analyses.[17]

As discussed in Embick 2007b, two PF processes in French interact in a way that appears to implicate cyclic Spell-Out. The first process is seen with (singular) definite articles, which exhibit a close phonological union with following vowel-initial elements:

(33) a. le chat 'the cat' (masc)
          la mère 'the mother' (fem)
      b. l'arbre 'the tree' (masc); *le arbre
          l'abeille 'the bee' (fem); *la abeille

I refer to this process as *Article Cliticization*, even though it might be more general; it operates under linear adjacency and is sensitive to the phonology of the target. *Article Cliticization* is a rule of *local dislocation*, which adjoins definite D to vowel-initial elements when they are concatenated (see (35a)).

The second process is one that creates what are sometimes called "fused" prepositions/determiners. Such forms are found with the prepositions *à* and *de* and with the masculine and plural definite articles:

(34) Examples of prepositions and determiners

		"Fused"	*Separate*	*Gloss*
a.	(Fem)	*	de la mère	'of the mother'
		*	à la mère	'to the mother'
		aux mères	*à les mères	'to the mothers'
b.	(Masc)	du chat	*de le chat	'of the cat'
		au chat	*à le chat	'to the cat'
		aux chats	*à les chats	'to the cats'

The use of the term *fused* here is descriptive, and not technical. The analysis of this effect could posit either one or two VIs in *du*; only the former case would involve Fusion in the technical sense. These matters are clarified below.

Given the patterns in (34), there must be a rule of *Preposition-Determiner Affixation* that affixes certain prepositions to masculine and plural definite determiners.

The two rules discussed above are stated in (35), in a formulation that treats each as an instance of local dislocation:[18]

(35) PF rules: French

    a. Article Cliticization
    $\text{D[def]} \frown X \rightarrow \text{[D[def][X]]}$, X V-initial
    b. P-D Affixation
    $P^+ \frown \text{D[def]}^+ \rightarrow [P^+[D^+]]$
    where $^+$ is a diacritic for the particular terminals that are subject to this process

These two rules interact in cases where either process could apply: namely, with masculine nouns that are vowel-initial. In such examples, Article Cliticization applies, and P-D Affixation thus does not apply:

(36) a. de l'arbre
    b. *du arbre

As discussed in Embick 2007b, the fact that Article Cliticization is found here appears to be natural in a cyclic theory: specifically, the correct results are derived if the DP is spelled out prior to the cycle in which P and D are processed together.

Implementing a cyclic analysis in detail implicates the questions posed at the beginning of this section, concerning which nodes constitute cyclic domains. The first stage in the analysis is a structure, (37), in which D is merged with the nP:

(37) Stage 1

DP
├── D
└── nP
    ├── n
    │   ├── √ROOT
    │   └── n
    └── ...

In determining how this DP is spelled out, whether P is a cyclic or noncyclic node is critical; possible analyses of the interaction of the rules in (35) differ depending on whether or not P is present in the same PF cycle in which D undergoes Vocabulary Insertion.

Before addressing further the status of P, we must look at the specifics of how different types of DPs are spelled out. These are as follows. When a DP is spelled out, PF computes linearization statements that contain the information that D is concatenated with the noun:

(38) $D^\frown [_n \sqrt{\text{ROOT}}\ n]$

At this point, one of two things can happen: either Article Cliticization applies, or it does not, depending on the phonological properties of the nominal. With V-initial nouns, Article Cliticization affixes D to N. The output of this rule is shown in (39a). This structure is then linearized to produce (39b) (recall that $\oplus$ is shorthand for M-Word-internal concatenation and that $^+$ picks out those Ps and Ds subject to the rule):

(39) PF: Cliticization
    a. $D^{+\frown} [_n \sqrt{\text{ARBRE}} \oplus n] \rightarrow [D^+ [_n \sqrt{\text{ARBRE}} \oplus n]]$
    b. $D^+ \oplus \sqrt{\text{ARBRE}},\ \sqrt{\text{ARBRE}} \oplus n$

When Article Cliticization does not occur—that is, when the noun is C-initial—the PF representation for the DP is that given in (38), where D is concatenated with the noun but not affixed to it.

The next step is to consider what happens when a DP is the complement of a preposition. Syntactically, the object in question is as shown in (40):

(40) Stage 2

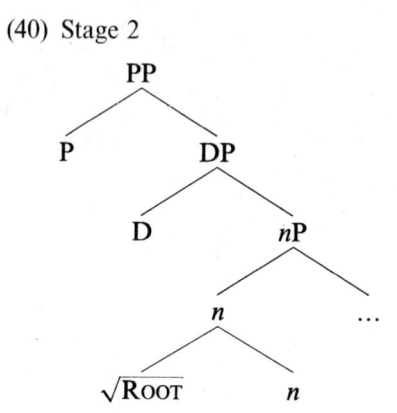

Regarding how Spell-Out of this object proceeds, there are two scenarios to consider:

(41) a. *Scenario 1:* P is a cyclic node. Thus, the DP is spelled out without reference to P's presence.

b. *Scenario 2:* P is not a cyclic node. Thus, the DP is spelled out in a cycle in which P is also present.

Assuming Scenario 1, D must be spelled out in a way that shows no sensitivity to P. This means that in the case of (e.g.) a masculine singular noun, the exponent *le* is inserted at D. Thus, there is no possibility of positing a VI for the prepositional environment with a "reduced" exponent, like *-e* or *-u*, and having this beat *le* when necessary. Relatedly, it would be impossible to fuse D and P prior to Vocabulary Insertion and have (e.g.) *du* realize a single node. Instead, the morphophonology must, evidently, be capable of deriving *du* from *de* and *le*.

Assuming Scenario 2, P is not a cyclic node. This might weaken certain syntactic predictions, but it does not complicate the morphophonology as much as Scenario 1 does. The most important aspect of Scenario 2 for these purposes is that Vocabulary Insertion at D could be made sensitive to the presence of P. Thus, for example, a PF rule could adjoin P and D so that they were in the same complex head, and then specific "head-internal" allomorphs of D would be inserted in this particular environment. There are several different ways of doing this, depending on how much burden is put on the Vocabulary versus the morphophonology. For example, one possibility would be to simply have "vocalic" allomorphs of D inserted in a complex head with P:

(42) D[def, masc] $\leftrightarrow$ e/$P^+\oplus$__

D[def, masc] $\leftrightarrow$ le

In this way, the more specific "head-internal" allomorph -*e* wins out over the less fully specified ones. After insertion of *d(e)* and *à* in the P position, the (morpho)phonology must operate to produce the effects in (43):

(43) d(e)-e → du

d(e)-e-s → des

à-e → au (/o/)

à-e-s → aux (/oz/)

The first of these processes is clearly "unnatural" (as opposed to the others), but there is really little to say about it except that it must be stated somewhere in the grammar. If it is not the result of a readjustment rule, as it is on the account just sketched, it would be possible to form an analysis with an -*u* allomorph of D[def, masc] and have this beat the other allomorphs in the relevant environments:

(44) D[def, masc] $\leftrightarrow$ u/$P^+\oplus$__

D[def, masc] $\leftrightarrow$ le

While either of the analyses just sketched might be simpler morphophonologically than what falls out of Scenario 1, treating P as noncyclic has syntactic consequences that must be considered.

There are other possibilities that are worth exploring in this type of case. For example, one that avoids some of the difficulties mentioned earlier in the text would be to say that prepositions have an internally complex structure (see, e.g., Svenonius, to appear). If this were the case, then it could be argued that *de*, for example, is the Spell-Out of the noncyclic head P between a cyclic *p* head and the DP, in which case P and D would be spelled out in the same cycle. Such a proposal would allow a simple morphophonological analysis along the lines of Scenario 2, while maintaining the idea that prepositional phrases in the broad sense are cyclic domains, as in Scenario 1.

The cyclicity of derivations plays an important role in all of the analyses outlined above. An important empirical question for future work is whether there are other reasons for assuming P to be cyclic or not. If for example both P and D are cyclic, then it is predicted that there P and D should never fuse in the technical sense. Given that P-D interactions are not uncommon crosslinguistically, this suggests an interesting avenue for further investigation.

3.3 Case Studies: Inner/Outer Affixation

In chapter 2, patterns of allomorphy in two types of English nominals were used to illustrate basic points about the behavior of cyclic heads. In that preliminary discussion, the central pattern was the contrast between "special" or "derived" nominals, with a number of different n allomorphs (*laugh-ter*, *marri-age*, etc.), and gerunds, where n is realized as *-ing* (*laughing*, *marry-ing*, etc.). The way in which outer cyclic heads are insensitive to Roots is an important facet of the theory. As discussed in detail in chapter 2, there is a basic asymmetry in allomorphy that is illustrated in structures like (45):

(45) $\dots \sqrt{\text{ROOT}}]\ x]\ W]\ y]\ Z$

The (cyclic) head x and attached W can show allomorphy determined by elements in the complement of x, but y and Z cannot. These effects follow from the $\mathbb{C}_1$-LIN theory, as summarized in the Activity Corollary:

(46) Activity Corollary

In $[[\dots x]\ y]$, x, y both cyclic, material in the complement of x is not *active* in the PF cycle in which y is spelled out.

In the empirical patterns studied in chapter 2, a head like n takes different affixes in the Root-attached and outer domains. Another question that arises when the same type of cyclic head attaches in both inner and outer domains concerns identity in form. In some cases, identical exponents for (e.g.) n are inserted in both inner and outer environments. For example, the exponent *-ing* occurs across the board in English gerunds; but at the same time, there is also an *-ing* that appears in the inner domain, for nouns like *fill-ing* and *lin-ing* on their nongerund interpretations. In cases like this, questions arise about how the Vocabulary represents this identity in form (see also Embick 1996 on a related pattern in the Athabascan language Hupa). These points are illustrated in a look at Japanese causatives in section 3.3.1 and in a more detailed examination of English nominals in section 3.3.2.

3.3.1 Preliminary Predictions: Japanese Causatives

The idea that the same exponent can be inserted in both inner and outer heads was touched on earlier in this chapter, in the discussion of Hindi causatives. Recall that while the Voice[ag] head in Hindi shows Root-determined allomorphy in transitives, the same Voice[ag] head shows only the default *-aa* in the outer domain, with causatives. That is, there is no Root-determined allomorphy; this is what the Activity Corollary predicts.

Another illustration of cross-domain identity in form, one with very similar properties, is found in the behavior of causatives in Japanese, which have been studied in a large literature reviewed in Harley 2005. The points to be made here with reference to allomorphy relate directly to Miyagawa 1994 and references cited there.

For Japanese verbs that participate in transitivity alternations, the intransitive and transitive alternants show different patterns of morphological marking (examples selected from Harley 2005, in turn from Jacobsen 1992):

(47) Sample patterns

Affixes	*Intransitive*	*Transitive*	*Gloss*
-e/-Ø	hag-e-ru	hag-Ø-u	'peel off'
-Ø/-e	ak-Ø-u	ak-e-ru	'open'
-ar/-e	ag-ar-u	ag-e-ru	'rise'
-ar/-Ø	hasam-ar-u	hasam-Ø-u	'catch between'

Each verb in (47) stands in for sets of different sizes that alternate in this way. Moreover, there are many other classes as well, but they all show the same basic point: in intransitives and transitives, the allomorphy of this head is Root-determined. For concreteness, I take the exponents seen in (47) to be realizations of v (see also Pylkkänen 2002; for what is presented below, it would be possible to treat these exponents as instantiations of Voice as well).

The patterns in (47) connect with an important pair of observations that are discussed in Miyagawa 1994 and related work. In syntactic causatives—causatives in which a v takes some sort of verbal complement—the causative v head is always realized as -*sase*. However, there are also some -*sase*-affixed forms that have the properties of "lexical" causatives. The latter type of -*sase* form has a v head in the inner domain, where it is Root-attached.

Miyagawa observes that -*sase* is possible as a lexical causative for some Root only when there is no "special" affix of the type illustrated in (47) for that Root. In other words, -*sase* is the default (agentive) v head; it is (i) often blocked in the Root-attached domain, where a more specific VI applies, as in (47), and (ii) invariably found in the outer domain.

The fact that -*sase* is found in inner and outer domains is accounted for by positing a VI that is the overall default for the causative v:

(48) $v \leftrightarrow$ -sase

This VI applies in the Root-attached domain when there is no more specific VI with a contextual condition that beats it. In the outer domain, it appears across the board because (i) Roots are not visible for outer *v* heads, and (ii) there is no VI that is specified to occur in this context, that is, one that is specific to causatives.

According to this analysis, *-sase* appears in both inner and outer domains, because the VI with this exponent is a default. In this way, the Japanese pattern is quite similar to what is found in Hindi. Beyond this type of pattern, where the default occurs in both inner and outer domains, identical exponents are also found with nondefaults; a case of this type is examined next.

3.3.2 Nominal Affixes: The Outer Cycle

In the discussion of English nominalizations above, Root-attached *n* with its many allomorphs is contrasted with outer *n* in gerunds, where the *-ing* allomorph occurs without exception. While it is true that all nominalizations with the syntax of a gerund show *-ing*, it is not the case that *-ing* is the only exponent found for *n* in the outer cycle. Examples like those in (49) show an outer *n*, outside of a Root verbalized by *v* as shown in (50). The overt exponent *-ize* signals verbalization; *n* in these cases is realized as *-ation*, not *-ing*:

(49) Outer *-ation*

Root	*Verb*	*Nominalization*
$\sqrt{\text{COLOR}}$	color-ize	color-iz-ation
$\sqrt{\text{ITEM}}$	item-ize	item-iz-ation
$\sqrt{\text{LEGAL}}$	legal-ize	legal-iz-ation
$\sqrt{\text{VAPOR}}$	vapor-ize	vapor-iz-ation

(50) *colorization*

Unlike in the case of Japanese *-sase*, in English there is more than one exponent that appears in the outer domain: both *-ation* and *-ing* appear there. There are two factors to consider in analyzing this effect. The first is that the forms like *color-iz-ation* do not have the syntax of gerunds: gerunds with -*ing* can be formed on *color-ize*, and they are different syntactically from the -*ation* forms (e.g., gerund *John's colorizing the movies* vs. nongerund *John's colorization of the movies*). One way of thinking about this is that the cases in (49) have an intransitive Voice head, whereas gerunds possess *v* and the agentive head Voice[ag].

As an abbreviation for these analyses, I will represent the -*ize*-type cases—*Z-nominals* for convenience—with a head v^z, which stands for *v* (and the Voice head) found with this type of nominalization; the *n* head attaches outside of these heads. In gerunds, the *n* attaches outside of what I abbreviate as v^g: a *v* head and the (transitive) Voice[ag] head:

(51) Heads in nominals

    a. *Z-nominal:* $[[\sqrt{\text{Root}}\ v^z]\ n]$
    b. *Gerund:* $[[[\sqrt{\text{Root}}\ v^g]\ n]$

The second factor in the analysis is the one that accounts for the appearance of -*ation* in the structure in (51a). This can be treated as a case of potentiation, of the type found with, say, -*able* and -*ity*; recall section 2.2.3. In the example employed there, the idea was that the *a* head that is pronounced -*able* is on the list of objects that condition insertion of -*ity*, making the latter affix fully productive after the former. The VI with the -*ity* exponent appears both in the Root-attached domain in *atroc-ity*, *curios-ity*, and so on, and in the outer domain, after suffixes like -*able* and -*al*:

(52) $n \leftrightarrow$ -ity/X___
    X = Roots ($\sqrt{\text{Atroc}}$, $\sqrt{\text{Curious}}$ ...); [*a*, -able], [*a*, -al]

The allomorphy of *n* in Z-nominals can be treated in the same way; the Vocabulary contains a VI that has -*ation* as an exponent, and one of the contextual elements that appears in this VI is the head v^z:

(53) $n \leftrightarrow$ -ation/LIST⌢___
    LIST = {Roots, ... v^z ... }

That is, in addition to whatever Roots condition the insertion of -*(a)tion* into Root-attached *n*, this exponent is also inserted into *n* that is attached to the v^z pronounced -*ize*. When *n* occurs in the outer cycle outside of v^z, this VI wins over the one with the -*ing* exponent that is seen with gerunds.

To this point, three types of formation with *n* have been considered: special nominalizations, with Root-attached *n*; Z-nominals, with *n* outside of v^z; and gerunds, where *n* appears outside of the structure abbreviated with v^g.

Taking this part of the English nominal system as a whole, it appears that many VIs apply only in the Root-attached domain, as might be expected in a theory of the type presented in chapter 2. There are also some exponents that appear in both the inner and outer domains: for example, *-ation* and *-ity*, as well as *-ing*. The last of these is the realization of Root-attached *n* in cases like *lin-ing*, *fill-ing*, and *hold-ing* (as in *John's holdings are extensive*).

The appearance of *-ing* in the inner and outer domains could be treated as another case of potentiation. The VI with the *-ing* exponent would have to be specified with a list that includes a set of Roots along with v^g:

(54) Nominalizations

$n \leftrightarrow$ -al   /LIST1⌒__
$n \leftrightarrow$ -age /LIST2⌒__
$n \leftrightarrow$ -tion /LIST3⌒__
$n \leftrightarrow$ -ing /LIST4⌒__
$n \leftrightarrow$:   :
$n \leftrightarrow$ -Ø   /$\sqrt{\text{Root}}$⌒__
LIST4 = {$\sqrt{\text{Line}}$, $\sqrt{\text{Fill}}$, ..., v^g, ...}

Treating *-ing* along the lines of *-ity* might be supported by other facts as well. It is not the case that *-ity* is a default in the outer domain; rather, as is well-known, *-ness* appears to be the default for *n* when it attaches outside of *a*. Both *-ing* and *-ness* are thus "defaults" of *n* in some sense. What distinguishes them is the morpheme to which the *n* attaches: *a* in the case of *-ness*, v^g in the case of *-ing*.[19] In some sense, the relationship between *-ness* and *-ing*—coupled with the fact that *-ing* appears in the inner domain—precludes a simple treatment in which *-ing* is the global default for *n*. Further research is required to see if there are alternatives in which the default status of *-ing* can be maintained. There are a number of options that could be explored along these lines. One possibility mentioned in note 19, which is attractive because it maintains the default status of *-ing*, would be to say that *-ing* and *-ness* realize different types of *n* heads.

In sum, there are two types of cases in which the same exponent can be inserted into inner and outer heads. In one type, illustrated with Japanese causatives, the exponent in question is a default. In the second type, illustrated with English nominalizations, the exponents that appear in the outer domain could be treated as potentiated by inner functional heads, although other options could be explored as well.

3.4   Morphology and Phonology

Having presented several predictions of the C_1-LIN theory for allomorphy, I turn now to questions that center on morphology-phonology interactions. While the theory of morphology developed in this part of the book does not necessarily force the details of a phonological theory, some phonological theories fit much better with it than others, as discussed in chapter 1. In particular, to the extent that there is no evidence for competition among multiple derived objects in syntax and morphology, the most natural assumption would be that the phonological component also functions without competition among multiple complex objects.

This section focuses on three aspects of the interface between morphology and phonology. Section 3.4.1 looks at the status of readjustment rules: morphophonological rules that are triggered by particular features, such as the rule that changes *break* to *broke* in the context of the past tense head T[past]. It is argued that, all other things being equal, such rules should show cyclic locality effects of the type defined by the C_1-LIN theory. At the same time, these morphophonological rules might not obey the linear constraint on allomorphy that is found with Vocabulary Insertion.

Section 3.4.2 I examines some aspects of phonologically conditioned allomorphy from the perspective of the C_1-LIN theory. The basic point is that Vocabulary Insertion may be sensitive to the phonological properties of inner nodes, namely, those that have undergone Vocabulary Insertion. Additional questions concern whether *derived* phonological properties could be visible to Vocabulary Insertion.

Finally, section 3.4.3 looks at a case in which it appears that the linear condition on contextual allomorphy is violated: a morpheme in the language Palauan that seems to show Root-determined allomorphy, even though another morpheme intervenes between it and the Root. In fact, however, this case shows a phonological process that masks a relationship that is local in the morphology, when Vocabulary Insertion occurs. The analysis of this effect requires a theory in which the representations employed for Vocabulary Insertion are not those found in the surface phonology.

3.4.1   Competition for Insertion versus Morphophonology
Distributed Morphology implements a difference between (i) "piece-based" affixation, in which nodes in a syntactic structure are realized via Vocabulary Insertion, and (ii) *readjustment rules*, which are

morphosyntactically triggered phonological rules that change the phonology of Roots (and exponents of functional heads as well). The effects of readjustment rules are seen in the derivation of the past tense of the Root √SING, that is, *sang*. Prior to Vocabulary Insertion, the structure is (55), where the Root is combined with *v* and T[past]:

(55) Structure for *sang*

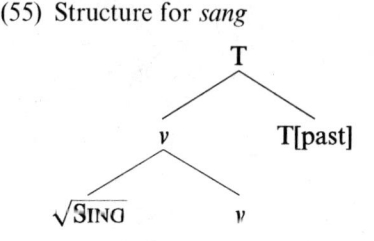

The Vocabulary Insertion process inserts a -Ø affix for *v*, which is then pruned as described in chapter 2. Vocabulary Insertion at T[past] can see the Root, and √SING is on the list for the VI that inserts a -Ø exponent for T[past], so that -Ø is inserted into this node. In addition to this, √SING is on the list for a readjustment rule that is triggered in the context of T[past] (see Halle and Mohanan 1985 for one view). This rule has the effect of changing the vowel of the Root, yielding *sang*.

Competition for insertion and readjustment are distinct in two ways.[20] First, a single VI has a coherent distribution, which means that a VI cannot contain a "disjunctive" list of features that are not compatible with one another. A single readjustment rule, on the other hand, can be *one rule* at the level of what it does phonologically, but be triggered in a range of environments that do not necessarily have anything in common. German Umlaut has this property, as discussed in Embick and Halle 2005, following Lieber 1980. Of course, it is possible for a readjustment rule to apply in a coherent environment, but this is not a defining property of such rules.

A second difference is that contextual allomorphy is subject to the considerations of locality outlined in chapter 2. Readjustment rules—and, more generally, phonological rules—are not subject to the same *linear adjacency* (LIN) condition that restricts allomorphic interactions. Exactly what this means remains to be explored, but there appear to be cases in which a readjustment rule "skips" intervening, overt morphemes. Carstairs-McCarthy (1992) provides an illustration of this point from Zulu, where the passive morpheme -*w* triggers palatalization of labials in the verb stem (56a); this rule applies even when a morpheme like causative -*is* intervenes between the passive and the Root (56b):

(56) Zulu palatalization of labials (Carstairs-McCarthy 1992, 70)

	Active	*Passive*	*Gloss*
a.	bamb-a	banj-wa	'catch'/'be caught'
	boph-a	bosh-wa	'tie'/'be tied'
b.	bamb-is-a	banj-is-wa	'cause to catch'/'be caused to catch'
	boph-is-a	bosh-is-wa	'cause to tie'/'be caused to tie'

Palatalization of this type is a readjustment rule triggered by the passive morpheme. Its effects are manifested across intervening morphemes, unlike what is seen with contextual allomorphy, whose effects are limited to concatenated pieces.

In the examples in (56), the passive morpheme that triggers palatalization is able to skip the intervening causative morpheme. However, while this rule is a readjustment rule, in that it is triggered by the passive head, it does not refer to the identity of specific undergoers: it is not Root- or morpheme-specific.

In other cases, it appears that a readjustment rule triggered by a particular morpheme only applies to specific elements. One example of this type is the behavior of the Classical Greek aorist morpheme, an Asp head.[21] As seen in column (57a), the exponent of the aorist morpheme, which appears penultimate in the word, is *-sa*; the only exception is the 3sg form, which shows *-se*. In the aorist optative active, column (57b), the optative has the exponent *-i* after the aorist morpheme; the optative morpheme is followed by an Agr node. As (57b) shows, *-sa* appears for the aorist in only a subset of the person/number combinations; in the 2sg, 3sg, and 3pl, *-se* appears instead of *-sa* (forms from Smyth 1920):

(57) Aorist forms (*lu* 'to loose')

	a.	b.	c.
P/N	*Indicative*	*Optative*	*Optative middle*
1sg	é-lū-sa	lú-sa-i-mi	lū-sa-í-mēn
2sg	é-lū-sa-s	lú-**se**-i-as	lú-sa-i-o
3sg	é-lū-**se**	lú-**se**-i-e	lú-sa-i-to
2du	e-lú-sa-ton	lú-sa-i-ton	lū-sa-i-st^{h}on
3du	e-lū-sá-tēn	lū-sa-í-tēn	lū-sa-í-st^{h}ēn
1pl	e-lú-sa-men	lú-sa-i-men	lū-sa-í-met^{h}a
2pl	e-lú-sa-te	lú-sa-i-te	lú-sa-i-st^{h}e
3pl	é-lū-sa-n	lú-**se**-i-an	lú-sa-i-nto

There is no reason to expect *-se* for *-sa* in any of these cases as part of the phonology. Rather, it seems that *-se* appears as the result of a readjustment rule that changes -*sa* when certain Agr nodes are present. The rule is highly specific to the 2sg, 3sg, and 3pl aorist optatives; even more specific is the fact that it applies only in actives, and not in middles, as shown in column (57c).

From the perspective of locality, this readjustment rule applies in configurations in which the triggering morpheme, the Agr head, is not adjacent to the aorist morpheme. In the aorist indicative, Agr and the Aorist head are adjacent, but this is not the case in the forms of the aorist optative in (57b): the optative -*i* intervenes. Thus, the rule that readjusts -*sa* has to see elements that are not adjacent to -*sa*.

Some alternatives to the readjustment rule analysis are possible. For instance, reducing the -*se* versus -*sa* effect to Vocabulary Insertion is conceivable, but not entirely promising. For example, the optative morpheme could be spelled out by a special VI whose exponent has a mystery segment -*?* in the relevant contexts, -*?i*, which beats -*i* and causes the -*sa*/-*se* alternation phonologically. The hypothesized /?/ component would trigger the -*sa*/-*se* alternation locally. However, there seems to be little to gain from this maneuver, in the sense that the putative -*?* component has no other effects.

Another possibility is to put -*se* in competition with default -*sa* as the exponent of the Aorist head. In the optative forms, the Aorist head would not be adjacent to the Agr node, so the only way to condition the -*sa*/-*se* alternation would be to make -*se* sensitive to φ-features on T placed by Agree. It is difficult to see how this could account for the active/middle contrast, however.

It appears that the most straightforward analysis of this effect changes -*sa* to -*se* via a readjustment rule, along the lines discussed above, although other possibilities, with different segmentations, might work as well.

While readjustment rules do not appear to respect the linear condition that is found with contextual allomorphy, it seems reasonable to expect that Root-specific readjustment rules are subject to phase-determined conditions on *activity*, in the same way that contextual allomorphy is. These restrictions apply to those readjustment rules that must refer to the identity of a specific Root or morpheme in order to apply, like the readjustment rule that creates *sang*, which has to see $\sqrt{\text{SING}}$ in the structure [[$\sqrt{\text{SING}}$ *v*] T[past]]. This type of rule has to see the identity of the Root in order to apply; it is not triggered by the phonological matrix alone. This property is similar to what is found with grammatically conditioned allomorphy, where particular Roots or morphemes are visible for contextual allomorphy. The expectation under the theory in chapter 2 is that the "activity" of elements should be the same, whether for contextual allomorphy or for readjustment rules. That is:

(58) Readjustment Activity Hypothesis

A readjustment rule triggered by morpheme X can effect a Root- or morpheme-specific change only when X and the Root/functional head are in the same PF cycle.

According to this hypothesis, the cyclic conditions on what a readjustment rule can target are subject to C_1 locality. Thus, noncyclic heads outside of the first cyclic head can trigger Root-specific readjustment rules, but outer cyclic heads cannot, and so on.

3.4.2 Sensitivity to Phonology

Chapter 1 contains some initial illustrations of phonologically conditioned allomorphy. This is a type of suppletive allomorphy in which the factor that determines the choice of allomorphs is not a particular morpheme in the environment of the node being spelled out, but is instead some aspect of the local phonological representation. The passive morpheme in Seri, for example, has the forms in (59):

(59) Seri passive

Allomorph	Env.	Example	Gloss
-p-	/__V	-p-eši	'be defeated'
-aː?-	elsewhere	-aː?-kašni	'be bitten'

Whereas allomorphy in, say, the English past tense refers to the identity of specific Roots, allomorphy of this passive morpheme [pass] refers only to a phonological property: whether the object next to [pass] begins with a vowel or a consonant.

In terms of the theory of chapter 2, this kind of allomorphy is subject to C_1-LIN locality. In the case of (59), this means that there must be VIs in which the contextual condition refers to the phonology of the linearly adjacent element:

(60) [pass] ↔ -p-/__⌒V-
[pass] ↔ -aː?-

In this particular case, it is segmental material that is visible. In cases in which the suppletive allomorphy is determined by metrical structure, the foot structure of the object next to the morpheme undergoing Vocabulary Insertion is visible (more precisely, perhaps, a foot boundary is visible).[22]

In the way just described, the theory allows Vocabulary Insertion to see phonological representations. In the Seri example, the phonological property that conditions allomorphy is a property of the underlying representation of the Root. However, Vocabulary Insertion could in principle refer to derived phonological structure as well. The details of this type of interaction depend on specific claims about when phonological cycles occur with respect to Vocabulary Insertion. That is, there are different possible models of when "inner" material is processed phonologically in the course of cyclic (inside-out) Vocabulary Insertion. Questions of this type are familiar in phonological theory. An important question that arose following *The Sound Pattern of English* concerns *interactionism*: the extent to which morphology and phonology are interleaved. A strong form of interactionism considered in different versions of Lexical Phonology and Morphology (see Hargus 1993; Odden 1993) holds that morphological cycles can see the output of earlier phonological cycles. Not only can morphological processes be sensitive to phonological properties, but they may also detect *derived* phonological properties, as long as these occur in an earlier stratum (see Hargus 1993 for illustration).

While phase-cyclic derivation may force certain positions on phonological interaction—for example, by specifying where Spell-Out occurs—many aspects of the interface between morphology and phonology could in principle be implemented in different ways that are all compatible with the theory of chapter 2. Take, for example, a structure that consists of a Root, a cyclic head x, and noncyclic affixes Y and Z, $[[[\sqrt{\text{ROOT}}\ x]\ Y]\ Z]$. Aside from phonological cycles triggered by cyclic Spell-Out, it is perhaps also the case that individual exponents trigger a cycle of phonological rule application (this is one take on part of Halle and Vergnaud's (1987) analysis of "Level 1" versus "Level 2" affixes in English). To the extent that cycles of phonology are followed by Vocabulary Insertion, the theory then allows "interactionism," in which Vocabulary Insertion at outer nodes is in principle capable of being conditioned by the *derived* phonology of inner pieces.

For the purposes of this book, the most important point is that while morphology (Vocabulary Insertion in particular) and phonology might be interleaved, they are distinct systems, so that output or subsequent phonology cannot drive Vocabulary Insertion. This point is discussed in detail in part II.

While the exact phonological details implicated in the discussion immediately above cannot be explored here, an important point about phonologically conditioned allomorphy is that allomorphic sensitivity to phonological representations is not bound in the same way that allomorphic sensitivity to a particular Root or morpheme is. The phonological representations of elements that are derivationally "closed off" by the Activity Corollary are visible for later stages of derivation. When a Root or a particular functional head is active, it is visible *qua Root*, or as a functional head of that particular type. This means that for either morphophonological or semantic purposes, there could be Root- or morpheme-specific interactions during the derivational window in which these elements are active.

In later stages when these elements are closed off by the Activity Corollary, these elements cannot be seen as Roots or as particular functional heads. However, these elements possess a phonological matrix, and this representation may be visible to subsequent operations. For example, it is in principle possible for phonologically conditioned allomorphy at outer nodes to refer to a phonological matrix associated with a Root. A rule of this type could not, however, target certain Roots to the exclusion of others; it would have to apply to any phonological representation meeting its structural description.

Relatedly, elements that are *inactive* because of the cyclic structure nevertheless must enter new statements of linearization. When, for instance, a DP is merged into a larger syntactic structure as (e.g.) a subject, the rightmost element of that DP must ultimately be linearized with respect to elements that are outside of the DP cyclic domain. In other words, even though that particular element is *inactive*, it still has to enter some new PF relations that account for the order of elements.[23] What this means is that, in some sense, PF cyclic derivation cannot be completely "done" with elements that are *inactive*.

3.4.3   An Illustration: Palauan Verb Marker Allomorphy
The Austronesian language Palauan provides an interesting case study for the interaction of locally conditioned allomorphy with a complex morphophonology. An apparent counterexample to the adjacency-based view of allomorphy—a case where a morpheme sees a Root despite the presence of an *overt* intervening morpheme—turns out to be a case where the phonology obscures what is a local linear relationship when Vocabulary Insertion takes place. The case study thus illustrates the basic point that the generalizations about locality of allomorphic relations are clear in a theory in which morphology (Vocabulary Insertion) and phonology are separate systems.

The discussion here draws on Flora 1974 and Josephs 1975, 1990. Palauan has a morpheme called a "verb marker" (VM) in the literature; it resembles morphemes found in many other Austronesian languages that express transitivity, voice, aspect, and related notions. This morpheme, whose basic form is mə-, shows up as a prefix (and also as an infix) in many verb forms, in a way correlated with (i) verbhood and (ii) (in)transitivity. This suggests a treatment of this morpheme as a *v* or a Voice head.

The VM surfaces in two forms: *mə-* (61a) and *o-* (61b). The cases in (61b) are all labial-initial Roots, and it appears that the VM undergoes dissimilation in these cases:

(61) VM-verb

	Verb	*Gloss*
a.	mə-rael	'walk, travel'
	mə-ngədub	'swim'
	mə-ləʔo	'bathe'
	me-ʔiuaiu	'sleep'
b.	o-bəkall	'drive'
	o-bail	'clothe'
	o-boes	'shoot'
	o-bes	'forget'

The phonological dissimilation seen in (61b) is not, however, the only source of surface /o/-realizations of the VM. For a small class of verbs, this morpheme appears as *o-*, even though the stem does not begin with a labial:

(62) Exceptional *o-* verbs (Josephs 1975, 148)

Verb	*Gloss*
o-ker	'ask'
o-klukl	'cough'
o-koad	'fight'
o-sus	'greet'
o-ʔərʔur	'laugh'
o-siik	'look for'
o-kor	'refuse'
o-kiu	'go by way of'

In these cases, it appears that the Roots in question condition the insertion of an underlying *o-* allomorph of the VM; there is no way to derive the *o-* phonologically. This means that the language must have the following two VIs:

(63) VM $\leftrightarrow$ o-/__$\frown$LIST
     VM $\leftrightarrow$ mə-

When additional verb forms are taken into account, a problem appears to arise for the adjacency-based theory of allomorphy, as instantiated in the first VI in (63). In the past tense, an overt tense morpheme -*il-* occurs between the VM and the verb Root. Thus, using so-called middle verb forms to factor out some morphophonological complications, we find patterns like these:

(64) Past tense of *mə-* verbs

Present	Past	Gloss
mə-nga	m-il-ənga	'eat'
mə-ngəlebəd	m-il-əngəlebəd	'hit'
mə-lim	m-il-lim	'drink'
mə-lu?əs	m-il-lu?əs	'write'
mə-tabək	m-il-tabək	'patch'

The same effect is found with the verbs that take *o-* as their VM. In both types of *o-* verb—those where /o/ is underlyingly *mə-* (65a), and those that take the *o-* allomorph of VM (65b)—this /o/ is found when the -*il-* morpheme appears between the VM and the Root. I represent these cases with the sequence *o-il-verb*:[24]

(65) Examples

	Present	Past	Gloss
a.	o-balə?	o-il-balə?	'shoot'
	o-basə?	o-il-basə?	'count'
	o-bunt	o-il-bunt	'curl'
	o-bes	o-il-bes	'forget'
	o-mes	o-il-əmes	'see'
b.	o-siik	o-il-siik	'look for'
	o-ker	o-il-əker	'ask'
	o-kiu	o-il-əkiu	'go by way of'
	o-mu?əl	o-il-əmu?əl	'begin'

The surface order of the morphemes in these verbs is shown in (66):

(66) Surface form
     VM-T-Root

Crucially, the VM and the Root are not adjacent in the surface form. If the linear part of the theory advanced above is correct, then the surface form cannot be the one that is relevant for the locality conditions on allomorphy. Rather, at the stage when Vocabulary Insertion occurs, the VM must be concatenated with the Root, so that it can have its allomorphy conditioned accordingly.

Closer examination of the morphophonology reveals that there is evidence for such a representation. The argument is that the *-il-* past tense morpheme is infixed *phonologically* to whatever is on its right. This infixation takes place after Vocabulary Insertion has occurred.

The structure that underlies the past tense verbs is (67), where VM is a *v*/Voice head structurally lower than T(ense):

(67) Past tense verb

In the concatenation statements derived from this structure, the Root is adjacent to the VM, that is, VM⌢Root. This statement is present when Vocabulary Insertion occurs, and the Root-determined allomorphs can be inserted when necessary. After Vocabulary Insertion takes place, the *-il-* morpheme that realizes the Tense node is infixed in the phonology to yield the surface representations shown above:

(68) *o-il-siik (ulsiik)* 'look for-PAST'
   a. Structure: [T [VM √Sɪɪk]]
   b. PF
      i.   Concatenation: T⌢VM, VM⌢√Sɪɪk
      ii. Vocabulary Insertion: [T, -il]⌢VM, [VM, o-]⌢√Sɪɪk
      iii. Chaining: -il-o-√Sɪɪk
      iv. Phonology: o-il-√Sɪɪk

Evidence for this analysis comes in a few steps. First, it can be shown that past tense *-il-* is infixed into whatever element is on its right. Thus, it does not originate between the VM and the Root. Second, the infixation is phonological in nature: it sees phonological entities (segments, etc.), not morphosyntactic ones like the Subword. This means that it must take place after Vocabulary Insertion occurs.

Different types of examples illustrate the point that *-il-* is an infix. One type consists of verbs in the perfective aspect/tense. In the nonpast perfective, the VM appears infixed into the root. In the past perfective, where the VM never surfaces, the past tense -*il*- is infixed after the stem-initial consonant, as is expected if this element is infixed in the phonology:

(69) Perfective forms

Stem	Perfective	Past perfective	Gloss
dasə?	d-m-asə?	d-il-asə?	'carve'
deel	d-m-eel	d-il-eel	'nail'
kiis	k-m-iis	k-il-iis	'dig'
leng	l-m-eng	l-il-eng	'borrow'

A similar point can be made with some stative verbs that do not take a VM. With these verbs, the past tense -*il*- appears infixed into the Root as well (70b); regular statives, in which past -*il*- follows VM, are provided for illustration in (70a):

(70) Some statives

Stem	Past	Gloss
a. mə-kar	m-il-kar	'be awake'
me-?iuaiu	m-il-ə?iuaiu	'sleep'
b. dəng?okl	d-il-əng?okl	'sit'
kie	k-il-ie	'live'

As seen in (70a), the past tense marker surfaces after the VM, which makes it look like the morpheme order is VM-T-Verb; however, -*il*- also appears after Root-initial segments, as seen in (70b). This kind of infixation is not definable in terms of morphosyntactic nodes. Rather, it is the result of a phonological rule.

Putting these points together, the behavior of the "exceptional" class of verbs with the *o*- VM is not a counterexample to the adjacency-based view of allomorphy. In the representation where allomorphy is determined, the VM is concatenated with the Root and can see it for allomorphic purposes. Subsequent action in the phonology infixes the past tense morpheme -*il*-, but this happens after the point that is relevant for Vocabulary Insertion.[25]

The analysis of this effect illustrates many aspects of the localist theory: both local relationships and different stages of a serial derivation play a crucial role. In particular, morphology (here, structural relations from the syntax, and Vocabulary Insertion) must be distinct from phonology. The important generalizations about allomorphic locality are, if this analysis is correct, not always found in surface forms. Rather, the phonology has the potential to obscure a relationship that is local when Vocabulary

Insertion occurs. Making sense of patterns of this type in a way that retains a restrictive account of allomorphy requires a theory in which morphology and phonology are distinct, along the lines proposed above.

3.5   Conclusion to Part I

The core of chapters 2 and 3 develops the localist theory of syntax and morphology, makes specific proposals about how cyclic derivation works, and articulates a theory of allomorphy that derives from the interaction of cyclic and linear factors. Taken on its own, this part of the book illustrates the strong predictions that are generated when a cyclic theory of derivations is extended into morphology and phonology.

This work also provides a foundation for addressing the broader range of questions raised in chapter 1, which highlight the different factors that localist and globalist theories allow to influence how phonological forms are derived. While the localist theory of syntax and morphology does not, in the end, force a full-fledged phonological theory, it places sharp constraints on interactions of the type that are the focus of this book. It does this by making specific claims about the types of information that can play a role in the derivation of some object's phonological form.

The details of the $\mathbb{C}_1$-LIN theory are subject to investigation and (dis)-confirmation. The overall picture that emerges from the next part of the book is that, even if this particular localist theory is incorrect, morphology and phonology do not interact in the ways that would require a globalist architecture.

II Phonologically Conditioned Allomorphy

4 Phonologically Conditioned Allomorphy: The Globalist Intuition

Chapter 1 of this book highlights the fundamental tension between localist theories of the type developed in chapters 2 and 3 and the prevailing view in phonological theory, the globalist framework of Optimality Theory (OT). This part of the book compares the empirical predictions of these theories in the domain of (phonologically conditioned) allomorphy. This comparison, which relies on the specifics of allomorphic interaction, implicates a larger question: *how do morphology and phonology interact?*

In the current theoretical context, where syntactic theories of morphology have advanced considerably, the architectural scope of this question is quite broad. Questions about morphology and phonology implicate syntax as well; this point is emphasized in Embick and Marantz 2008 and recognized in some form in a number of theories that seek to account for putative competitions between words and phrases. Thus, what is at issue here goes well beyond morphology in the narrow sense: the general question is how the sound form of complex expressions relates to the system(s) responsible for generating such expressions.

A central focus of the following chapters is whether there is evidence for any sort of global interaction between morphology and phonology. In the terms employed in chapter 1, a theory that allows morphology and phonology to interact globally shows *global-MP*. The primary result of part II of this book is that even theories with a "limited" form of globalism make predictions about allomorphy that are (i) distinct from those made by localist theories and (ii) importantly, not borne out by the data.

This line of argument is quite general. In many globalist theories, some limitations on global interaction are assumed. For example, mission statements like those provided in McCarthy 2002 point to a "standard assumption" to the effect that phonological and syntactic computations are different in OT terms, which makes for a kind of limited modularity (see 2002, 142, in particular). The same work, however, recognizes that arguments *for* OT's architecture would be stronger to the extent that all such modular boundaries were found to be epiphenomenal. More recent moves in globalist theories have been made in the opposite direction, toward cyclic or serial architectures. As discussed in chapter 6, however, it appears that even the "restrained" global-MP allowed in such theories makes incorrect predictions about allomorphy.

4.1 Morphology-Phonology Relations

The question of how morphology and phonology interact has a long history, one that predates generative theories of language. To a large extent, research in the generative tradition has taken the position that morphology and phonology constitute separate systems of grammatical competence, the most important research question being the exact manner in which these components interact. Another important set of questions concerns putative "dividing lines" between these two domains: for example, can phonological rules be morphologically conditioned, and vice versa?

Answers to these questions rely crucially on assumptions about the nature of morphology, the nature of the morpheme, and so on. In Chomsky and Halle's (1968) *The Sound Pattern of English* (*SPE*), for example, morphological structure is built before phonological rules apply, so that phonological rules do not begin to interpret an internally complex word until it has been completely built. In accordance with the principles of the transformational cycle, however, the phonological rules operate "inside out" on bracketed structures, in a way that makes the domains for phonological interaction isomorphic to the domains for morphological composition in the default case. In this theory, (i) morphology and phonology are distinct components of the grammar, and (ii) interaction between them is limited, in the sense that phonological rules can see morphological structure, but not vice versa: no morphological rule can see the output of any phonological rule, because all of the morphological rules apply to create such structures before the phonology begins to operate on them. It is for this reason that theories like that of *SPE* are sometimes called *noninteractionist*.

The particular form of noninteractionism that is found in *SPE* derives from specific assumptions about the nature of the morpheme and the nature of the processes that assemble morphemes into complex objects (labeled bracketings). Stepping back from the details of this particular approach, it is clear that in general, there are two questions about morphology that different theories account for in different ways:

(1) Two parts of morphology

    a. *Combinatorics:* What is the nature of the system that assembles morphemes into complex objects?

    b. *Allomorph selection:* What is the nature of the system that provides morphemes with their phonological form?

In *SPE*, it is assumed that "morphological rules" combine morphemes into labeled bracketings, thus answering the first question. To answer the second question, it is assumed that the morphemes that are combined by morphological rules possess a phonological underlying representation. In this theory, then, the fact that phonology cannot "feed" morphology derives from the fact that both aspects of (1) are determined before the phonological rule system begins to apply.

Some theories that follow *SPE* deviate from this view of phonology and morphology by allowing interactions in which morphological rules follow phonological rules. To take the most salient example, Lexical Phonology (see Pesetsky 1979; Kiparsky 1982; and related work) proposes that cycles of morphology and phonology are interleaved in a way that allows morphology to see the output of phonology under some circumstances, not just vice versa; this is an *interactionist* position. Whether the general rule is that each morpheme triggers a cycle of phonological rule application, or that sets of morphemes are followed by phonological cycles (*stratal* organization), the general principle is the same: morphological operations that build structure and introduce the phonological underlying representations of morphemes are interleaved with phonological rules.

The theory presented in part I, in which syntactic structures are built and then operated on in the PF component, allows certain interactions between morphology and phonology, and not others. It answers the question in (1a) by holding that morphemes are composed in syntactic structures. The functional morphemes that appear in such structures do not have a phonological representation underlyingly. Rather, this information is provided in the process of Vocabulary Insertion. Thus, while (1a) occurs before the phonology, it is possible for (1b), the Vocabulary Insertion process, to be sensitive to the earlier application of phonological rules (some different possibilities along these lines are outlined in chapter 3).

Structurally, the theory of part I allows Vocabulary Insertion to refer to local phonological properties of elements that are inside of the node being worked on. Overall, however, the types of interaction that are allowed are quite restricted in scope. While there might be phonological sensitivities encoded in the contextual conditions on Vocabulary Insertion, this process is locally encapsulated and operates without reference to subsequent actions of the phonological component, which in turn must deal with whatever Vocabulary Insertion serves up to it. In short, the theory allows (limited) phonological sensitivity in allomorphy, but it allows no outright selection of allomorphs by the global or surface phonology.

The restricted type of phonological sensitivity that is possible in a localist theory contrasts sharply with what is allowed in a theory with a globally interacting morphology and phonology (global-MP). Global-MP offers one of the most extreme types of interactionism that can be formulated: not only can morphology see the output of earlier cycles of phonology, but in fact morphology and phonology are one system, such that any aspect of the phonology of an entire derived word could in principle affect the shape of a morpheme anywhere in that word. While specific theoretical proposals in the OT context might restrain possible interactions in different ways, in principle the framework allows any aspect of the (output) phonological representation to *determine* either the combinatorics (1a) or allomorph selection (1b). To the extent that the combinatorics are done by the syntax—as argued for in Distributed Morphology and related approaches—this means that there would be a globally interacting syntax, morphology, and phonology, in which phonological well-formedness of surface forms could conceivably play a decisive role in many competitions. The prospects for this kind of approach to morphosyntax, however, seem rather poor; see Embick and Marantz 2008 for discussion. The question addressed below is whether there is any evidence for globalism in phenomena that are more morphophonological in nature, where allomorphy provides the crucial information.

4.2 Allomorphy and Globalism

In the domain of allomorphy, a sort of best-case scenario for globalism— one that would provide a strong argument that the grammar has to be organized in those terms—would be one in which all allomorphic selection in a language could be predicted on the basis of the constraint system required for the "normal" phonology of that language. In this hypothetical universe, the grammar generates all host-allomorph combinations and variations on these, and the winners (the correct allomorphs) are selected · via the phonology.

This kind of intuition is found in a qualified form in the P≫M theory of McCarthy and Prince (1993), which hypothesizes that in certain types of interactions, phonological constraints must outrank morphological constraints. The role played by this ranking schema is seen clearly in the analysis of infixation, where, for example, prosodic constraints that require an affix to adjoin to a prosodic unit like the foot outrank "morphological" constraints that make that affix either a prefix or a suffix.[1]

The P≫M theory is restricted, so that phonology is predicted to trump morphology with "prosodic morphology"; in cases of "normal" affixation, morphological constraints may prevail. However the restriction to prosodic morphology is to be defined, the globalism that is central to OT predicts that there should be many cases in which the effects of P≫M are visible. Phonologically conditioned allomorphy (PCA) in particular is predicted by the P≫M approach to be defined by phonological surface well-formedness. It is thus expected to be phonologically optimizing.

The P≫M theory makes other predictions as well, although these are of limited interest to the current discussion. A wide range of phenomena covered by the P≫M approach have been examined by others; Paster (2006) and Bye (2008), in particular, have argued that the empirical predictions of this theory are not borne out. While these arguments appear to be sound, it must be stressed that P≫M is only one specific theory that can be formulated within a globalist framework. There are many, many predictions that derive from globalism that do not require the details of the P≫M approach but that would be impossible to state on a localist view. The comparison between localist and globalist theories executed below assumes this more general orientation, and it looks for any type of interaction that could provide empirical evidence for global interaction between morphology and phonology.

4.2.1 Phonologically Conditioned Allomorphy: The Globalist Intuition

The predictions for allomorphy that derive from a theory with global-MP can be approached in a few steps. Starting at the most general level, it is clear that phonology cannot play a role in *all* cases of allomorph selection. In particular, there is no reason to think that phonological considerations should play a role in *grammatically* conditioned allomorphy. For example, the "regular" phonology of English is not the reason why

Vocabulary Insertion selects the exponent -*t* for the past tense of *bend*, but -*ed* for the past tense of *mend*.[2] This is a "morphological" fact, one that, from the perspective of almost any grammatical theory, simply has to be memorized. This is the reason that McCarthy and Prince (1993) restrict P≫M to cases of prosodic morphology; in grammatically conditioned allomorphy, morphological constraints can dominate phonological ones, such that the phonological constraints do not play a role in determining allomorph choice (see McCarthy and Prince 1993, chap. 7).

For obvious reasons, the clearest differences between the predictions of localist and globalist architectures are seen in PCA. While the details of the predictions are important, and will be fleshed out in the rest of this book, a basic prediction of a theory with even restrained global-MP is that at least some cases of allomorphy should be determined by global interactions in a complex word: interactions in which surface phonology plays the decisive role.

While the emphasis of the next two chapters is on empirical predictions of the type just mentioned, many comparisons of localism and globalism in the literature operate on a conceptual level, and these must be acknowledged before the discussion proceeds.

On the conceptual front, globalist theories are committed to the idea that patterns of allomorph selection in PCA are the way they are *for a reason* and that this reason must be stated in the grammar. In other words, a bare statement of the distribution of allomorphs is not enough: the grammar must explain distributions in phonological terms. This kind of argument is typically put forth with reference to cases of PCA that appear to "make sense" phonologically. Recall, for example, the Korean nominative morpheme, whose allomorphic distribution in terms of C-final and V-final hosts can be understood in terms of syllable-structure markedness:

(2) Korean nominative

-*i* after C: pap-i 'cooked rice'
-*ka* after V: ai-ka 'child'

While any theory can acknowledge that some nontrivial phonological patterns might be found in allomorph distribution, the conceptual part of the globalist program goes beyond this: it asserts that the grammar itself must say why this distribution is found. Stating "why" a distribution is found is something that requires global-MP, because only in such a theory can the output phonology of the whole word determine morphology.

Thus, the driving intuition behind the globalist research program in this domain is that (at least some) allomorph distributions are the way they are because the phonology plays the decisive role in allomorph selection. The further argument is that localist theories, even if they are capable of stating the distribution, are missing something essential, because such theories cannot say that the output phonology is what is responsible for that distribution.

4.2.2 Illustration and Implementation

Schematically, an approach that implements allomorph selection in terms of output properties needs two components in order to function properly. First, for any given HOST and allomorphs x_1, x_2, ... of some morpheme, the grammar must generate all possible combinations (3a); these are in competition. Then, some set of principles must determine which combination wins the competition, such that the rest are marked as ungrammatical:

(3) Schematization

    a. *GENERATION:* HOST, $\begin{Bmatrix} x_1 \\ x_2 \\ x_3 \end{Bmatrix} \rightarrow$ HOST-x_1, HOST-x_2, HOST-x_3

    b. *SELECTION:* pick winner, mark losers as ungrammatical

Clearly, the idea behind implementing allomorph selection in this way is that the constraints of the (normal) phonology are decisive in the SELECTION stage (3b). As should be clear from (3), one way of making the overall picture precise in OT terms is to have (3a) performed by GEN and (3b) performed by EVAL.

The line of reasoning embodied in (3) is exploited in several early works on PCA. To take a specific example, another case of allomorphy from Korean that has been analyzed in this literature (see Lapointe 1999) illustrates important points about how the phonology could be employed to drive allomorph selection. The allomorphy is exhibited by the "topic/focus" morpheme, which appears with the allomorphs -*un* after C-final hosts and -*nun* after V-final hosts:

(4) Korean topic/focus morpheme

    -*un* after C: pap-un 'cooked rice'
    -*nun* after V: ai-nun 'child'

As noted by Lapointe (1999) and others, the type of C/-Ø alternation shown by this morpheme appears to follow naturally from a theory with the properties of (3). A generalized (and weakened) version of this type of reasoning is taken up by Bonet, Lloret, and Mascaró (2007) and Mascaró (2007); these authors analyze the data in (4) along the lines of (5):

(5) Analysis of allomorph selection

(i) pap-{un, nun}	ONSET	NOCODA
a. ☞ pap-un		*
b. pap-nun		**!
(ii) ai-{un, nun}	ONSET	NOCODA
a. ai-un	**!	*
b. ☞ ai-nun	*	*

The idea is that a candidate like *pap-nun* violates NOCODA more than *pap-un*, and *ai-un* violates ONSET more than *ai-nun*. In this way, the distribution of allomorphs is exhaustively determined by constraints with independent motivation. Moreover, the constraints are phonological (highlighting the idea that morphology and phonology are one system, as supposed by global-MP), and they are those associated with familiar patterns in syllable structure (highlighting the idea that selection of allomorphs is driven by optimization of the output phonology).[3]

4.2.3 Generalizing: Phonological Selection
I refer to theories in which globalism allows global properties of the phonology (or the surface phonology) to determine allomorph selection as implementing *Phonological Selection*. Along with the general idea that there are instances where some aspect of the phonology determines allomorph selection in this way, there is a strong version of this hypothesis according to which all (phonologically conditioned) allomorph selection is determined by the normal phonology:

(6) Types of Phonological Selection

 a. *Phonological Selection:* The constraints responsible for the (normal?) phonology play at least some role in determining allomorph selection in a way that requires reference to global properties (or properties of surface outputs).

 b. *Strong Phonological Selection:* In cases of PCA, the choice among competing allomorphs is determined exclusively by the normal phonology.

In chapter 3, it was shown that the $\mathbb{C}_1$-LIN theory allows phonological information to serve as a contextual condition on Vocabulary Insertion. However, in this theory only the phonology of "inner" nodes could potentially be visible to a node undergoing insertion. The effects of Phonological Selection schematized in (6) go far beyond this, by allowing the phonology of outer morphemes or the phonology of the entire word to determine which allomorph is chosen. This point of contrast—along with others—allows the predictions of localist and globalist theories to be compared directly.

As will be discussed in chapter 5, Strong Phonological Selection does not work, and this has driven various globalist theories to introduce different kinds of morphological ordering into the analysis of PCA. Since evidence for Phonological Selection in any form would be an argument for the globalist view, the empirical focus in the next chapters is on the status of (6a).

4.3 Generalizations and Formal Predictions

The next two chapters examine the intuition behind Phonological Selection and the formal predictions made by theories with global-MP. Before we move on to this part of the discussion, which concentrates on specific empirical expectations and predictions, further clarifications are in order regarding *conceptual* motivations for global-MP and Phonological Selection, expanding the introductory remarks in section 4.2.1.

The conceptual points can be illustrated with reference to the $\mathbb{C}_1$-LIN theory of part I. Recall that in this theory, cases of PCA are analyzed by means of VIs that refer to phonological properties of adjacent objects. For example, the allomorphy shown by the Korean topic/focus morpheme could be analyzed as follows:[4]

(7) [top/foc] $\leftrightarrow$ -un/C⌢__
    [top/foc] $\leftrightarrow$ -nun/V⌢__

The question raised in comparison with globalist frameworks is this: is a localist approach along the lines of (7) missing a generalization in exactly those cases where the allomorphy is apparently "optimizing," because it does not assert that the allomorphs are distributed the way they are for this reason? Clearly, the VIs in (7) account for the distribution of the exponents, but they do not say *why* this pattern is found; is this enough? A familiar claim in the debate between globalist and localist theories in phonology is that the latter type of theory is explanatorily inadequate because it does not explain why certain patterns are found, and not others. With reference to something like (7), the idea is that the localist theory is explanatorily deficient because it can say nothing about the fact that the distribution is nonarbitrary when viewed in terms of properties of the output forms.

The idea that localist theories have nothing to say about patterns of distribution is, however, misleading. A more accurate way of making the point is that the localist theory cannot state *within the grammar* that the distribution of allomorphs is the way it is *because* surface phonological properties are optimized. There is an important point here that is often overlooked. It is not true that a localist theory cannot be connected with any explanation of allomorph distributions; it can. However, it would assign the explanation of the putative generalizations about distribution to another part of the theory of language in the broad sense; after all, not every generalization about language is a generalization about the grammar. The net result of this line of reasoning is that the localist view does not assert that there are *no* generalizations about how allomorphs are distributed in surface forms; rather, it holds that if there is something to be said about why some distributions are found (and not others), these generalizations fall under the purview of diachrony, acquisition, phonetics, processing, and so forth—perhaps in some combination. Analyzing a generalization in these terms—that is, assigning it to a system that is not the grammar in the narrow sense—does not exclude it from principled explanation.

From the globalist point of view, the localist theory is explanatorily deficient. The reason for this is that the mechanisms used to derive the distribution of allomorphs, which are incapable of referring to properties of output forms, do not say *why* a particular distribution is the way it is. Most theories of allomorphy that assume a globalist framework begin with this point. McCarthy (2002, 154–155) offers a clear version of what is at stake: "Derivational approaches based on selecting an allomorph at the point of lexical insertion miss the connection between the constraint(s) responsible for allomorph choice and the constraints of phonology as a whole." That is, a localist theory in which allomorph selection does not make reference to global or output properties cannot connect patterns of allomorph distribution with (independently motivated) aspects of the phonology of the language.

This particular version of the argument takes for granted a view in which PCA results from the "normal" phonology alone, something that was shown not to work in early research on this topic (see chapter 5).

Nevertheless, the line of argumentation is clear, and could be deployed even if Strong Phonological Selection does not hold: in short, on the globalist view, stating distributions is not enough; what is needed is a statement *within the grammar* of why allomorphs appear where they do.

Conceptual arguments of this type figure prominently in the literature, and for convenience, I refer to this class of arguments as being centered on *putative loss of generalization*:

(8) Putative loss of generalization (PLG)

Localist theories are inadequate because in the cases in which allomorph selection optimizes the output according to some metric, the allomorph selection procedure does not explicitly state the fact that the distribution is driven by global or output properties of the phonology.

Discussion of PLG outside the domain of allomorphy—that is, in the domain of phonology proper—is extensive and quite charged. Arguments at this level of abstraction are notoriously difficult to assess; they often implicate different and conflicting "research intuitions" about what explanations should look like and where they should be sought, rather than being commensurable accounts that make different empirical predictions. To see exactly what role PLG plays in motivating globalism over localism, consider two types of effects:

(C1) Cases in which the localist theory is able to state the relevant distribution of allomorphs, but not why (in the PLG-relevant sense) this distribution is found

(C2) Cases in which the localist theory is not capable of accounting for the relevant distribution of allomorphs, because the distributional facts themselves require global-MP

In (C1) cases, PLG is the only objection that can be raised against the localist view. The goal of the following chapters is to put conceptual arguments to the side and look at empirical arguments, which center on (C2). The hypothetical (C2) cases go beyond PLG; they are, by hypothesis, simply not derivable in a localist theory (at least, not without missing the key generalization about distribution).

4.4 Outline

The argument of the following two chapters is straightforward. A theory with the capacity to "explain" distributions in the way described above must have certain formal properties. The empirical predictions of this type of theory go beyond what can be expressed by a localist theory. Even in cyclic or serial versions of OT, as long as more than a few morphemes are worked on in the same computational domain, the predictions about what can drive allomorphy are significantly different from what is allowed in a localist view. Theories that have even limited global-MP, and thus allow PLG-compatible *explanations* of (C1), predict (C2) effects as an architectural consequence. However, there seems to be no evidence for global interactions of the (C2) type. The conclusion I draw from this is that the globalist architecture for morphology and phonology fails in its empirical predictions.

The argument proceeds in two steps. Chapter 5 looks at Phonological Selection and examines the intuition behind it. It turns out that the motivation for Phonological Selection is weakened considerably when artificially restricted examples are replaced by complex systems of allomorphy. At a minimum, this means that globalist theories do not generalize empirically; a further point is that there are cases in which such theories, because of their focus on surface effects, actually miss important morphophonological generalizations. Chapter 6 moves beyond the intuition and its conceptual motivations to the specific empirical predictions that globalism makes for allomorphic interactions. It shows that in cases where localist and globalist views make different predictions, the localist predictions are correct, and there is no evidence for global interaction.

5   On the Intuition behind Phonological Selection

Chapter 4 outlines the intuition that globalism extends to phonologically conditioned allomorphy (PCA). As noted there, the strongest confirmation that this intuition is correct would be found if all cases of PCA could be analyzed with the constraint system required for the normal phonology of a language.

There are many arguments in the literature showing that this view— Strong Phonological Selection—is incorrect. Some illustrations of this point are given in section 5.1. It must be stressed, though, that the failure of Strong Phonological Selection does not mean that the globalist architecture as a whole makes incorrect predictions about morphology-phonology interactions. Rather, the most that can be concluded is that one particular type of theory that can be formulated within the broad confines of a globalist architecture does not work. This conclusion leaves open the possibility that Phonological Selection is required in some weaker form; as noted in chapter 4, *any* clear empirical evidence for Phonological Selection would be an argument in favor of globalism and against localism.

Finding empirical arguments in which the strong predictions of globalism are identified and tested is difficult. One reason for this is that globalist theories that have detected the failure of Strong Phonological Selection have primarily attempted to account for the distribution of phonologically conditioned allomorphs by combining phonological constraints with different types of morphological ordering. These theories do not provide empirical arguments that the predictions of the globalist framework are superior to those stemming from localism; they are fixes to a particular kind of globalist theory, not arguments in favor of that architecture.

As a way of sharpening the empirical issues that are at stake, this chapter examines and evaluates the *intuition* behind Phonological Selection.

This is the intuition that, in some form or other, surface or nonlocal phonological factors can play a decisive role in determining allomorph selection of any morpheme in a word. The main thrust of the argument is that when an analysis in these terms moves beyond limited examples, the intuition that underlies Phonological Selection is misguided, or at least misleading. It is possible in almost any language with PCA to find at least some cases in which it looks like Phonological Selection is operative, as long as attention is restricted to a subpart of the morphology. However, when systems of PCA are examined in more detail, the questions that come up center on the interaction of stored information about morphemes with the generative process. It appears that while the morphological operation of Vocabulary Insertion and the (morpho)-phonological processes that affect morphemes when they are combined are central to this picture, nonlocal phonological factors are not relevant. The cases that make Phonological Selection look promising must be selected on an ad hoc basis, and the analyses of these subpatterns do not generalize.

The argument takes two forms. In section 5.2, an analysis of Djabugay shows that prima facie simple explanations of allomorphy based on Phonological Selection do not generalize, and that the generalizations about case allomorphy found in this language do not implicate properties of output forms in a systematic way. Section 5.3 presents an analysis of Yidiɲ case allomorphy that extends the conclusions from section 5.2 and makes a further point: important generalizations about the relationship between allomorph selection and vowel length are obscured in a surface-based analysis in which phonology and morphology interact globally, but can be accounted for directly in a localist framework in which morphology and phonology are distinct.

The points raised in this chapter are not direct arguments against the predictions of globalist models in the strict sense. Rather, the conclusions are that (i) analyses based on global-MP do not seem to generalize; (ii) the factors that must be taken into account in analyzing systems of allomorphy are not those that are expected if Phonological Selection is part of the grammar; and (iii) analyses based only on properties of output forms might in fact be missing key generalizations that are stated transparently in a localist model.

Taken together, these points raise serious doubts about the intuition that global phonological properties play an important role in allomorph selection. The next step in the argument, where formal predictions of globalism and localism are compared directly, makes up the substance of chapter 6.

5.1   Phonological Selection and Ordering Allomorphs

Strong Phonological Selection does not work. What this means is that simple phonological constraints operating on all possible host-allomorph combinations do not always make correct predictions about the selection of phonologically conditioned allomorphs. This point is evident in at least two types of cases. In one type, allomorphy is determined phonologically, but the resulting patterns are unexpected from the perspective of basic phonological constraints; this is illustrated with Haitian Creole determiner allomorphy in section 5.1.1. Another type of case involves phonological conditioning in which, for at least some hosts, basic phonological constraints are indifferent to the various allomorphic choices, because no constraints are violated by any of them. In such a case, the phonology by itself is unable to select a winner, and additional "morphological" constraints must be appealed to in order to account for the attested patterns. This is illustrated for genitive case affixes in Djabugay in section 5.1.2.

While cases of this type are arguments against Strong Phonological Selection, they nevertheless can be analyzed in a globalist theory. Importantly, though, none of the "fixes" to Strong Phonological Selection considered in the literature offer any evidence in favor of globalism, as discussed in section 5.1.3.

5.1.1   Haitian Creole Determiner Allomorphy

A morpheme referred to as a "definite determiner" in Haitian Creole (see Klein 2003; Paster 2006; Bonet, Lloret, and Mascaró 2007; Bye 2008) shows -*a* and -*la* allomorphs in a phonologically determined pattern.[1] The distribution is odd from the perspective of basic syllable structure markedness constraints. The -*a* allomorph appears after V-final hosts, and the -*la* allomorph after C-final ones:

(1) a. -*a* after V

	Noun	Noun-Definite	Gloss
	tu	tu-a	'hole'
	papje	papje-a	'paper'
	papa	papa-a	'father'
	lapli	lapli-a	'rain'
	chẽ	chẽ-ã	'dog'

b. -*la* after C

Noun	Noun-Definite	Gloss
liv	liv-la	'book'
pitit	pitit-la	'child'
ãj	ãj-la	'angel'
kay	kay-la	'house'

This distribution creates both VV hiatus (1a) and codas (1b). The reverse of the attested pattern does the opposite; that is, if the -*la* allomorph appeared after V-final nouns, and the -*a* allomorph after C-final nouns, the distribution would look like a clear case of phonological optimization, like the Korean examples discussed in chapter 4.

A "simple" sort of fix for the Phonological Selection approach to allomorphy could be formulated if the phonology of Haitian Creole treated the patterns in (1) as optimal, for reasons that are not obvious until the phonology of the language as a whole is considered; but this seems rather unpromising. It is not the case that onsets are somehow disesteemed in this language. This is evident from the fact that epenthesis takes place between [+ATR] vowels and the definite -*a*:[2]

(2) Glide insertion after [+ATR]-final vowels

Noun-Definite	Gloss
a. papje[j]-a	'the paper'
bato[w]-a	'the boat'
lapli[j]-a	'the rain'
tu[w]-a	'the hole'
b. papa-a	'the father'
bɔkɔ-a	'the sorcerer'

The problems for Strong Phonological Selection are fairly clear. As noted by Paster (2006) and Bye (2008), who concentrate on the predictions of the P≫M theory of McCarthy and Prince (1993), if both -*a*- and -*la*-affixed forms were potential candidates, then the phonology should select -*la* for V-final nouns. The language even epenthesizes in some cases; and clearly, inserting -*la* in the first place would remove the need for this.[3]

From the perspective of a theory that maintains Phonological Selection in a weakened form, it is in cases of the Haitian Creole type that *morphological* ordering of some sort is most motivated, even if, as will be shown, the need to order allomorphs morphologically arises in simpler cases (where allomorph distribution is not "perverse") as well. Considerations of this type are framed in Bonet, Lloret, and Mascaró 2007, where it is proposed that *allomorphic ordering* (developed as well in Mascaró 2007) establishes a partial order on the allomorphs of a particular morpheme, and a constraint called PRIORITY is violated by candidates that contain a nonprioritized allomorph.

The specific analysis of Haitian Creole proposed by Bonet, Lloret, and Mascaró (2007) is that the grammar contains a VI for the definite determiner morpheme D[def] that consists of a set of exponents. These exponents are ordered by the relation >, which establishes the priority relation among the allomorphs in the set:

(3) D[def] ↔ {a > la}

A form that has *-la* instead of *-a* violates the constraint PRIORITY. This has to be a "morphological" effect in the sense that there is no reason why *-a* should be better than *-la* for phonological reasons alone.

The challenge for theories implementing Phonological Selection is to make at least part of the definite determiner's distribution phonological. Since *-a* always beats *-la* on morphological grounds, other phonological constraints ranked higher than PRIORITY have to eliminate candidates with *-a* with C-final hosts. Bonet, Lloret, and Mascaró (2007) posit the following constraints to achieve this effect:

(4) Additional constraints

    a. *R-ALIGN STEM SYLLABLE:* Align right edge of stem $_s$] with right edge of syllable $_\sigma$].

    b. **C.V:* Avoid a syllable ending in a consonant followed by a syllable starting with a vowel.

The first constraint penalizes resyllabification of stem material, and the second penalizes the syllable contact that arises from the failure to resyllabify. Looking ahead, these constraints conspire to rule out *-a* with C-final hosts, since either resyllabifying or not incurs a violation of one of them.

The analysis using the constraints in (4) and PRIORITY is shown in tableaux (5a,b) (simplified slightly):

(5) Illustration

    a. *-a* after V

papa-{a>la}	R-ALIGN	*C.V	PRIORITY
papa.la			*!
☞ papa.a			

b. *-la* after C

liv-{a>la}	R-Align	*C.V	Priority
☞ liv.la			*
liv.a		*!	
li.va	*!		

Since the constraints ranked above Priority are phonological in nature and are meant to enforce Phonological Selection, it is worth reflecting for a moment on how this analysis achieves what it does. When *-a* appears, it is because it is prioritized morphologically; it does not win out over *-la* on phonological grounds. When *-la* appears, it is because *-a* creates phonological problems; that is, the *-a* form violates one of the constraints in (4). This analysis works mechanically because, as noted above, the two constraints that are ranked higher than Priority have the effect of making the preferred allomorph *-a* bad in C-final environments, whether it resyllabifies (R-Align) or does not (*C.V).

This is (in part) a "phonological" solution, but, as far as such solutions go, it is highly specific to the case at hand. Since the shape of the dispreferred allomorph *-la* renders R-Align and *C.V irrelevant, candidates with this allomorph win with C-final stems. These two constraints are irrelevant in other competitions as well. Other morphemes in the language trigger resyllabification with C-final stems, and steps must be taken in the phonological analysis to ensure that R-Align and *C.V do the work they are supposed to do with *-la* while not ruling out resyllabification across the board (see Bonet, Lloret, and Mascaró 2007 for details).

The net effect of these different facets of the analysis is clear: the two "phonological" constraints ranked higher than Priority that force *-a* to lose do the relevant work in competitions with definite *-a* and *-la*. Evidently, though, the *only* work done by these constraints is that they conspire to rule out *-a* with C-final stems; in other words, this solution is totally ad hoc.[4]

Taken as a whole, the analysis is one in which (i) there must be a stipulated ordering, one that is not in any obvious sense less stipulative than ordering VIs; and (ii) the role attributed to Phonological Selection involves constraints that are relevant only in accounting for the distribution of *-a* versus *-la*. These results are unimpressive; this kind of analysis is not superior in any obvious way to an account that achieves the distri-

bution in purely "morphological" terms (e.g., ordering of VIs). Phonological Selection is maintained in practice, but in a way that strips the intuition behind it of most of its content.

5.1.2 Djabugay Genitives

The position that surface prosodic optimization (partially) determines
allomorphic selection has been illustrated by Kager (1996) and others
with reference to genitive case allomorphy in Djabugay, a language of
the Cape York region of Australia (see Hale 1976a,c; Patz 1991). This
case study appears at the beginning of Kager 1996, where it is adduced
as an initial illustration of Phonological Selection's appeal and prospects.
In a way that connects with the PRIORITY theories examined above,
Kager's analysis recognizes that the phonology does not, by itself, suffice
to predict the distribution of allomorphs correctly, so that there is a role
for interaction with "morphological" constraints.

The facts considered in the works cited above are restricted in scope.
Djabugay has two genitive affixes: -:n after V-final stems and -ŋun with
C-final stems:[5]

(6) Genitive allomorphy

		Abs	Gen	Gloss
a.	V-final	guludu	guludu-:n	'dove'
		gurra:	gurra:-n	'dog'
b.	C-final	gaɲal	gaɲal-ŋun	'goanna'
		girrgirr	girrgirr-ŋun	'bush canary'

On Kager's analysis, the phonological force that determines (part of) this
distribution is exerted by a constraint that bans complex codas.[6] The
inputs to the competition consist of a noun and some abstractly specified
suffix like GEN for the genitive, and the competitors have the distinct
allomorphs of that morpheme. The phonology prevents -:n from attach-
ing to C-final hosts by *COMPLEX CODA (*CC), which makes the -ŋun-
affixed form the winner. However, if this constraint were the only active
force in allomorph selection, the grammar would not be able to rule out
-ŋun for V-final stems, since neither *guludu-:n* nor *guludu-ŋun*, for example, violates that constraint. Thus, Kager posits an additional constraint,
GENITIVE=/n/, that is violated when the genitive allomorph is not -:n.
This analysis is shown in (7):

(7) Competition between allomorphs

(i) {gaɲal-GEN}	*CC	Genitive=/n/
a. ☞ gaɲal-ŋun		*
b. gaɲal-ːn	*!	
(ii) {guludu-GEN}	*CC	Genitive=/n/
a. guludu-ŋun		*!
b. ☞ guludu-ːn		

The function of Genitive=/n/ is to establish a preference that prevents the -ŋun allomorph from winning across the board. In effect, it limits this "dispreferred" allomorph to environments where the preferred allomorph -ːn violates the higher-ranking phonological constraint *CC. The affinities that this analysis has with the Priority-type theory are clear.

Given the crucial role played by Genitive=/n/, it is important to consider how Kager's analysis might generalize, restricting attention for the moment to Djabugay. One obvious question concerns the specificity of this constraint. In response to the desideratum that constraints be universal and the fact that a constraint like Genitive=/n/ cannot have this property, Kager proposes that this constraint is an instantiation of the universal constraint that shorter things are to be preferred to longer ones. Thus, according to this hypothesis, the ordering effect derives from a kind of economy consideration, one that has analogues in other domains.[7]

The Djabugay genitive is revisited by Mascaró (2007), who, beyond just looking at -ːn and -ŋun, considers the additional roles of epenthesis and deletion. Mascaró notes that in order to rule out "fixes" to the syllable structure effected by the insertion or deletion of material, Max and Dep must be ranked higher than Priority, which operates with the ordering {-ːn > -ŋun}:

(8) Mascaró's analysis

(i) gaɲal-{:n>ŋun}	*CC	Max,Dep	Priority
a. ☞ gaɲal-ŋun			*
b. gaɲal-:n	*!		
c. gaɲal-na		*!	
(ii) guludu-{n>ŋun}	*CC	Max,Dep	Priority
a. ☞ guludu-:n			
b. guludu-ŋun		.	*!

The -na candidate has -n and epenthesis; it does not violate the condition on codas and thus has to be eliminated by other means, since it involves the prioritized allomorph. This is the role that is played by Dep.

The two analyses above are part phonological, part morphological. By allowing phonological and morphological constraints to interact in a single tableau, they clearly instantiate Phonological Selection. A natural question to ask is to what extent the constraints posited for the analysis of the genitive extend into the rest of the Djabugay case system, where numerous other cases of PCA are found. This question is addressed in section 5.2.

For the moment, the treatments in (7) and (8) illustrate the same kind of point made in the discussion of Haitian Creole. Even in "simple" cases of PCA, phonological constraints alone do not seem to determine the entire distribution of allomorphs; morphological constraints are needed as well.

5.1.3 Interim Assessment

The conclusions that can be drawn from the findings summarized here are relatively limited in scope. One conclusion is that Strong Phonological Selection—perhaps also the version of this called P≫M in McCarthy and Prince 1993—makes incorrect predictions; this is the main thrust of Paster's (2006) critique, among others. However, as noted above, Strong Phonological Selection is but one type of theory within the globalist framework, and the fact that it makes incorrect predictions does not rule out other theories framed within globalist assumptions.

Beyond this, the specific fix made to the globalist theories presented above—ordering of affixes—offers little of interest on its own. There is little reason to dwell on the details of the "hybrid" ordering theories, since there is no empirical argument that this type of approach is superior to a localist theory.

A more productive question, which can be raised with reference to Djabugay genitive allomorphy above, is whether the analyses that employ Phonological Selection in some form are able to generalize to other cases of PCA in the same language. The concern motivating this question is that the cases in which Phonological Selection is meant to apply can evidently be chosen on an ad hoc basis. This is not a fatal objection, but given that the "other mechanisms" that are invoked suffice to derive the correct distributions both in some cases of PCA and in all cases of grammatically conditioned allomorphy, the benefits of Phonological Selection are quite limited. That is, since morphological ordering mechanisms could account for the whole system, whether the allomorphy is grammatically or phonologically conditioned, why is it ever necessary or desirable to appeal to phonological constraints? In the absence of a strong empirical argument that Phonological Selection is required, there are only conceptual arguments, based on putative loss of generalization.

One way of allaying some of the concerns about the ad hoc application of Phonological Selection would be to demonstrate that the analysis of individual cases of PCA in some language generalized throughout the language in some interesting way. The next sections address this point, by looking at systems of PCA in detail.

5.1.4 Systems of Allomorphy: Some Questions
Many languages of Australia show PCA of different case endings. In analyzing these alternations, researchers often focus on the ergative case, for reasons made clear below. Beyond the details associated with this case in particular, the *systems* of case inflection provide a fertile ground for illustrating different frameworks and their differences in perspective on interactions between morphology and phonology. The systemic aspect of this is crucial. What looks "phonologically natural" with respect to one instance often looks much less so when other instances are brought into the picture. It is always possible to extract part of "the data" and construct a teleological explanation of why they are the way they are; in some sense, there should be no upper bound to the number of possible teleologies of this type. Part of the promise of Phonological Selection, though, is that an account in which phonology drives allomorph insertion should be able to extend throughout systems of PCA in the same lan-

guage in a straightforward way, thus offering explanatory advantages that reach beyond a limited subset of the facts.

Above, I reviewed two globalist analyses of genitive allomorphy in Djabugay. Even though analyses like these must be taken as "toy" illustrations, because they do not aspire to any level of detail either within one language's case system or across more than one language, the message they intend to convey is clear: allomorphic selection involves Phonological Selection in a way that accounts for generalizations that must be regarded as accidental from the localist point of view. Putting the conceptual part of this to the side, the discussion in the following sections takes the claim that Phonological Selection is necessary at face value by attempting to work through case systems in which PCA is abundant and asking to what extent significant generalizations are missed if Phonological Selection is ignored.

5.2 Djabugay Case Allomorphy

5.2.1 Basics of the Case System
Djabugay shows -:*n* and -*ŋun* allomorphs of the genitive morpheme, distributed according to the final segment of the host noun. The examples in (6) are repeated in (9) for convenience:

(9) Genitive allomorphy

	Abs	Gen	Gloss
a. V-final	guludu	guludu-:n	'dove'
	gurra:	gurra:-n	'dog'
b. C-final	gaɲal	gaɲal-ŋun	'goanna'
	girrgirr	girrgirr-ŋun	'bush canary'

As far as Phonological Selection goes, the degree to which the phonology of surface forms drives the selection of allomorphs is already somewhat compromised in the analyses of Kager (1996) and Mascaró (2007), in the sense that both analyses have to resort to nonphonological ordering in order to account even for this case. When the discussion moves to the rest of the case system, it becomes clear that the potential role for Phonological Selection is reduced even further.

The table in (10) shows the forms of ergative case affixes. The organization of allomorphs in (10) is centered on the admissible final consonants /m, n, ɲ, l, rr, r, y/ of the language:[8]

(10) Ergative allomorphy (Patz 1991, 264)

Env.	Allomorph	Noun	Erg	Gloss
a. stem/V/	-ŋgu	ɲumbu	ɲumbu-ŋgu	'father'
b. stem/rr/	-u	wumbarr	wumbarr-u	'puppy'
c. stem/l,r/	-ndu	baɖigal	baɖigal-ndu	'turtle'
d. stem/m/	-uŋgu	wulam	wulamu-ŋgu	'perch'
e. stem/n/	-ndu	buŋan	buŋa-ndu	'sun'
f. stem/C[+pal]/	-ɲɖu	ɖawarray	ɖawarra-ɲɖu	'thunderstorm'
f′.		murraɲ	murra-ɲɖu	'fever'

These facts raise several questions of interest for the analyses of genitive allomorphy presented above. For example:

• Kager's (1996) general prediction is that the "default" allomorph must be the smallest one. In (10), this means that the ergative should manifest a language-specific instantiation of this universal economy constraint in the form of the constraint ERGATIVE=/u/. The way that Kager's theory works, the dispreferred allomorph(s) should surface only when the preferred one violates higher-ranked syllable structure constraints. We should thus expect to find (e.g.) -u throughout the C-final forms in (10), contrary to fact.

• There is what looks like epenthesis in (10d). This raises the question why epenthesis cannot "rescue" any of the relevant genitive candidates—where -:n with C-final stems is eliminated by a constraint banning complex codas—while the evidently epenthesizing candidate (10d) can win in the case of /m/-final ergatives (recall that MAX and DEP are ranked above PRIORITY in Mascaró's (2007) analysis of the genitive in (8)). In addition to this, deletion is found in (10e–f′), where stem-final consonants are eliminated.

• Affixation in (10e–f′) is opaque, because the stem-final consonant is deleted. There is no reason why, in the analyses described to this point, the phonology should not have the "default" or prioritized allomorph (i.e., the one that occurs after V-final hosts) -ŋgu in these cases, since the "conditioning" stem-final consonant does not appear in the surface form.[9]

None of these facts are considered by Kager or Mascaró, who restrict their attention to the genitive. The intuitive appeal of something like Phonological Selection may or may not be felt when attention is restricted in this way. After all, the point of both Kager's and Mascaró's treatments is that phonology alone cannot account for the distribution of allomorphs.

In any case, the idea that simple phonological considerations account for
the attested patterns loses much of its force in the context of the ergative,
where the analysis required for the genitive cannot derive the facts without significant modification. This raises one of the concerns considered
above: if the "phonological" constraints required for allomorph distribution must be specified on a case-by-case basis, it is hard to see how an
item-specific analysis could be a success for Phonological Selection.

Additional points along these lines arise when other cases are taken
into account. As a first step toward a more comprehensive analysis of
the Djabugay case system, consider the "instrumental and locative"
(inst/loc) case forms:

(11) Instrumental and locative (Patz 1991, 265)

	Env.	Allomorph	Noun	Inst/Loc	Gloss
a.	σσ/V/	-:	mara	mara:	'hand'
b.	stem/V:/	-la	ḍina:	ḍina:-la	'foot'
b′.	not-(σσ)/V/	-la	digarra	digarra-la	'sand'
c.	stem/rr/	-a	biwurr	biwurr-a	'spear'
d.	stem/C/	-nda	diṉal	diṉal-nda	'egg'
e.	stem/m/	-unda	gurrŋam	gurrŋam-unda	'flame tree'
f.	stem/n/	-nda	ḍulbin	ḍulbi-nda	'tree, log'
g.	stem/C[+pal]/	-ɲḍa	guguy	gugu-ɲḍa	'center'
g′.			buḍaɲ	buḍa-ɲḍa	'beetle sp.'

Although certain effects are unique to this case, there are some clear parallels with what happens in the ergative, especially with assimilation of
the affixal consonants to adjacent segments: specifically, -nda and -ɲḍa
in the inst/loc correspond to -ngu and -ɲḍu in the ergative. From a comparative perspective, such correspondences between the ergative and the
inst/loc are unsurprising. Within the comparative study of Australian languages, it has long been observed that the locative case endings of the
type represented by Djabugay -nda are similar to or the same as the -ŋgu
set of ergative suffixes, the difference being that the locative ones have the
vowel /a/ in place of /u/.[10]

The series of affixes consisting of a nasal and a homorganic stop plays
an important role in this system. I refer to such morphemes with the abbreviation -^{N}C- affixes. The situation in Djabugay reflects the historical
connection between ergative and locative in part, except that the locative
never surfaces as -ŋga. For the purposes of the synchronic analysis of the
case system, there seems to be a single assimilation process that applies to
certain ergative and inst/loc endings (but not to other case endings; see

below), by which the -^{N}C- affixes acquire place features of consonants to their left.

Assuming this assimilation rule, and an additional epenthesis process (the latter for the /m/-final stems), the VIs needed for ergative can be reduced to -*ŋgu* and -*u*. The locative has -:, -*la*, -*a*, and -*nda*. I will assume for the moment that the first of these is a -∅ VI that triggers a lengthening readjustment rule, although nothing critical hinges on exactly this implementation; the notation -: is used to stand in for this analysis in the discussion below.

Further reduction and decomposition is possible in both the ergative and the inst/loc. In particular, the -^{N}C- component of -*ŋgu* and -*nda* is eliminated with /rr/-final stems, suggesting the following rule:

(12) -^{N}C- → ∅/stem/rr/-__

With the rule (12), there is no need for an -*u* exponent in the ergative, and the Spell-Out of this case can then be reduced to the VI with the exponent -*ŋgu*. Similarly, the -*a* in the inst/loc can be eliminated as a separate exponent.

In addition, it can be assumed that in some cases the -^{N}C- affixes also trigger the deletion of stem-final consonants.

Taking the description above at face value amounts to positing the following VIs:

(13) Case Spell-Out: Provisional

     a. Ergative
        ERG ↔ -ŋgu
     b. Instrumental/Locative
        INST/LOC ↔ -:/(...V)⌒__
        INST/LOC ↔ -la/V⌒__
        INST/LOC ↔ -nda

The full range of surface forms is derived from -*ŋgu* and -*nda* via assimilation and the other rules mentioned above. An obvious question is whether this assimilation is part of the normal phonology. The behavior of other case affixes shows that it is restricted to -^{N}C- affixes in the ergative and inst/loc. For example, the dative case is realized as -:*nda* after V-final stems and -*ɲunda* after C-final stems. This latter distribution includes C-final nouns that end in a palatal, where the ergative shows assimilation. The dative is not subject to the same assimilation (and other) processes that affect ergative -*ŋgu* and locative -*ndu*. Similarly, the genitive in -*ɲun* does not show assimilation. With assimilation versus nonassimilation in mind, the four cases discussed to this point can be arranged as follows:[11]

(14) Assimilating (a) versus not assimilating (b)

Case	Form	Env.	Noun	Affixed	Gloss
a. Ergative	-ŋgu				
Inst/Loc	-:	(σσV)/__	mara	mara:	'hand'
	-la	V(:)/__	ḍina:	ḍina:-la	'foot'
	-nda				
b. Genitive	-:n	V__	guludu	guludu-:n	'dove'
	-ɲun	C__	gaɲal	gaɲal-ɲun	'goanna'
Dative	-:nda	V__	yaba	yaba-:nda	'elder brother'
	-ɲunda	C__	ganaŋgirray	ganaŋgirray-ɲunda	'younger brother'

It is clear from these facts that the morphophonological assimilation rule cannot simply target nasal-initial affixes at syllable boundaries, because it would wrongly predict assimilation with genitives and datives, whose exponents are also nasal-initial. The process must be restricted to -^{N}C- affixes.

5.2.2 Case Decompositions

One question that arises at this point is whether, given a set of morphophonological processes that make specific reference to ergative and locative -^{N}C- exponents, there might be a loss of generalization if these particular case affixes are included by list in the morphophonological rules of assimilation and the like. That is, given that the exponents of ergative and inst/loc are quite similar to one another (-ŋgu for ergative, -nda for inst/loc), one way to account for the fact that parallel morphophonological behavior is found in exactly these cases would be to analyze them as sharing the -^{N}C- component as a morpheme. If the ergative were -^{N}C-u-, and the corresponding allomorph of inst/loc were -^{N}C-a-, then the various processes would all be applying to the same morpheme.

As a general point, the decomposition of case (or case-number) affixes has a precedent in the literature, particularly within the context of theories with *fission* of morphemes (see Noyer 1997; also see Halle 1997 and Halle and Vaux 1998 for slightly different views). The idea that at least some case endings in certain Australian languages are built out of other case endings (i.e., that they are internally complex) is also discussed in the literature (see Dixon 2002, sec. 5.2; this is not a proposal that has been made for the ergative and locative, as far as I am aware).

It appears that in the synchronic analysis of Djabugay, there is little motivation for positing a shared -^{N}C- morpheme for ergatives and inst/

loc. The inst/loc morpheme never surfaces as -ŋga, as would be expected if there were an -ŋg component common to ergative and inst/loc. In part, this is because -: and -la appear in the context of (different types of) V-final nouns; these are the environments in which the default (i.e., underlying) form of -ŋga should be found. Moreover, there are other places in the system where the locative does not pattern as predicted if the two cases in question shared an -ŋg component. For example, if the underlying form in the inst/loc were -ŋga, then -ŋga should surface after the epenthetic /u/ in the /m/-final nouns, in the same way that -ŋgu is found in this environment in the ergative. The inst/loc does not show this form, and there is no reason to think that the -/nd/- that is found in this environment for the inst/loc derives from -ŋga via some (morpho)phonological process, because if this were the case, we would equally expect to find undu in /m/-final ergatives.

Overall, it seems preferable to take the underlying representation of the relevant inst/loc morpheme to be -nda.

While there is no evidence for decomposing ergative and inst/loc in a way that makes them share a piece, breaking down case affixes is motivated in other parts of the system. In particular, the dative morphemes seen above are simply the genitive morphemes plus -da. This accounts for the fact that, in V-final and C-final environments, the first component of dative -:nda and -ŋunda mirrors the genitive -:n and -ŋun. Within a system of case features like that advanced in Halle and Vaux 1998, these two cases have the following features:

(15) Genitive and dative

	Gen	Dat
Oblique	+	+
Structural	+	+
Superior	−	+
Free	+	+

The mechanisms responsible for producing case features in the language create nodes with the feature specification of the dative and genitive in the appropriate syntactic contexts. The dative nodes undergo the rule of *Dative Splitting* (16a) prior to Vocabulary Insertion to yield two distinct nodes; then the VIs in (16b) produce the desired results:

(16) a. Dative Splitting

    [+obl +str +sup +free] → [+obl +str] [+sup +free]

  b. [+obl +str] ↔ -:n /V__

    [+obl +str] ↔ -ŋun /C__

    [+sup +free] ↔ -da

Rule (16a) is a fission rule that splits a node with the features for the dative case into two distinct nodes. Each of these nodes is then subjected to Vocabulary Insertion. The two morphemes -:*n* and -*ŋun* (called *genitive* above) thus win competitions for insertion under two sets of circumstances: first, with nodes that are "genitive" in the sense of (15) from the beginning; and, second, with nodes having the feature content [+obl +str] that are the product of (16a).

Continuing with the Spell-Out of the case morphemes, I assume that the case features involved in the system as a whole are as follows (see Halle and Vaux 1998, 225):

(17) Case features

	Nom	*Acc*	*Gen*	*Dat*	*Loc*	*Inst*	*Abl*	*Erg*
Oblique	−	−	+	+	+	+	+	−
Structural	+	+	+	+	−	−	−	+
Superior	+	−	−	+	−	+	+	+
Free	+	−	+	+	−	−	+	−

Putting the different aspects of the analysis together, the case inflections are inserted with the VIs in (18):

(18) [−obl +str +sup −free] ↔ -ŋgu   (ERG)
    [+obl −str −free]   ↔ -:   /(...V)__ (INST/LOC)
    [+obl −str −free]   ↔ -la /V__   (INST/LOC)
    [+obl −str −free]   ↔ -nda   (INST/LOC)
    [+obl +str]   ↔ -:n /V__   ("GEN")
    [+obl +str]   ↔ -ŋun /C__   ("GEN")
    [+sup +free]   ↔ -da   (DAT)

Other aspects of the surface forms of these morphemes are the product of rules that effect the changes described in (19), which apply to the affixes that begin with -^{N}C-:

(19) Morphophonological rules

    a. -^{N}*C- Assimilation:* -^{N}C- affixes assimilate in place.
    b. *Epenthesis:* -^{N}C- affixes have epenthetic /u/ after /m/.
    c. *Deletion1:* In -^{N}C- affixes, the -^{N}C- component is deleted after /rr/.
    d. *Deletion2:* C[+pal] → Ø/__-^{N}C-

There are two possibilities for the triggering of these morphophonological rules. One is that the affixes that undergo them must simply be marked, as in (20):

(20) $-\text{ŋgu}^+$, $-\text{nda}^+$

The other possibility—motivated perhaps only by looking at the assimilation effects—would be to attempt a phonological solution, in which the $-^N\text{C}-$ morphemes are underspecified to make $-^N\text{C}-$ Assimilation an automatic consequence. Whether this would work for that rule, it is not the case that the behavior of $-^N\text{C}-$ affixes with respect to Epenthesis and Deletion follows in the same way. In the end, the fact that some exponents are subject to these processes and others are not is something that does not seem to derive from other aspects of the phonology of the language.

5.2.3 Summary

The distribution of the Djabugay genitive allomorphs $-\!:\!n$ and $-\eta un$ is employed in the works cited at the beginning of this section (Kager 1996; Mascaró 2007) to generate the impression that there is strong motivation for Phonological Selection in cases of PCA. The questions that launched the more detailed investigation of Djabugay case inflections above are (primarily) whether, when this sort of case system is considered in detail, there is a role for Phonological Selection, and (secondarily) whether the claims made for Phonological Selection in the analyses of genitive allomorphy can generalize in any interesting sense.

In terms of these questions, the conclusions of this case study can be summarized as follows:

• *Making phonological sense:* According to Kager's (1996) and Mascaró's (2007) analyses, affixation of the genitive makes partial phonological sense, as brought out in the discussion above. In the ergative, however, there are many examples of affixation that create codas (e.g., all instances of $-ndu$ with C-final stems). On the surface, ergative case is realized as $-u$ with /rr/-final stems. If the $-u$ exponent of the ergative were inserted after other C-final nouns, the phonological markedness created by the resulting coda would be avoided (similar points come up in the inst/loc case). This does not happen. There are ways of avoiding this expectation—for example, grafting on ordering solutions in which $-u$ is dispreferred—but these are simply fixes that prevent the strong expectations of Phonological Selection from being instantiated.

• *Phonological consistency:* As noted earlier, the pattern of genitive allomorphy with $-\!:\!n$ and $-\eta un$ only makes sense if there is no epenthesis/ deletion. This is what motivates ranking DEP and MAX above the constraint banning complex codas in Mascaró's analysis in (8). However, in the ergative there is both epenthesis and deletion. On the whole, the system requires morphophonological rules that are specific to certain case affixes. This is unavoidable on any analysis, but as a result there is little potential role for Phonological Selection when the details of the system are considered.

• *Transparency:* Affixation of *-nda* in the inst/loc of /m/-final stems is found with epenthetic /u/, just like in the ergative. In the inst/loc, the epenthesis renders insertion of *-nda* opaque, since, in V-final contexts, *-la* (or *-:*) is inserted. This kind of opacity raises general questions for theories with global-MP. The issues connected with opaque interactions are examined in chapter 6.

Overall, it is clear that the analysis of genitive allomorphy based on the phonological constraint against complex codas cannot be extended to the rest of the Djabugay case system in any obvious way. As acknowledged in chapter 4, and in the introductory remarks to this chapter, it is impossible to argue against Phonological Selection by showing that it is not relevant in some system or other. At the same time, analyzing systems like Djabugay in detail is important because it provides some insight into how intuitions about Phonological Selection line up with complex systems of allomorphy. The factors identified in the analysis above are (i) a limited set of allomorphs, whose distribution is determined by elements in the local phonological context of the node showing allomorphy, interacting with (ii) a number of morphophonological rules that apply subsequent to this, changing the shapes of the morphemes and their hosts.

My claim is not that these facts can be analyzed only by a localist theory (although it remains to be seen what form a globalist account would take); rather, the point is that there is little in this system to suggest that important generalizations are missed by a theory that makes no use of Phonological Selection.

5.3 Yidiɲ Case Allomorphy

The language Yidiɲ—closely related to Djabugay—is described and analyzed in work by Dixon (1977a,b). The case morphology in this language shows PCA that in some ways looks very similar to some of the patterns analyzed above. There are, however, other factors that make Yidiɲ an important case study for the relationship between morphology and phonology. The patterns of case allomorphy interact with a set of (morpho)-phonological processes in a way that produces a complex pattern of vowel length alternations and alternations between "long" and "short" allomorphs of particular morphemes. Crucially—and this is Dixon's insight into this system—these patterns can be stated in a clear and simple fashion if morphological and (morpho)phonological processes interact serially, in a way that makes the connection between the vowel length and the allomorphic patterns opaque in the surface forms.

The relationship between allomorphy and vowel length provides an important illustration of the strengths and weaknesses of Phonological Selection. Looking only at the surface manifestations of case allomorphy, an account based on Phonological Selection appears very promising for Yidiɲ. A theory that makes use of a constraint that prefers exhaustive footing is able to predict many allomorphic alternations. However, this method of accounting for allomorphy makes the vowel length alternations impossible to state in a simple way. Thus, when the system as a whole is considered, the motivation for Phonological Selection disappears.

5.3.1 Preliminary View of the Cases

The ergative case in Yidiɲ shows the forms in (21), which are organized according to V-final nouns (21a,b), stop-final nouns (21c), rhotic-final nouns (21d), and glide-final nouns (21e):

(21) Ergative

	Root = Abs	Erg	Gloss
a.	yabi	yabi:-ŋ	'gray possum'
b.	waguḍa	waguḍa-ŋgu	'man'
c.	ḍuḍum	ḍuḍu:m-bu	'father's sister'
	guban	guba:n-du	'big butterfly'
	ŋurbirbiɲ	ŋubirbiɲ-ḍu	'leech'
	wagal	waga:l-du	'wife'
	warabal	warabal-du	'flying squirrel'
d.	wuḍar	wuḍa:-du	'dew, frost'
	gugaɽ	guga:-du	'large guana'
	maŋgumbar	maŋgumba(r)-du	'leaf grub'
	buliyiɽ	buliyi(ɽ)-du	'chicken hawk'
e.	gunduy	gundu:(y)-(ɲ)ḍu	'brown snake'

V-final stems show -ŋ alternating with the familiar -ŋgu, on the basis of even versus odd syllable count, as seen in (21a) versus (21b). Despite appearances, this alternation does not involve distinct VIs; below, I follow Dixon in accounting for it in terms of a deletion rule that applies throughout the language. In C-final stems, the nasal component is either absent (21c) or absent along with deletion of the stem-final sonorant consonant (21d).[12]

Taking (21) as a whole, it is possible to posit a single -*ŋgu* allomorph for the ergative and derive the surface forms in the morphophonology. This requires phonological rules that delete the nasal component and assimilate the stop component to the stem-final consonant. Other phonological alternations seen throughout (21), which involve deletion of word-final material and lengthening of vowels, are analyzed in detail in later sections.

The locative, instrumental, and allative cases syncretize for nouns in Yidiɲ. I use *locative+* as a cover term for this case form. The allomorphs of locative+ forms are shown in (22):

(22) Locative/Allative/Instrumental

	Root = Abs	*Loc+*	*Gloss*
a.	buɽi	buɽi-:	'fire'
b.	gabuḏu	gabuḏu-la	'white clay'
c.	muḏam	muḏa:m-ba	'mother'
	warḏan	warḏa:n-da	'boat'
	yidiɲ	yidi:ɲ-ḏa	'language name'
	muygal	muyga:l-da	'hole, trap'
d.	baŋguɽ	baŋgu:-da	'fish spear'
	maŋgumbar	maŋgumba(r)-da	'leaf grub'
	guŋgambuɽ	guŋgambu(ɽ)-da	'butterfly sp.'
e.	gabay	gaba:(y)-ɲḏa	'path, track'

With V-final stems, locative+ is marked by final lengthening alone in disyllabics (22a); in trisyllabic nouns, the affix -*la* appears (22b). This pattern is related to the -*ŋ*/-*ŋgu* alternation in the ergative; the distributional conditions under which the alternation occurs are identical. However, the alternation between lengthening and -*la* is in some sense unpredictable as far as the phonology goes, since it is predicted that "long" -*la* will alternate with "short" -*l*, parallel to the way -*ŋgu* and -*ŋ* alternate in the ergative.[13] In C-final stems, locative+ is realized as an assimilating stop (22c), as -*da* plus deletion of the stem-final consonant with rhotics (22d), and with assimilated -*ɲḏa* and variable deletion of the stem-final consonant with final /y/ (22e).[14]

In a way that parallels the Djabugay case system, other case endings do not assimilate to adjacent consonants as the ergative and locative+ exponents do. Sets of inflected forms illustrating this and a number of additional points of morphophonological interest are shown in (23), where nouns are organized by V-/C-final stems and odd/even syllable count:

(23) Nouns/Case endings (Dixon 1977a, 57)

	$\sigma\sigma V$ 'kangaroo sp.'	$\sigma\sigma\sigma V$ 'initiated man'	$\sigma\sigma C$ 'hornet'	$\sigma\sigma\sigma C$ 'tortoise'
Abs	mabi	mula:ri	biɲḍin	baḍi:gal
Erg	mabi:-ŋ	mulari-ŋgu	biɲḍi:n-du	baḍigal-du
Dat	mabi:-nda	mulari-nda	biɲḍi:n-da	baḍigal-nda
Purp	mabi:-gu	mulari-gu	biɲḍi:n-gu	baḍigal-gu
Loc	mabi:-Ø	mulari-la	biɲḍi:n-da	baḍigal-da
Abl	mabi-m	mulari-mu	biɲḍi:n-mu	baḍigal-mu
Com	mabi:	mulari-yi	biɲḍi:n-ḍi	baḍigal-ḍi
Gen	mabi:-n	mulari-ni	biɲḍi:n-i	baḍigal-ni

Throughout these forms, there are alternations between long and short versions of the case affix: along with *-ŋgu/-ŋ* in the ergative, there are *-mu/-m* in the ablative and *-ni/-n* in the genitive.[15]

In addition to this alternation in the affixes, the forms in (23) show changes in vowel length. With the exception of a few words, vowel length does not exist in underlying forms in Yidiɲ; it appears as the result of a phonological rule. Crucially, this lengthening rule interacts with the principles governing the allomorphic effects in the case system, as can be seen by considering the morphophonology of Yidiɲ in greater detail.

5.3.2 Morphophonological Interactions

Dixon's (1977a,b) rules accounting for long/short allomorphy refer to syllable count, and subsequent analyses in the metrical framework like those of Nash (1979) and Hayes (1982) treat this factor in terms of foot structure.

I assume that Yidiɲ words are footed from left to right, with the insertion of] (here and below, I assume a theory like that proposed in Idsardi 1992; Halle and Idsardi 1995; and related work):

(24) Footing

Insert] iteratively from left to right, binary.

Subsequent rules refer to foot boundaries and, in the case of deletion, to whether or not a particular part of the representation is footed. When footing occurs with respect to Vocabulary Insertion is an important issue; see below.

Dixon's analysis involves two rules for the vowel-length and long/short allomorph alternations. The first rule, *Penultimate Lengthening* (*PL*), accounts for the long vowels seen in the forms above: it creates long vowels in the penults of odd-syllabled words. As recognized by Hayes (1982) and others following him, this process refers to foot structure; it can be stated as follows:[16]

(25) Penultimate Lengthening

$$\sigma\sigma]\sigma\# \to \sigma\sigma\text{:}]\sigma\#$$

Clearly, this rule follows the footing rule in (24).

The second rule of the phonology is *Final-Syllable Deletion* (*FSD*), which accounts for long/short alternations in affixes, both in noun inflection and elsewhere in the language. The effects of PL and FSD together are illustrated in (26), which shows the present tense affix -*ŋ* and the past tense affix -*ɲu* in combination with even- and odd-syllabled hosts:

(26) Final-Syllable Deletion (Dixon 1977a, 44)

	Even	*Odd*
	'go'	'walk up'
Stem	gali-	maḍinda-
Present	gali-ŋ	maḍi:nda-ŋ
Past	gali:-ɲ	maḍinda-ɲu

Present tense shows the exponent -*ŋ*. The exponent of past tense has the form -*ɲu*, and it surfaces in this form in quadrisyllabic *maḍinda-ɲu*. In the case of the verb *gali* 'go', the nucleus of the final syllable is deleted, yielding /ɲ/ on the surface. This is the same rule that applies throughout the case system, for example yielding the alternation between -*ŋgu* and -*ŋ* in the ergative case.

The interaction of PL and FSD accounts for a significant part of the morphophonological system of the language. An important component of Dixon's analysis of Yidiɲ phonology is the proposal that FSD is ordered after PL, as (27) shows with reference to some different hosts and affixes:[17]

(27) Illustration of Penultimate Lengthening and Final-Syllable Deletion

	Verb-Past	*Verb-Dat-Sub*	*Noun-Erg*	*Noun-Gen*
	'go'	'walk up'	'woman'	'woman'
Input	gali-ɲu	maḍinda-ɲu-nda	buɲa-ŋgu	buɲa-ni
Footing	gali]-ɲu	maḍi]nda-ɲu]-nda	buɲa]-ŋgu	buɲa]-ni
PL	gali:]-ɲu	maḍi]nda-ɲu:]-nda	buɲa:]-ŋgu	buɲa:]-ni
FSD	gali:-ɲ]	maḍi]nda-ɲu:-n]	buɲa:-ŋ]	buɲa:-n]

When FSD applies after PL in this way, it renders the distribution of long vowels opaque. This is a significant point for assessing the potential contributions of Phonological Selection in the analysis of this system; see section 5.3.5.

The details of FSD are complicated; Dixon's formulation of the rule, which involves a number of conditions that must be unpacked, is as follows:

(28) Final-Syllable Deletion (Dixon 1977a, 48)

$XV_1C_1(C_2)V_2\# \rightarrow XV_1C_1\#$

a. if $XV_1C_1(C_2)V_2\#$ is an odd-syllabled word;

b. and C_1 is one of the set ($l, r, ɾ, y, m, n, ɲ, ŋ$) of allowable word-final consonants;

c. and there is a morpheme boundary between V_1 and C_1.

The condition (28a) specifying the syllable count is statable in terms of foot structure, exactly as with PL (cf. Nash 1979; Hayes 1982). Beyond sensitivity to foot structure, three other aspects of the deletion process require comment. The first is that the rule applies only to *open* final syllables. The second and third are (28b,c): the "acceptable final consonant" condition and the "morpheme boundary" condition, respectively.

Dixon motivates the need to restrict the rule to deletion of open syllables with examples like these:

(29) Examples

a. gali 'go'
   gali-COMITATIVE+CONJUGATION-l   gali:-ŋa-l, *gali:ŋ
b. gali 'go'
   gali-CAUSAL SUBORDINATE   gali:-ɲu-m, *gali:ɲ
c. maḍinda 'walk up'
   maḍinda-PRESENT   maḍi:nda-ŋ, *maḍi:n

In each of these cases, affixation produces a closed word-final syllable that is not deleted by FSD. It is possible that some of the examples that are intended to illustrate this particular restriction derive from other factors. However, I will assume for present purposes that only open syllables are deleted, and build this directly into the structural description of the rule. This assumption could potentially be simplified, but it is not critical for the interaction of PL and FSD.

The "acceptable final consonant" condition (28b) and "morpheme boundary" condition (28c) are more important for the general set of phonology/morphology issues under consideration here. The statement of the former condition makes it look like deletion is blocked when it would create a problem for syllable structure: only possible word-final segments may precede deleted material. In this way, it appears to require a kind of lookahead, in which the application of the deletion process is determined by properties of the output. The kind of example that motivates this condition is seen in (30):

(30) mabi 'kangaroo sp.'
      mabi:-gu, *mabi:-g 'kangaroo sp.-PURP'

That is, /g/ is not possible word-finally, and there is no deletion of final /u/.

The morphological boundary referred to in (28c) also implicates connections between morphology and phonology. The motivation for this restriction is not as easy to see as the motivation for the other conditions. Its effects are seen in cases in which phonologically identical words show different behavior with respect to FSD, in a way that correlates with differences in morphological structure. The example in (31) illustrates this restriction:

(31) biɲḍin 'hornet'
      biɲḍi:n-gu, *biɲḍi:n 'hornet-DAT'

There is no problem with the final consonant here, since -*gu* occurs after a C-final noun and could be deleted as a whole to leave admissible /n/ in word-final position. However, the morpheme boundary condition is not met in this form: there is no morpheme boundary between V_1 (the second /i/ of *biɲḍin*) and C_1 (the final /n/). There *is* a morpheme boundary between C_1 and C_2 (the final /n/ of the Root and the initial /g/ of the purposive affix), but this fact is irrelevant to Dixon's rule, and now it is clear why. Evidently, there must be a morpheme boundary between the consonant to the left of the deleted material and the material to that consonant's left.

One possible response to the effect in (31) would be to say that the failure to delete is the result of another factor, which prohibits the deletion of entire morphemes. In all of the other deletion cases seen to this point, an overt piece remains of the morpheme that is partially deleted (recall the "short" case and tense forms). In the hypothetical deletion in (31), the deletion process eliminates the entire -*gu* morpheme, which might suggest that the morpheme boundary condition actually reflects a ban on the deletion of entire morphemes.

Additional forms show that there is at least one type of case where an entire -CV affix is deleted by FSD. (26) shows past tense verbs, which have the affix -*ɲu*. With disyllabic verbs like *wawa:-l* 'see', where the -*l* is the conjugation marker, the past tense form shows no overt Tense affix. This follows from FSD as formulated by Dixon:

(32) wawa-l-ɲu $\xrightarrow{\text{PL}}$ wawa:-l-ɲu $\xrightarrow{\text{FSD}}$ wawa:-l

Notice that in the case of *wawa:-l*, there is a morpheme boundary between V_1 (the final vowel of the stem) and C_1 (the conjugation marker *-l*).

An alternative to positing FSD in this type of case, such as treating the *-ɲ/-Ø* alternation in the past tense as suppletive allomorphy, requires an analysis in which the past tense morpheme has a *-Ø* allomorph only with verbs of a particular phonological size, such that this allomorph appears in environments that are associated with FSD elsewhere in the language. It also makes the vowel length on the second syllable of *wawa:l* mysterious, since, it being a final syllable, PL cannot have applied to give this length. On the other hand, positing a *-ɲu* that is deleted by FSD allows a straightforward treatment of the vowel length in terms of PL.

In sum, it appears that a ban against "whole morpheme deletion" is not responsible for the nondeletion of *-gu* in (31).[18]

5.3.3 (Re)analysis

From the above review of Dixon's deletion rule, the two aspects of FSD that need to be accounted for are (i) the effect that bans deletion after impossible word-final consonants and (ii) the (somewhat odd-looking) morpheme boundary condition.

The first restriction can be reduced directly to factors that do not involve lookahead. In particular, the fact that FSD does not apply when it would produce an impossible word-final consonant derives from the fact that deletion occurs only after sonorants. This can be written directly into the deletion rule, as a contextual condition.

The second condition, which seems to directly implicate the morphological structure, reduces to the way in which deletion is sensitive to foot structure and syllabification. The effects of this condition can be captured if the deletion rule eliminates unfooted material that appears after unsyllabified sonorants.

Taking these points into consideration, I formulate FSD as in (33), where the notation $\sigma°$ is employed for a syllable that is not footed, and material linked to x is unsyllabified:[19]

(33) Final-Syllable Deletion

$$
\begin{array}{ccc}
\sigma° & & \text{x} \\
| & \rightarrow \emptyset/ & | \quad \_\# \\
\text{(C)V} & & \text{C[+son]}
\end{array}
$$

The derivation of the ergative case forms for V-final disyllabic and tri-syllabic nouns is illustrated in (34). In these derivations, it is assumed that the Root is syllabified and footed before Vocabulary Insertion applies to functional heads attached to the Root. Following Vocabulary Insertion at these nodes, a second round of syllabification and footing applies to the exponents of the nodes that have undergone Vocabulary Insertion, and then the phonological rules PL, FSD, and Resyllabification apply:[20]

(34) Derivation of *-ŋ* affixation (*yabi* 'gray possum', *mula:ri* 'initiated man')

yabi-ERG	mulari-ERG	Input
yabi]-ERG	mula]ri-ERG	Syllabification/Footing
yabi]-ŋgu	mula]ri-ŋgu	Vocabulary Insertion
yabi]-ŋgu	mula]ri-ŋgu]	Syllabification/Footing
yabi:]-ŋgu	—	PL
yabi:]-ŋ	—	FSD
yabi:ŋ]	mula]riŋ-gu]	Resyllabification

The syllabification that takes place after Vocabulary Insertion looks at the phonological representation of affixal material. In sequences of affixes like *-l-ɲu* 'Conjugation-Tense', or for affixes like *-ŋgu* 'ergative', syllab-ification after Vocabulary Insertion produces a representation in which the initial segment is unsyllabified. As shown in the derivation in (34), Resyllabification—integration of these segments with the already syllabi-fied Root—occurs late in the derivation, after PL and FSD have applied. This is crucial in explaining the cases that motivated Dixon's morpheme boundary condition.

To illustrate how this proposal captures the effects of Dixon's mor-pheme boundary condition, I will employ the pair *wawa-l-ɲu* 'see-CONJ-PAST', which surfaces with the final syllable deleted as *wawa:l*, and *guygal-du* 'bandicoot-ERG', which does not show FSD and surfaces as *guyga:ldu*, not **guygal*. In the analysis that implements deletion with (33), the difference between these forms has to do with the way in which material is footed, depending on whether it is part of the Root's pho-nology or the exponent of a morpheme that undergoes VI. Prior to Vocabulary Insertion the *wawa* form and the *guygal* form have the repre-sentations in (35):

(35) Representations prior to Vocabulary Insertion

    a. wawa]-CONJ-T[past]

    b. guygal]-ERG

When Vocabulary Insertion occurs, the exponents of the morphemes CONJ, T[past], and ERG shown in (36) are inserted, and Syllabification and Footing apply:

(36) Representations after Vocabulary Insertion

    a. wawa]-l-ɲu

    b. guygal]-du

In each of these examples, no new feet are created in the second cycle, because the footing process groups only sequences of two syllables (i.e., it creates binary feet). The affixal material -ɲu and -du is unfooted and thus potentially able to undergo FSD.

The important asymmetry that accounts for why deletion occurs with the *wawa* form but not the *guygal* form is that in (36a), the sonorant is unsyllabified, whereas in (36b), it is syllabified as part of the root. It follows that Root-final sonorant consonants, like the final /l/ of *guygal*, cannot trigger deletion, since FSD is triggered only by *unsyllabified* sonorants. On the other hand, affixal sonorants, like the conjugation /l/ in *wawa:-l*, are outside of the foot boundary. This consonant is not syllabified with the Root, and FSD applies accordingly.

The analysis of the different rules of Yidiɲ discussed above, and incorporating (33), is illustrated in (37) for nouns and verbs of different sizes; *Syll/Foot* abbreviates *Syllabification and Footing*:[21]

(37) Final-Syllable Deletion and "morpheme boundaries"

'bandicoot'	'see'	'tortoise'	'go'	
guygal-ERG	wawa-CONJ-PAST	badigal-ERG	gali-COM-CONJ-PAST	Input
guygal]-ERG	wawa]-CONJ-PAST	badi]gal-ERG	gali]-COM-CONJ-PAST	Syll/Foot
guygal]-du	wawa]-l-ɲu	badi]gal-du	gali]-ɲa-l-ɲu	Vocabulary Insertion
—	—	badi]gal-du]	gali]-ŋa-l-ɲu]	Syll/Foot
guyga:l]-du	wawa:]-l-ɲu	—	—	PL
—	wawa:]-l	—	—	FSD
—	wawa:l]	—	—	Resyll

To summarize, the work done by Dixon's morpheme boundary condition is done on this analysis by the requirement that an unsyllabified sonorant precede the deleted material. Sonorants that are part of the Root are syllabified early, in the first application of Syllabification and Footing. In some cases, affixal sonorants cannot be syllabified with other affixal material; moreover, these consonants are not resyllabified as codas until late in the derivation. These sonorants trigger FSD when the other conditions on this rule are met, whereas Root-final sonorants do not. This produces an asymmetry with respect to FSD that is derivative of morphological structure.

5.3.4 Putting the Components Together

Although the phonological processes required in this system are complex (for deletion in particular), the overall analysis is one in which the surface complexity reduces to an analysis in which there is a small set of VIs, along with a set of phonological operations that apply to these. The VIs required for Yidiɲ are as follows (for simplicity, the cases are not decomposed into features):[22]

(38) Vocabulary items for case

ERG   ↔ -ŋgu
LOC   ↔ -la
PURP ↔ -gu
DAT   ↔ -nda
ABL   ↔ -mu
COM ↔ -yi   /V⌢__
COM ↔ -ḍi   /C⌢__
GEN   ↔ -ni

In addition, the phonological rules posited above must be applied, in the order shown in (37).

   Beyond this, a few additional points must be noted:

· For the locative+ of a V-final disyllabic host, the rules given above produce final -l; so, for (e.g.) buṛi 'fire', the locative+ should be buṛi:l. As noted earlier, these forms surface with final lengthening: for example, buṛi:. The final /l/ has to be deleted by some additional rule, on any analysis.

· Forms with the ablative do not undergo PL unless the syllable in question is closed prior to affixation. Thus, we find buɲa-m 'woman-ABL' rather than the expected *buɲa:-m, but guyga:l-mu 'bandicoot-ABL' with a long vowel.

· The dative morpheme -nda is not subject to FSD. Thus, we find mabi:-nda 'kangaroo sp.-DAT', not *mabi:-n.

Overall, the analysis of Yidiɲ looks very much like the analysis of Djabugay advanced above.

5.3.5 Phonological Selection Obscures Generalizations

An important aspect of the analysis presented above, one that follows
Dixon's rule-based treatment, is that morphology—specifically, Vocabulary Insertion—and phonology are distinct. This architectural assumption
allows for a uniform explanation of (i) the distribution of vowel length
and (ii) the alternation between "long" and "short" allomorphs of the
case affixes. It is not clear how these two effects can be correlated in a
surface-based treatment, because deletion renders the distribution of long
vowels opaque: long vowels that derive from PL often appear in word-
final position because of the application of FSD.

The correlation between these rules is important because part of the
Yidiɲ case system might appear to be a promising arena for Phonological
Selection. If attention is restricted to the long/short allomorph alternation, the choice of allomorphs of the ergative case in, for example,
mabi:-ŋ versus *baɟigal-du* might suggest an analysis in terms of syllable
structure constraints: choose the -CV allomorph when the -C allomorph
would produce an unacceptable word-final cluster or a violation of a constraint against complex codas *CC. Moreover, the "long" alternants are
affixed to hosts with an odd number of syllables, to yield words that can
be exhaustively parsed into binary feet. This suggests a role for PARSE-
SYL, which penalizes representations with unfooted material. As shown
in (39), PARSE-SYL must be trumped by the condition against complex
codas, *CC, which is distinct from the general NoCODA constraint that
appears lower in the ranking (nouns here are *mabi* 'kangaroo sp.', *muygal*
'hole, trap', and *mula:ri* 'initiated man'):[23]

(39) Phonological selection in Yidiɲ

		*CC	PARSE-SYL	NoCODA
a.	☞ mabi:-ŋ]			*
	mabi:]-ŋgu		*!	
b.	muyga:l-ŋ]	*!		**
	☞ muygal]-du		*	**
c.	mula:]ri-ŋ		*!	*
	☞ mula]ri-ŋgu]			*

Looking just at the case morpheme alternations, (39) derives the correct results for this particular allomorph alternation, and it does so with phonological constraints. Thus far, the prospects for Phonological Selection are good. However, this type of analysis encounters immediate difficulties elsewhere in the system: specifically, it precludes a straightforward metrical treatment of PL. The simple conditioning environment for this process—penultimate syllables of the type specified above—cannot be appealed to, since, on an analysis like the one given in (39), the long vowels in (39a) and similar cases are word-final.

Appealing to some other metrical factor to account for length—for example, the idea that (final) iambs have lengthening, framed in terms of a preference for uneven iambs—does not look promising. Absolutive forms that are disyllabic and phonologically identical to those with lengthening do not show long final syllables: *guban* 'big butterfly', for example. Nor, for that matter, do quadrisyllabic words (e.g., *baḍigaldu* 'tortoise-ERG') show lengthening of the final vowel.

One possible attempt at fixing this problem would be to divide the nouns of the language into distinct noun classes, on the basis of their behavior with respect to vowel length. The nouns would fall into one of the following two classes: an "even" class in which a long vowel appears in affixed forms, and an "odd" class in which a long vowel appears in the base form (i.e., the absolutive). The idea would be to make the length alternation (at least in some cases) "morphological," so that there are two "declension classes" in which class membership is marked by length in the ways described above.

This type of approach does not appear to be on the right track. At the most basic level, it would fail to explain why there should be two distinct noun classes defined morphologically, with long vowels being found word-finally in one class and in penultimate syllables in the other class. Given that verbs show a similar set of alternations, in the same phonological environments, trying to make length a morphological manifestation of noun class membership is missing the point.[24]

Thus, while it looks like Phonological Selection might have something to say about the allomorphy of case affixes, it can do this only at the expense of an analysis of PL. The localist analysis presented here takes allomorph selection and morphophonology to be distinct. It accounts for the facts, and it does so in a way that accounts simultaneously for generalizations about affix allomorphy and the length distributions.

5.4 Conclusions

This chapter examines Phonological Selection, as one way of looking at
the architectural premise that morphology and phonology are computed
in the same global system (global-MP). Strong Phonological Selection—
the idea that the phonology alone suffices to determine all cases of
PCA—was shown to be untenable in the early literature on allomorphy
in OT. It is simply not the case that the "regular phonology" suffices to
produce the right patterns in PCA. The broader question addressed in
this chapter is whether there is any evidence that Phonological Selection
is nevertheless required, even in "hybrid" theories that introduce morphological ordering into the picture. The answer seems to be negative: the
only arguments in favor of these globalist approaches are conceptual;
that is, they stem from putative loss of generalization.

Moving beyond this into the more complex case studies of Djabugay
and Yidiɲ case inflections, the discussion centers on the intuition behind
Phonological Selection and the question of whether globalist analyses of
allomorphy can generalize. It is proposed that the proper analysis of these
systems involves an architecture in which competition for insertion (morphology) is sharply distinguished from subsequent phonology. As shown
in the analysis of Djabugay cases, the idea that Phonological Selection is
necessary fades when the treatment moves past a few carefully selected
forms. Even where there appears to be prima facie support for "output"
considerations, as in Yidiɲ, careful consideration of the relevant facts
shows that the surface phonology does not drive allomorph selection
and that surface-based analyses of allomorph selection miss important
generalizations.

One possible move for a globalist theory would be to say that all of the
effects studied in this chapter are simply morphological in nature and that
globalist theories like OT are not responsible for them, because such
theories are instead directed at (mostly markedness-related) phonological
patterns. This is a sort of nonanswer. A theory of phonology must take
morphology into account, because phonological effects are seen in complex forms.

In the end, arguments about intuitions are inconclusive in comparison
with arguments about empirical predictions. The most important predictions concern cases in which local and global formulations of the principles driving a particular alternation conflict with one another. These are
the topic of the next chapter.

6 Potentially Global Interactions Are Resolved Locally

This chapter looks directly at the empirical predictions that distinguish globalist and localist theories; in particular, it is centered on possible forms of evidence in favor of global computation of morphology and phonology. In the abstract, this means an argument showing that the morphological and phonological properties of some structure in some language are computed in a way that cannot be analyzed in a localist theory.

The type of argument that dominates the discussion below is based on scenarios in which global requirements effectively "override" other, more local considerations. Schematically, this type of case is stated in (1) in a way that is tailored to the discussion of phonologically conditioned allomorphy (PCA):

(1) Global instead of local interactions

These are cases in which local phonological considerations favor one allomorph, whereas global considerations—for example, brought about by the phonological form of "outer" affixes, or the phonology of the entire word—favor another allomorph, where it is the latter that is chosen.

More specifically, (1) refers to cases in which there is more than one allomorph for some morpheme—say, x_1, x_2, x_3—such that (i) the distribution of these allomorphs is phonologically conditioned; and (ii) in a case where "local" conditioning requires x_1, and global optimization requires x_3, the language shows x_3.

When cases of this type are examined in greater detail, it is possible to identify different types of effects that fall under the general heading of (1). The following subcategories are examined in detail below:

(2) Possible instantiations of (1)

    a. *"Unconditioned" allomorphs/phonological effects:* Theories with (at least some) global interaction between morphology and phonology (global-MP) allow for what look like locally "unconditioned" allomorphs to be inserted, or locally "unconditioned" phonological effects to be found, in cases in which this results in globally optimal outputs.

    b. *(Phonologically driven) allomorphic vacillation:* Globalist theories predict that there should be cases in which the allomorph chosen for part of the paradigm of some Root differs from the allomorph chosen in another part of the paradigm. In such a case, different allomorphs are inserted for the same Root in a way that depends on the global phonological context. The head showing the different allomorphs can be said to show *allomorphic vacillation* in this scenario. Crucially, these hypothesized effects could go beyond the local types of outward-sensitive allomorphy predicted by the theory of part I.

The search for (1) and its manifestations in (2) connects with another point. In many cases of PCA, phonological processes make selection *opaque* by removing from the surface form the phonological factor that determines the choice among competing allomorphs. Questions about opacity are natural in the discussion of globalist versus localist theories, for reasons that dominate discussion in the phonological literature on parallel versus serial rule/constraint interaction (see Idsardi 2000 for one overview).

The introduction of opacity into the discussion of allomorphy highlights the architectural predictions of globalist theories. While it is true that opaque allomorphy presents certain challenges for theories that deny serialism (see, for different perspectives, Vaux 2003; Aranovich et al. 2005; Łubowicz 2005; Paster 2006; Bye 2008), there is a sense in which globalist theories also predict global effects that go far beyond normal opacity. Cases of the latter type are crucial to understanding the strong predictions of globalism. The discussion below therefore advances via a general discussion of opacity in PCA in section 6.1, with the two types of "global over local" effects outlined in (1)—unconditioned allomorphy and allomorphic vacillation—at the center of sections 6.2 and 6.3. The main thrust of these sections is that there are situations in which the strong predictions of globalist theories—those in (1) and (2)—could be seen, but that the interactions found in actual languages are those expected in a localist framework. In particular, there is no evidence for unconditioned allomorphy, and in cases where a morpheme is expected to vacillate given the shape of outer morphemes, no such alternation is found. Thus, the strong predictions of globalism are not borne out.

In cases where allomorphic vacillation perhaps should occur, but does not, it could be argued that this is the result of constraints that force the same allomorph to be chosen throughout a "paradigm": PARADIGM UNI-FORMITY, in the sense of Kenstowicz 1996 and related work. In section 6.4, this point is addressed with reference to cases of "outward-sensitive" allomorphy. Cases of this type show "nonuniform" paradigms. At the same time, these cases show allomorphy conditioned by local, adjacent morphemes, not by phonological properties of the word. In other words, the strong predictions of globalism are not attested, whether paradigms are uniform or not.

6.1 From Opacity Effects to Global Interactions

Opaque interactions are generally held to be problematic for Optimality Theory (OT), for reasons that have been amply detailed in the phonological literature. Thus, the idea advanced above—namely, that effects that are related to opacity are important for understanding the strong predictions of globalism—requires some unpacking.

Opaque allomorphic selection is in evidence in several of the examples studied in preceding chapters, including Haitian Creole definite allomorphy (section 5.1) and many of the case affixes seen in Djabugay and Yidiɲ (sections 5.2 and 5.3). The defining property is that these cases involve (i) PCA conditioned by some element in the host, and (ii) additional phonological processes (often, but not always, deletion) that render the allomorphic conditioning opaque.

In the Haitian Creole definite, for example, -a is inserted after V-final nouns and -la after C-final nouns. In the subset of the V-final nouns that have epenthesis—that is, those nouns that end in [+ATR] vowels—a glide is inserted. Viewed sequentially, this looks as follows for *bato* 'boat':

(3) Sequence

bato-DEF	Input
bato-a	Vocabulary Insertion
batow-a	Glide Insertion

In a theory without serial steps, however, there is a prima facie difficulty with *batowa*. The presence of the glide in the surface form makes it effectively C-final, such that, all other things being equal, the *-la* allomorph is expected. Put slightly differently, the surface distribution of allomorphs is complicated by this effect: the *-a* allomorph appears on the surface after both consonants and vowels, whereas *-la* appears only after consonants.

In a serialist theory with intermediate derivational steps, this kind of interaction is expected. Specifically, in the representation that is accessed for Vocabulary Insertion *-a* is inserted, since at that stage of the derivation, the definite morpheme is next to a V-final host. In this type of analysis, it can be said that the definite morpheme is in the *local conditioning environment* for the insertion of *-a* when Vocabulary Insertion takes place. In serialist theories, then, the fact that the conditioning factor for some change is not "local" to the locus of the change in a *surface form* is irrelevant; the point is that at an earlier derivational stage where the relevant computation (in this case, Vocabulary Insertion) is executed, the local conditioning environment for the computation is found.

The notion of local conditioning environment is crucial to understanding the predictions of different frameworks. In the domain of phonological interactions, globalist and parallelist theories like OT effectively dispense with the idea that being in a local conditioning environment is what determines that a form changes in a particular way. Instead, whether or not a surface form is changed relative to the input is determined by the globally interacting system of constraints. This makes the notion of local conditioning environment epiphenomenal; to the extent that local interactions take place, they are entirely derivative of the global system of constraint interaction.

This architectural claim of globalist theories makes clear predictions about which factors are potentially visible for the purposes of allomorphic selection. Globalist theories allow for a multitude of nonlocal interactions, of which standard cases of opacity are a subtype. Although surface-oriented theories might have difficulties with "standard" cases of opacity, the other types of allomorphic interaction that are predicted to exist if local conditioning environments are epiphenomenal are crucial for testing the predictions of globalism.

6.1.1 Opacity and Global Interactions

Some initial points about opacity and its relation to global effects can be made concrete with reference to a textbook example of opacity: epenthesis in Turkish (see, e.g., Lewis 1967; Kager 1999). The first person singular possessive morpheme has the form *-m*. It surfaces as such after V-final nouns (4a); after C-final nouns, affixation of *-m* is accompanied by epenthesis, so that, as seen in (4b), a vowel is inserted between the final consonant of the host and the *-m* suffix:

(4) Epenthesis in Turkish

Noun	Noun-1SG.POSS	Gloss
a. ölçü	ölçü-m	'measure'/'my measure'
b. el	el-im	'hand'/'my hand'

The opacity involving the *-m* morpheme arises in cases in which the epenthetic vowel appears after a velar consonant. Turkish has a phonological rule of Velar Deletion that deletes such consonants intervocalically. So, for *ajak* 'foot', the 1sg possessive form is *ajaɪm*. In a theory with ordered rules, this effect is analyzed with a derivation in which Epenthesis is ordered before Velar Deletion:

(5) Example

ajak-m	Input
ajak-ɪm	Epenthesis
aja-ɪm	Velar Deletion

Putting to the side various ways in which surface-oriented theories could produce *ajaɪm* over (e.g.) **ajam*, there is a general point here for the study of global interactions. The effect seen in (5) is one in which an epenthetic vowel appears in an environment in which it is not locally conditioned on the surface. The localist theory accounts for this with ordering: the structural description for Epenthesis is found at an intermediate stage of the representation, so that the epenthetic vowel is, in the terms employed above, locally conditioned.

While this particular type of surface-unconditioned effect is difficult for OT, the broader point is that locally "unmotivated" effects are in principle not a problem for theories that espouse globalism. As stressed above, one of the defining properties of such theories is the ease with which they dispense with the notion of local conditioning environment. Thus, the fact that a "change" occurs in a way that does not seem locally motivated in surface forms is not problematic in general. Rather, the problems in the specific case of Turkish epenthesis (and other cases like this) are the following. First, there are no obvious, phonologically natural factors in the surface form of the word that would produce the actual form (i.e., that would motivate epenthesis).[1] Second, by ordering Epenthesis before Velar

Deletion, the serialist theory provides an obvious answer to the question of why the epenthetic vowel appears in spite of not being between consonants on the surface.

6.1.2 Over-/Underapplication in Allomorphy?

Whatever solution is offered for "standard" opacities of the type discussed immediately above, the crucial point for present purposes is that theories with global-MP predict *overapplication* and *underapplication* in allomorphic selection, in the same way that overapplication and underapplication are predicted in the phonology. This can be seen when the intuition behind standard OT treatments of overapplication in reduplication are extended to allomorphic interactions.

Recall that the general idea in globalist theories is that what is relevant for surface phonological form is not whether a particular element is in a configuration that triggers a change. Instead, the change happens when the overall constraint ranking prefers the candidate with the change, even if the local conditioning environment for the change is not found in the surface form. This type of reasoning is illustrated in (6), which shows McCarthy and Prince's (1995) analysis of overapplication in Tagalog /paN-RED-pu:tul/, which surfaces as *pa-mu-mu:tul* 'a cutting in quantity'. In this example, the stem-initial /p/ surfaces as /m/, even though it is not adjacent to the *paN-* affix that triggers nasalization. The analysis involves the interaction of three constraints: a phonological Constraint that forces "mutation" of /p/ to /m/, a constraint requiring base-reduplicant identity (IDENT$_{BR}$), and the standard input-output faithfulness constraint (FAITH$_{IO}$):

(6) McCarthy and Prince's (1995) analysis

/paN-RED-pu:tul/	Phono-Constraint	IDENT$_{BR}$	FAITH$_{IO}$
a. pam-pu-pu:tul	*!		
b. ☞ pa-mu-mu:tul			*
c. pa-mu-pu:tul		*!	

The stem-initial /p/ surfaces as /m/ in the winning candidate because base-reduplicant identity outranks the faithfulness constraint that penalizes candidates with changes to the underlying form. Thus, even though the relevant /p/ is not in the local conditioning environment associated with the /p/ → /m/ mutation, it surfaces as /m/ because of the identity constraint. In this way, the global constraint ranking enforces a change that is not locally expected given the surface form.

The general effect seen in this type of analysis can be called *nonlocal (NL) application*:[2]

(7) NL-application

An effect is found in a surface form even though the effect is not constrained to its (typical) local conditioning environment, because the constraint system allows global forces to override local ones.

The example from Tagalog analyzed in (6) does not directly involve globalism in the global-MP sense. While it involves apparent "action at a distance," in the way described in (7), it is not the same kind of allomorph selection that is studied throughout this book. However, the type of interaction that it shows can easily be formulated in a way that implicates global-MP as well, to yield predictions about PCA; this is the topic of the next section.

6.2 Allomorphy and Nonlocal Application

"Standard" opacity effects are a subcase of NL-application, namely, the subset in which the serialist theory would have the effect derive from local conditioning by an element at an intermediate stage of a derivation. While standard cases of opacity are congenial to localist/serialist theories, the general type of NL-application allowed by globalist theories—that is, the general principle that global effects can trump local conditioning in ways that do not involve local interaction at intermediate stages—defines a range of cases that cannot be analyzed on a localist approach. Identifying the properties of these cases is a crucial step in understanding the predictions of globalism.

6.2.1 Turkish Third Person Singular Possessive

A case of allomorphic selection that illustrates the possibility of NL-application is found in the Turkish 3sg possessive morpheme (see Lewis 1967; Carstairs 1987; Kornfilt 1997; Aranovich et al. 2005; Paster 2006). This appears to be a relatively straightforward case of (C)V allomorphy, with -*sɪ* after vowels and -*ɪ* after consonants (vowel harmony also affects the vowel component; examples from Paster 2006):

(8) Two allomorphs: *-ı* (after C); *-sı* (after V)

	Noun-3SG.POSS	Gloss
a.	bedel-i	'its price'
	ikiz-i	'its twin'
	alet-i	'its tool'
b.	fire-si	'its attrition'
	elma-sı	'its apple'
	arı-sı	'its bee'

The alternation between *-sı* and *-ı* interacts with the process of Velar Deletion, described above. Recall that this rule deletes velars intervocalically:[3]

(9) Velar Deletion

$$k \rightarrow \emptyset / V\_\_V$$

The 3sg possessive allomorph *-ı* is inserted after /k/-final stems. This produces the environment for Velar Deletion, which then applies to yield forms that have hiatus and that are opaque in terms of allomorph selection:

(10) Possessives of velar-final nouns

Noun	Noun-3SG.POSS	Gloss
açlık	açlı-ı	'hunger'/'its hunger'
bebek	bebe-i	'baby'/'its baby'
gerdanlık	gerdanlı-ı	'necklace'/'its necklace'
ekmek	ekme-i	'bread'/'its bread'

Assuming a localist theory like the one in part I of this book, and on the further assumption that the *-sı/-ı* alternation involves competition between two distinct allomorphs, Turkish has the VIs in (11):[4]

(11) [poss] ↔ -sı/V__
      [poss] ↔ -ı/C__

After Vocabulary Insertion, Velar Deletion applies in the phonology.

For OT, these facts present a general challenge, as is typically the case with opacity. Whatever solutions might be proposed for this particular case, the Turkish 3sg allomorphy—and some hypothetical variants of Turkish in particular—illustrate the predictions that globalist frameworks make concerning NL-application.

6.2.2 NL-Application: "Overriding" Local Concerns

Informally, localist theories are incapable of accounting for lookahead conditioning, of the type in (12):

(12) Insert affix x in a particular environment, unless doing so creates an undesirable representation because of interaction with other phonological or morphological processes that occur later in the derivation.

In the terms employed above, a theory with NL-application could easily derive such effects. They would not involve lookahead, obviously, but instead a constraint ranking in which the global system produces a result that looks surprising from the perspective of a theory in which computations are restricted to apply in local conditioning environments.

Schematically, the specific manifestations of NL-application that are expected by globalism can be seen as types of overapplication:

(13) a. Allomorphic overapplication

A locally "unconditioned" allomorph is inserted instead of the expected one, because when the whole word is taken into account, the net result is better.
Example (Turkish'): In the Turkish case above, -*sı* is inserted after velar-final stems, in order to avoid the hiatus created by Velar Deletion. This would yield, for example, *bebek-si*. (Viewing this as allomorphic *underapplication* of the -*ı* allomorph amounts to the same thing.)

   b. Allomorph-driven phonological overapplication

Rather than inserting an "unexpected" allomorph to avoid a problem, it should also be possible to see the surface results of a phonological change, even though its environment for application is not met locally.
Example (Turkish'): In the Turkish case above, the velar /k/ is deleted and -*sı* is inserted to yield *bebe-si.*

The specific analyses of the patterns in (13) can be sketched in a way that illustrates the basic point. Beginning with Turkish' in (13a), if a constraint penalizing hiatus, *HIATUS, is ranked higher than the *VκV constraint that enforces velar deletion, then the -*sı*/-*ı* alternation could be analyzed directly as a case of Phonological Selection, where, exclusively with velars, the "local" effect that selects -*ı* with C-final hosts is overridden. This analysis is shown in (14), where (14i,ii) show the simple cases of allomorphy, and (14iii) shows the *HIATUS-driven allomorphic overapplication effect:[5]

(14) Turkish′

(i) fire-sɪ/-ɪ	*HIATUS	*VKV	MAX(C)	NoCODA
a. ☞ fire-sɪ				
b. fire-ɪ	*!			
(ii) bedel-sɪ/-ɪ	*HIATUS	*VKV	MAX(C)	NoCODA
a. bedel-ɜɪ				*!
b. ☞ bedel-ɪ				
c. bede-sɪ			*!	
(iii) bebek-sɪ/-ɪ	*HIATUS	*VKV	MAX(C)	NoCODA
a. ☞ bebek-sɪ				*
b. bebek-ɪ		*!		
c. bebe-ɪ	*!		*	
d. bebe-sɪ			*!	

In the analysis of Turkish′, the simple cases of allomorphy between -sɪ and -ɪ emerge from the interaction of the constraints *HIATUS and NoCODA. The constraint MAX(C) prevents deletion of consonants and rules out other conceivable surface forms like *bede-sɪ. Because of the way the constraint driving Velar Deletion, *VKV, interacts with these constraints, the optimal candidate for velar-final stems is bebek-sɪ, with -sɪ instead of -ɪ. The net result of this constraint ranking is a version of Turkish in which -sɪ is optimal for velar-final stems, because this allomorph choice avoids both hiatus and intervocalic velars.[6]

The Turkish′ example shows the insertion of what is, in effect, a locally unconditioned allomorph, as outlined in (13a). The Turkish″ (13b) type of case, in which a phonological process overapplies, is easy to formalize as well. In particular, it is also possible to rank the constraints so that bebe-sɪ is optimal:

(15) Turkish[″]

bebek-sɪ/-ɪ	*HIATUS	*VKV	NoCODA	MAX(C)
a. bebek-sɪ			*!	
b. bebek-ɪ		*!		
c. bebe-ɪ	*!		*	
d. ☞ bebe-sɪ				*

Naturally, the constraint rankings involved in either of the two hypothetical languages just considered would have to be supported by larger analyses of the language. At the same time, these two possible systems clarify the types of phenomena that would provide evidence for globalism.

A localist theory has some difficulties producing the hypothetical forms. The generalization for Turkish[′] is that -ɪ is inserted after nonvelar consonants, and -sɪ elsewhere. It is not clear that VIs could refer to a phonologically unnatural class in this way. The VIs required would have to be these:

(16) [3sg] ↔ -ɪ/C[−vel]⌢__
     [3sg] ↔ -sɪ

Reference to an unnatural phonological environment (nonvelar consonants) might be impossible, depending on how this part of the theory is configured.

The situation with *bebe-sɪ* is similar, although slightly more is required of a localist theory. The VIs in (16) could be employed to state the distribution of these exponents. In the case of velar-final stems, an additional (readjustment) rule is required that deletes the stem-final velar in front of the -sɪ suffix.

6.2.3 A More Extreme (Hypothetical) Case

The examples from hypothetical Turkish might be salvageable on a localist theory, as just indicated. The reason that some potential localist analyses of these effects can be formulated is that allomorph choice can still be made on the basis of something that is locally visible to the 3sg possessive morpheme. But it is also possible to construct examples in which the factors forcing allomorph selection are not adjacent to the morpheme in question. This kind of effect is easy to formulate in a globalist theory, but goes beyond what a localist theory can express.

One type of example along these lines has an additional morpheme intervening between two other morphemes that show allomorphy. Consider, for example, a language in which Roots may be followed by three morphemes, $-X$, $-Y$, $-Z$, where these have the allomorphs listed:

(17) Structure

(18) Root-X-Y-Z

a. X: -tak; -ilub
b. Y: -o
c. Z:
   i. Z_1: -bat
   ii. Z_2: -tarag

In the simple cases—that is, in examples where $-Y$ and $-Z$ are null or not present—the $-X$ morpheme shows PCA based on the metrical properties of the host:

(19) -*tak* after odd-syllabled host
    -*ilub* after even-syllabled host

Suppose further that the $-Z$ morpheme is not subject to contextual allomorphy at all, so that, for example, $-Z_1$ -*bat* and $-Z_2$ -*tarag* are associated with different feature combinations.[7]

With global interaction, it is possible to set things up so that the allomorph of the $-X$ morpheme *vacillates* depending on what is inserted into the outer and nonadjacent $-Z$ morpheme. Beginning with the simple cases with only $-X$, it can be hypothesized that a PARSE-σ constraint favoring even-numbered words accounts for the pattern of allomorph selection shown by $-X$ (footing shown):

(20) Root-X cases; Roots = blik, golut

  a. (blik-tak)
     *(blik-i)lub (violates PARSE-σ)
  b. *(golut)-tak (violates PARSE-σ)
     (golu)(t-ilub)

In the more complex structures, with the additional $-Y$ and $-Z$ morphemes, what is optimal at $-X$ depends on which morpheme appears in the outer and nonadjacent $-Z$ position. This is illustrated in (21), where foot boundaries are again shown for expository purposes; the two subcases show how -X varies depending on whether -*bat* or -*tarag* is inserted at -Z:

(21) a. i. blik-X-o-bat: -*tak* inserted at -X
            *(blik-i)(lub-o)-bat
            (blik-ta)(k-o-bat)
      ii. blik-X-o-tarag: -*ilub* inserted at -X
            (blik-i)(lub-o)-(tarag)
            *(blik-ta)(k-o-ta)rag
   b. i. golut-X-o-bat: -*ilub* inserted at -X
            (golu)(t-ilu)(b-o-bat)
            *(golut-)(tak-o)-bat
      ii. golut-X-o-tarag: -*tak* inserted at -X
            *(golu)(t-ilu)(b-o-ta)rag
            (golut)-(tak-o)-(tarag)

Clearly, the way these examples work involves global considerations. The superficially "local" requirement that -*tak* appear after odd- and -*ilub* after even-syllabled hosts is overridden by the global pressure exerted by the phonology of -Z's exponent. The (output) phonology determines the morphology of allomorph selection, and the properties of the whole word have to be visible simultaneously for this to be done properly.

In a localist theory, this effect cannot be derived. In the theory of chapter 2, there are two reasons for this. The first is that an inner morpheme cannot be sensitive to the phonology of an outer morpheme, by the assumption of cyclic or "outward" Vocabulary Insertion. The second reason is that the -X morpheme is not adjacent to the -Z morpheme and therefore cannot see it for allomorphic purposes. The most that could be stated is the part of the distribution that is seen in the "basic" cases, where -*ilub* is inserted for -X next to a foot boundary:

(22) $[X] \leftrightarrow$ -ilub/...]⌢__
     $[X] \leftrightarrow$ -tak

This analysis predicts that -X's allomorphy should depend only on the metrical properties of what is to its left, whatever form -Z may ultimately take. It is incapable of stating the pattern described above.

There are two points to be made about the kind of example examined here. The first is that such cases would be a clear argument in favor of a globalist theory. The second is that there appears to be no evidence that this type of effect is found in any language; in actual cases where something like this hypothetical scenario can be found, the facts are those expected in the localist model; they show no evidence for global computation.

6.2.4 Local and Cyclic Interactions

The literature has to a limited extent addressed predictions of globalist theories along the lines schematized above. In one type of case, the point has been made that a localist or cyclic theory makes the correct predictions. Some shorter cases of this type are reviewed below, followed by some comments on cyclic OT in section 6.2.5. Another type of case involves explicit arguments for surface phonology determining allomorph selection. In section 6.3, I examine in greater detail arguments along these lines from Mester 1994 for global allomorph selection in Latin. I show that when the relevant facts are analyzed in detail, the argument for global interaction collapses.

6.2.4.1 Affix Placement in Huave An early clarification of the predictions of globalism is made by Noyer (1993), who discusses the behavior of "mobile" affixes in Huave. Some affixes in this language, like -t- past tense, attach to an element that is analyzed as a theme vowel. The theme vowel is sometimes a prefix, sometimes a suffix, in ways that correlate with transitivity: the theme is a prefix with transitive verbs and a suffix with intransitive verbs. The set of affixes to which -t- belongs attaches to the theme in either case (i.e., whether the theme is a prefix or a suffix):

(23) a. t   -a   -wit'
        PAST -TH -raise
        'he/she raised (it)'
     b. wit' -i   -t
        raise -TH -PAST
        'he/she rose up'

Affixes like -t- are "mobile" in the sense that they may occur either as prefixes or as suffixes.[8]

Noyer explores the possibility that this distribution results from the requirement that Huave words must have final codas. This is a version of Phonological Selection in which output phonology determines not allomorphy, but the placement of morphemes in a word.

On the assumption that the theme vowel's status as a prefix or a suffix depends on morphosyntactic factors, the phonology determines the placement of the mobile affix. Specifically, candidates like *t-a-wit'* and *a-wit'-t* and *t-wit'-a* and *wit'-a-t* are considered for the prefixal and suffixal theme cases, respectively. The constraint system selects the candidates that meet the phonological condition requiring final codas.

Noyer goes on to discuss a further set of examples that implicate the questions about globalism raised above. In some forms, the mobile affixes can occur inside of other affixes; this is seen in (24a) for past tense *-t-*, and in (24b) for 1sg *-n-*, which is also mobile:

(24) a. wit' -i   -t   -as -on
       raise -TH -PAST -1 -AUG
       'we-INCL rose'
     b. sa   -wit' -i   -n -on
        (1)FUT -raise -TH -1 -AUG
        'we-EXCL will rise'

As Noyer points out, if the whole word is evaluated in these types of cases, there is no reason for the mobile affixes to appear where they do. As far as the condition on final codas is concerned, the 1sg *-n-* morpheme in (24b) could be realized as a prefix, as in *sa-**n**-wit'-i-on*. The solution Noyer offers is that evaluation of well-formedness occurs cyclically. In the case of (24b), for example, this means that when the placement of *-n-* is determined, "outer" suffixes are not present in the computation.

Examples of this type are important: they are cases in which the strong predictions of globalism could conceivably be manifested, but instead what is found is what is expected from a cyclic point of view. A fully global theory predicts that there should be interactions that do not show this kind of cyclic effect—that is, where the full globality discussed in the preceding sections is required. In such a theory, it is possible to model this type of interaction, either indirectly or directly (in the latter case, by assuming cyclic or stratal OT; see section 6.2.5); however, placing restraints on the theory in this way is not an argument for globalism.

6.2.4.2 Saami Moving past affix placement to allomorph selection, the literature provides additional cases in which global considerations allow for a type of allomorph selection that is not possible in the localist view, and, once again, the globalist theory must be "restrained" to produce the correct results, that is, to exclude other cases that might be expected to arise.

The sensitivity of various allomorphs in Saami (Lappish) to metrical structure is addressed in Dolbey 1997 and Orgun and Dolbey 2007 (also see Bergsland 1976; Hargus 1993), which discuss the interaction of cyclic and local factors versus global optimization in Saami verbs. The allomorphy in question appears to be phonologically optimizing in the sense that it yields surface forms that contain an even number of syllables; the examples here are drawn from the person/number system, along with a passive morpheme:

(25) Person-marking/Passive allomorphy

    a. Allomorphs by host syllable count

P/N	Even	Odd
1du	-Ø	-tne
2du	-beahtti	-hppi
2pl	-behtet	-hpet
3pl pret	-Ø	-dje
Passive	-juvvo	-vvo

    b. Examples: *jearra* 'ask', *veahkehea* 'help'

P/N	Even	Odd
1du	je:r.re.-Ø	veah.ke.he:-t.ne
2du	jear.ra.-beaht.ti	veah.ke.hea-hp.pi
2pl	jear.ra.-beh.tet	veah.ke.he:-h.pet
3pl pret	je:r.re.-Ø	veah.ke.he:-d.je
Passive	je:r.ro.-juv.vo	veah.ke.hu-v.vo

From the perspective of the phonology, this pattern of allomorphy creates even-syllabled forms that can be exhaustively parsed into binary feet.

    Dolbey (1997) makes the point that the evaluation that results in this distribution appears to be local rather than global in character. In cases in which more than one of these affixes is added to a host, there is more than one possible outcome that optimizes the syllable count. For example, with a 2du passive form, adding two monosyllabic affixes results in an even syllable count, just as adding two disyllabic affixes does. A localist theory predicts that the disyllabic affix must be inserted in the inner morpheme position, since this is what the local context demands; following this, the local environment forces selection of another disyllabic affix.

    The facts show that in the cases in question, two disyllabic affixes are selected:[9]

(26) je:rro-juvvo-beahti; *je:rru-vvo-hppi
     veahkehu-vvo-beahtti; *veahkehu-juvvo-hppi

Again, this is the type of situation in which the strong predictions of globalism could be manifested. If in the cases where two metrically conditioned allomorphs are found, two monosyllables were inserted, the putative phonological "target" of allomorph selection—exhaustively parsable structures—would be achieved; and it would be achieved in a way that could not be stated in the localist theory, where lookahead to outputs is impossible. Instead, however, the interaction appears to be local, in a way that follows naturally from the localist theory. It is, of course, possible to state such a pattern in a globalist theory, but that is not at issue. Rather, the point is that a case in which the strong predictions of globalism *could* conceivably be found functions in terms that can be analyzed in the more restrictive localist architecture.

6.2.5 Some Comments on Cyclic Optimality Theory

The idea that local concerns trump global ones is, in some sense, the motivation for cyclicity. Some theories have sought to restrain the predictions of a fully globalist architecture by proposing that constraint evaluation is cyclic, in the sense familiar from Lexical Phonology (see, e.g., Kiparsky 2000 and subsequent work).

It is important to note that while cyclic OT is able in principle to account for (at least some of) the cases examined above, it still makes predictions that are very different from those of a localist theory. In particular, a cyclic OT theory is still globalist *within any given stratum of affixation*. While this type of theory restrains predictions about allomorphy in comparison with a fully globalist model, there appears to be no evidence for this limited amount of global interaction between morphology and phonology.

The specific predictions made by a stratal or cyclic OT model depend on how cycles of affixation are defined. The primary point to be made is that, in any theory that allows three morphemes to have their morphology and phonology computed in the same cycle, NL-application is predicted. This point is schematized in (27):

(27) Root-X-Y-Z

If the heads X, Y, and Z are processed in the same cycle (perhaps in a way that excludes other, outer heads), the theory predicts that allomorph insertion at X could be sensitive to the phonology of Z, or the phonology of the whole object containing Z. These types of effects cannot be stated in the localist theory; but they do not seem to be found. Other effects, such as those involving the phonological form of two morphemes, as in the Saami example above, would also be predicted to show global behavior as long as the two morphemes are in the same stratum. Again, there is no clear evidence that this kind of limited global interaction is attested.

Thus, while appealing to stratal or cyclic OT might rule out some of the (unattested) cases predicted by a fully globalist model, it makes predictions about morphology-phonology interactions that are evidently not found.

6.2.6 Interim Assessment

A number of cases, both hypothetical and real, were examined above in order to specify and test the predictions of globalist theories. A basic point where globalism and localism differ is that globalism predicts allomorphic effects in PCA that are locally unconditioned, but that make sense when the global, surface phonology is taken into account.

There appears to be no clear evidence that interactions of this type are found in natural languages. In the cases that have been studied, selection appears to proceed step by step, in a way that is expected from the point of view of a cyclic localist theory.

The same points are made by a more detailed examination of certain patterns of allomorphy in Latin verbs, to which I now turn.

6.3 Case Study: Arguments for Global Optimization in Latin

The predictions of globalist theories can be seen quite clearly in two case studies from Latin, drawn from Mester 1994. Each one involves the distribution of allomorphs in the verbal system: perfect -u versus -s in conjugation II verbs, and theme vowel -ī- versus -i- in the so-called io-verbs. In each case, standard handbooks of Latin allude to metrical patterns that correlate with the allomorphic patterns. Whatever status these claims might have within Latin historical phonology and morphology, Mester goes one step further than this, by arguing that the distribution of allomorphs in the synchronic grammar of Classical Latin requires a globalist framework in which selection of (certain) host-allomorph combinations is computed by generating all of the relevant combinations and letting the phonology determine the winner.

Closer examination of both cases shows that Mester's arguments for globalism fail to provide any convincing evidence for such a framework. The proposals apply only to a carefully selected set of forms and make incorrect predictions when extended beyond these. The two cases do, however, pave the way for discussion of a further strong prediction of globalism, called *allomorphic vacillation* above: a "switch" in the selected allomorph for a particular root, based on (phonological) properties of outer morphemes. This strong prediction is not borne out in Latin; nor, to my knowledge, is it manifested elsewhere.

Part of this section is thus devoted to a negative demonstration. In addition, though, these cases show important patterns to attend to—in perfect formation in particular—and these patterns show the kind of locality effect discussed in section 6.2.

6.3.1 Latin Perfect Allomorphy in the Second Conjugation

Mester's (1994) influential discussion of the perfect forms of (some) Latin verbs is often cited as an example in which global prosodic considerations play a decisive role in allomorph selection.

Conjugation II Latin verbs show the theme vowel -ē- in the present tense system: thus, we find infinitives like *mon-ē-re* 'to warn' and *aug-ē-re* 'to increase, enlarge'. The argument that Mester makes for phonology determining allomorphy is based on the perfect forms of (some) verbs from this conjugation.

Throughout the Latin verbal system, the perfect tenses show a great deal of allomorphy. I will assume here that, in addition to stem changes, what is at issue is the allomorphy of the Aspectual head Asp[perf]; recall the discussion of section 3.1.1, where the structure in (28) is assumed:

(28) Structure

The Asp[perf] head in finite forms shows different allomorphs, including the vowel -u (often written -v), -s, and -i (1sg citation form employed here):[10]

(29) Perfect allomorphs in Latin

	Conjugation	Form	Gloss	Perfect
a.	I	laud-ā-re	'praise'	laud-ā-**v**-ī
b.	II	mon-ē-re	'warn'	mon-**u**-ī
c.	II	aug-ē-re	'increase'	aug-**s**-ī
d.	II	strīd-ē-re	'whistle'	strīd-**i**-ī

The case that Mester concentrates on is in conjugation II, where the distribution of -*u* and -*s* in the (29b,c) types is, according to the traditional literature (see Meiser 1998, 2003 for overviews), correlated with metrical factors: light stems take -*u*, and heavy stems -*s*.[11]

Whether or not the prosodic correlations connected with this pattern of allomorphy are descriptively accurate, the interesting point for present purposes is how Mester accounts for this effect in terms of competition in the synchronic grammar of Classical Latin. Mester's primary focus is on sets of effects correlated with *trapping* configurations—more precisely, instances of *medial* trapping, where an unparsed light syllable appears after footed material:[12]

(30) Medial trapping

    ... [ō̄]ŏ⟨ō̄⟩

This sort of configuration arises in a moraic theory where trochees are both minimally and maximally bimoraic.[13] The essential idea behind Mester's proposal is that it is the avoidance of medial trapping that determines the choice between -*u* and -*s*. This means that for any given verb of the type under consideration (i.e., conjugation II with -*u* or -*s* perfect), the input, consisting of a Root and a perfect morpheme, is associated with candidates with different allomorphs; thus, for *monēre*, *mon-u-ī* is competing with (among other things) *mon-s-ī*. The constraint or constraints that disfavor medial trapping or its equivalent (i.e., a trimoraic trochee) do the rest, effectively selecting one allomorph and rejecting the other:

(31) a.   [monu]⟨ī⟩
     b. *[au]gu⟨ī⟩ (trapping)
        [aug]⟨sī⟩

Mester does not formalize the competition, but explains the intuition guiding his analysis by remarking that "a lexical selection process ... is driven by a prosodic criterion choosing the best among several alternatives" (1994, 46). The *u*-perfect is given "default" status, appearing where selection plays no role; for Mester, this is the case with verbs that he classifies as denominal, which appear with the *u*-perfect without regard to Root phonology.

To this point, the proposal looks exactly like many of the cases discussed above. When we consider entire sets of inflected perfects, moreover, it is possible to see the strongest predictions of the globalist view. Consider, to begin with, the two types of verbs analyzed above, inflected for the perfect indicative; for reference, the metrical structure of the output is presented:

(32) Types: Perfect indicative active

P/N	Light Root	Metrical structure	Heavy Root	Metrical structure
1sg	monuī	[ŏŏ]⟨ō⟩	augsī	[ō]⟨ō⟩
2sg	monuistī	[ŏŏ][ō]⟨ō⟩	augsistī	[ō][ō]⟨ō⟩
3sg	monuit	[ŏŏ]⟨ō⟩	augsit	[ō]⟨ō⟩
1pl	monuimus	ŏ[ŏŏ]⟨ō⟩	augsimus	[ō]ŏ⟨ō⟩
2pl	monuistis	[ŏŏ][ō]⟨ō⟩	augsistis	[ō][ō]⟨ō⟩
3pl	monuērunt	[ŏŏ][ō]⟨ō⟩	augsērunt	[ō][ō]⟨ō⟩
3pl	monuerunt	ŏ[ŏŏ]⟨ō⟩	augserunt	[ō]ŏ⟨ō⟩
3pl	monuēre	[ŏŏ][ō]⟨ō⟩	augsēre	[ō][ō]⟨ō⟩

The crucial form to consider in (32) is the 1pl of the heavy verb *augēre*.[14] This appears with the *s*-perfect, which, in combination with the 1pl agreement morpheme, results in the configuration with medial trapping [ō]ŏ⟨ō⟩. This point is crucial because of the competition logic that underlies the optimization approach to allomorphic selection. Within this kind of theory, the medial trapping perfect with -*s* is generated and compared with other possible perfects. The *u*-perfect for *augēre, auguimus* has the metrical structure ŏŏŏŏ and, according to Mester's assumptions, can be exhaustively parsed: [ō][ŏŏ]⟨ō⟩. Thus, if prosodic well-formedness is really the driving factor in selecting allomorphs, *auguimus should be grammatical, contrary to fact.

It would always be possible to appeal to the force of other constraints to account for the presence of -*s*, by invoking (e.g.) UNIFORM EXPONENCE constraints, as in Kenstowicz 1996 and related work. Such constraints enforce identical allomorphy across the different forms. However an analysis in these terms might be implemented, this type of solution subverts the strongest predictions of the globalist approach. Since the globalist theory allows the entire word's phonological properties to be taken into account in determining the winner of the competition, it—unlike the localist theory—predicts that there should be cases of suppletive allomorphy that show allomorphic vacillation, where the chosen allomorph depends on outer, global properties. There is no vacillation, and the pattern found with Latin *augēre* is clearly compatible with the localist theory; it can, of course, be made compatible with the globalist theory, but it provides no arguments for that (more expressive) view.[15]

The failure of the strong prediction is not restricted to 1pl perfects. The same point can be made for the pluperfect indicative, with a lot more force, it appears:

(33) Pluperfect indicative of *augēre*

P/N	Pluperfect	Metrical structure	-u *form*	Metrical structure
1sg	augseram	[σ̄]σ̆⟨σ̄⟩	augueram	[σ̄][σ̆σ̆]⟨σ̄⟩
2sg	augserās	[σ̄]σ̆⟨σ̄⟩	auguerās	[σ̄][σ̆σ̆]⟨σ̄⟩
3sg	augserat	[σ̄]σ̆⟨σ̆⟩	auguerat	[σ̄][σ̆σ̆]⟨σ̆⟩
1pl	augserāmus	[σ̄]σ̆[σ̄]⟨σ̄⟩	auguerāmus	[σ̄][σ̆σ̆][σ̄]⟨σ̄⟩
2pl	augserātis	[σ̄]σ̆[σ̄]⟨σ̄⟩	auguerātis	[σ̄][σ̆σ̆][σ̄]⟨σ̄⟩
3pl	augserant	[σ̄]σ̆⟨σ̆⟩	auguerant	[σ̆][σ̆σ̆]⟨σ̄⟩

In the perfect indicatives in (32), selection of the -*s* allomorph avoids medial trapping for heavy verbs like *augēre*, except in the 1pl. In the pluperfect, the selection of the -*s* allomorph creates trapping configurations in the entire paradigm of inflected forms. Crucially, these trapping configurations are not created by the *u*-perfect, where the light syllable with -*u* can be footed across the board. If all the different host-allomorph combinations were generated, with the phonology selecting the winner on the basis of metrical felicity—that is, if the strong predictions of Mester's theory were correct—this pattern would not be found; pluperfects with these stems should show -*u*. However, the -*s* forms are the grammatical ones.

In sum, something must be added to a globalist theory in order to make prosodic optimization the determining factor for allomorphy in only some contexts. It should be clear by this point that such an addition would not compromise such a theory directly. As noted above, it would be possible to posit additional constraints to ensure that *augsimus* wins the competition; for example, a constraint requiring that allomorphy be held constant for a particular root could be ranked above the constraints that enforce prosodic well-formedness.[16] This would penalize *auguimus for taking a different allomorph from the rest of the paradigm, so that the prosodically worse *augsimus* would then win. The fact that the globalist theory can be altered in this way or other ways to yield the correct output is not really what is at issue, however. If there were cases in which something like *auguimus* did surface because of global prosodic considerations, then it would be a clear argument in favor of a globalist theory. As with other examples shown above, it is clear exactly what sort of effect would be a strong argument for globalism in the Latin case, and we do not see such effects.

6.3.2 Generalizations about Latin Perfect Allomorphy

While the prospects for a globalist approach to Latin perfect allomorphy look quite unpromising, there are important generalizations about this system that relate directly to themes developed throughout this book.[17] As a first step, consider the classification of Latin verbs in (34), which divides the verbal system into conjugation classes and shows the theme vowel that is found in each class:[18]

(34) Conjugations and theme vowels

Conjugation	Example	Theme vowel
I	laud-ā-mus	-ā-
II	mon-ē-mus	-ē-
III	dūc-i-mus	-i-
III(i)	cap-i-mus	-i-
IV	aud-ī-mus	-ī-
Athematic	es-Ø-se	-Ø-

It will be assumed here that the theme vowel is the Spell-Out of a head Th, attached to the *v* head in the PF component (Oltra-Massuet 1999). The reason for approaching the perfect in terms of conjugation is that there are basic associations between conjugation class and what happens in the perfect. Putting aside various readjustments that apply to the stem, there are two pieces of information that are central to these patterns: first, whether or not there is a theme vowel in the perfect form; and second, what allomorph of the head Asp[perf] appears, -*vi*, -*si*, or -*i* (henceforth, these forms are used rather than -*u* and -*s*; recall the discussion of chapter 3). The basic associations between conjugation and perfect type are as follows (here and below, I use orthographic -*v*- in the exponent of Asp[perf] that has both vowel and glide surface forms):

(35) Perfect type by conjugation: Basic associations

Conjugation	Perfect type
I	thematic with -*vi*
II	athematic with -*vi*
III	athematic
III(i)	athematic
IV	thematic with -*vi*

The associations are "basic" in the sense that most verbs in the relevant conjugations behave accordingly. At the same time, there are departures from these norms. The following chart summarizes attested patterns:[19]

(36) Perfect types by conjugation

	Conj.	Verb	Perfect	Gloss	Theme?		Exponent
a.	I	laudāre	laud-ā-v-ī	'praise'	thematic	+	-vi
b.	I	crepāre	crep-v-ī	'rattle'	athematic	+	-vi
c.	I	iuvāre	iūv-ī	'help'	athematic	+	-i
d.	II	monēre	mon-v-ī	'warn'	athematic	+	-vi
e.	II	sedēre	sēd-ī	'sit'	athematic	+	-i
f.	II	manēre	man-s-ī	'remain'	athematic	+	-si
g.	III	vomere	vom-v-ī	'vomit'	athematic	+	-vi
h.	III	vertere	vert-ī	'turn'	athematic	+	-i
i.	III	dūcere	dūc-s-ī	'lead'	athematic	+	-si
j.	III(i)	rapere	rap-v-ī	'seize'	athematic	+	-vi
k.	III(i)	capere	cēp-ī	'take'	athematic	+	-i
l.	III(i)	-spicere	spec-s-ī	'peer'	athematic	+	-si
m.	IV	audīre	aud-ī-v-ī	'hear'	thematic	+	-vi
n.	IV	aperīre	aper-v-ī	'open'	athematic	+	-vi
o.	IV	venīre	vēn-ī	'come'	athematic	+	-i
p.	IV	farcīre	far-s-ī	'stuff'	athematic	+	-si

Despite the large number of filled cells in this chart, which suggests a highly disorderly pattern, the formation of the perfect is, by and large, determined systematically by conjugation class.[20] My analysis of these patterns builds directly on the idea that aspects of perfect formation, in particular whether or not a Root is thematic or athematic in the perfect, are correlated directly with conjugation class features. In particular, all verbs of conjugations II, III, and III(i) are athematic in the perfect, along with a handful of verbs from conjugations I and IV (list in (37)). For concreteness, I assume that there is a rule that deletes (or does not assign) the Th node to such verbs in the perfect:

(37) Athematic perfect rule

$$v \text{ is athematic } / \left\{ \begin{array}{l} [\text{II}] \\ [\text{III}] \\ [\text{III(i)}] \\ \text{LIST} \end{array} \right\} \underline{\quad} \text{Asp[perf]}$$

$$\text{LIST} = \{\sqrt{\text{CREP}}, \sqrt{\text{VEN}}, \dots\}$$

Simply listing the conjugation features in this manner might seem arbitrary, but it is more or less necessary. There is no overarching generalization that unites the verbs of conjugations II, III, and III(i). There is, moreover, no generalization that unifies conjugations I and IV, those conjugations that are by default thematic in the perfect. This means that the information regarding the presence or absence of a theme in the perfect must be stated in terms of processes that refer to the conjugation features [II], [III], and [III(i)], along with the additional Roots from the other conjugations.

The presence or absence of a theme vowel interacts with the second aspect of perfect formation, the allomorphy of the head Asp[perf]. Here the generalizations are as follows:

(38) Generalizations about perfect formation

    a. Perfects with -*si* are always athematic.

    b. Perfects with -*i* are always athematic.

    c. If there is a theme vowel in the perfect, it is

        i. always long (i.e., -*ā*- or -*ī*-);

        ii. always followed by the -*vi* exponent of Asp[perf].

These generalizations are accounted for with the following VIs:

(39) Asp ↔ -si/{$\sqrt{\text{MAN}}$, $\sqrt{\text{DŪC}}$, $\sqrt{\text{FARC}}$, ...}⌒__
     Asp ↔ -i/{$\sqrt{\text{SED}}$, $\sqrt{\text{VERT}}$, $\sqrt{\text{CAP}}$, $\sqrt{\text{VEN}}$, ...}⌒__
     Asp ↔ -vi

In these VIs, -*si* and -*i* require particular Roots to be inserted. Significantly, the rules for inserting these exponents only apply when the Asp[perf] node is linearly adjacent to the Root. In this way, the insertion of these exponents can only take place in athematic forms. Beyond this, the system defaults to the insertion of -*vi*. This VI does not have a list associated with it. It will be inserted in environments in which (i) the Root is adjacent, but not on the list for either -*si* or -*i* (athematic formation), or (ii) the Root is followed by a theme vowel—either -*ā*- or -*ī*-.

In short, there are important generalizations about allomorphy in the Latin perfect: generalizations that take into account local relations, in the way predicted by the theory of part I.

6.3.3 Latin Verbs of Conjugations III/III(i)/IV

A long-standing question in Latin morphology and phonology concerns the behavior of two classes of verbs in the language that, because they have 1sg forms that end in *-iō*, are often simply referred to as *-io* verbs. The notable property of these verbs is that they fall into two types, which can be seen in other verb forms: those with a short theme vowel, like *capĭmus* 'take, etc.', and those with long *-ī-*, like *audīmus* 'hear'; I use 1pl forms here because some other forms involve morphophonological rules that obscure this basic pattern. The *capimus* class—henceforth, conjugation III(i)—is quite small, consisting of fewer than twenty verbs, while the *-ī-* class—conjugation IV—is very large.

The traditional literature has faced in many forms the question of how these classes are related to one another, since there are clear diachronic connections. The typical approach is to try to derive (in the historical sense) the verbs of conjugation III(i) from what were earlier conjugation IV verbs—that is, to account for theme vowel shortening with a subset of conjugation IV verbs, in a way that eventually became "morphologized."

A point often discussed in such accounts is that there is a phonological subregularity unifying the verbs of III(i): their stems are light. This correlation is potentially enlightening, and many traditional works have sought to derive *-ī-* shortening as a metrical effect, with varying degrees of success.[21]

The traditional accounts mentioned above are interested in the historical relationship between these classes of verbs. Mester's (1994) analysis goes beyond the historical and pushes the quantity differences in the theme vowel into the synchronic grammar; his position is that the III(i) and IV groups show "underlying unity," because "for primary verbs the quantity of the theme vowel is to a large extent predictable from the prosodic pattern of the root" (1994, 24). The unified approach is implemented with a "single" theme vowel at a morphological level; this single morphological object has two allomorphs (1994, 26):

(40) Theme vowel /i/

    a. *Primary allomorph:* -ī-
    b. *Secondary allomorph:* -ĭ-

For verbs that belong to either conjugation III(i) or conjugation IV (minus certain exceptions, such as those that are denominal), selection is determined by prosody: "the secondary allomorph *-ĭ-* is chosen ... in situations where short quantity results in more optimal prosodic organization" (1994, 26–27). Mester illustrates the effects of this selection along the lines of (41), for *audīre* 'hear', *aperīre* 'uncover', and *capere* 'take':

(41) Host-allomorph selection by phonology

 a. -ī-   [σ̄][σ̄]⟨σ⟩   [σ̆σ̆][σ̄]⟨σ⟩   σ̄[σ̄]⟨σ⟩
           [au][dī]⟨mus⟩   [ape][rī]⟨mus⟩   ca[pī]⟨mus⟩
           audīmus   aperīmus   *capīmus

 b. -i-   [σ̄]σ̆⟨σ⟩   σ̄[σ̆σ̆]⟨σ⟩   [σ̆σ̆]⟨σ⟩
           [au]dĭ⟨mus⟩   a[perĭ]⟨mus⟩   [capĭ]⟨mus⟩
           *audĭmus   *aperĭmus   capĭmus

Mester seeks additional evidence for prosodic selection elsewhere in the verbal system—in particular, in effects found with unprefixed and prefixed verbs, where, in the cases he discusses, there appears to be an alternation in theme vowel length (1994, 27–28). These cases are important in light of the discussion above, since, if one adopts the spirit of the proposal under consideration, changes in a theme vowel's quantity driven by the addition of a prefix could constitute an instance of allomorphic vacillation:

(42) Prefixation

No prefix	*Light prefix*	*Heavy prefix*
a. [σ̆σ̆]⟨σ⟩	b. [σ̆σ̆][σ̄]⟨σ⟩	c. [σ̄][σ̆σ̆]⟨σ⟩
-ī-	-ī-	-ī-
parĭmus	re-perīmus	
sapĭmus	re-sipīmus	dē-sipĭmus

Taking the proposal as a whole, there are different ways to approach its predictions. One of the basic tenets of the theory is that the -ī- theme of conjugation IV verbs appears because of metrical optimization. Thus, the theory predicts allomorphic vacillation in other forms of the same verb, in a way that depends on the phonology of outer morphemes (e.g., Tense and Agreement). Here there are fewer cases than there were with conjugation II perfect allomorphy, but there is at least one case where a prediction is made: the 2pl passive, where the agreement ending is disyllabic. This is shown with long and short *i* in (43):

(43) 2pl present indicative passives

 a. audī-minī   [σ̄][σ̄]σ̆⟨σ⟩
 b. audĭ-minī   [σ̄][σ̆σ̆]⟨σ⟩

Clearly, the (43b) form should be selected, because the (43a) form traps a light syllable. Again, though, this is not what is found; as with perfect allomorphy, there is no vacillation.

An extension of this type of prediction is behind Mester's take on the prefixed verbs in (42). The idea is that the verb forms differ only in the quantity of the prefix, and, when this can result in suboptimal footing as in (42b), the -ī- allomorph wins out over the expected -i- theme. The general prediction here is as follows:[22]

(44) Optimization prediction

Verbs of conjugation III(i) when prefixed by a single light syllable should switch to the -ī- theme.
Rationale: [ŏ̄ŏ̄][ō̄]⟨σ⟩ is better than ŏ̄[ŏ̄ŏ̄]⟨σ⟩.

While this prediction is supposed to account for pairs like those in (42), it does not generalize. For many of the conjugation III(i) verbs, there are examples with the light prefix *re-* employed in (42); none of these show the predicted change in theme vowel:

(45) *re*-prefixed verbs with -*i*-

capĭmus	'take, etc.'	re-cipĭmus	'retake'
facĭmus	'make, etc.'	re-ficĭmus	'make again'
fodĭmus	'dig'	re-fodĭmus	'dig again'
gradĭmur	'step, walk'	re-gredĭmur	'go/come back'

In these verbs, the theme vowel is the same in the unprefixed and the prefixed forms. While many things are going on in Latin prefixed verbs, the prediction in (44) is not borne out.

What, then, can be said about the cases adduced by Mester in (42)? The triplet *sap-ĭ-mus, re-sip-ī-mus, dē-sip-ĭ-mus* from (42) is taken by Mester to be "particularly telling," since the same Root is involved (historically, in any case). Here the facts are simply unclear, for the *re*-prefixed form in particular. Lewis and Short's (1969) Latin dictionary shows an infinitive in -*ĕre*, which means that it is treated as a verb of conjugation III(i). For the -*ī*- theme that his argument is based on, Mester cites Niedermann 1908. Niedermann includes the form in a footnote, attributing it to the post-Classical grammarian Charisius; there is, moreover, apparently a text by Charisius in which the vowel is short. As far as I know, there is no other evidence than this for a long-vowel form.

This leaves the verb *reperīre* 'find, discern', which is (at a minimum, historically) related to conjugation III(i) *parere* and shows the -*ī*- theme expected on Mester's account. Given the facts adduced above, this single form is certainly not evidence in favor of the globalist theory. The putative base of this prefixed form, *parere*, means 'bear, beget'. It is possible that despite the historical connection, speakers did not analyze these forms as possessing the same Root.[23] Whatever there is to say about this single case, the point that it provides no argument for the globalist theory is clear.

Overall, the facts adduced by Mester that would support the predictions of the globalist theory are at best isolated and sporadic. The clear predictions of the theory—those that would support the globalist view and show that the localist view is problematic—are not found.

6.4   Paradigm (Non)uniformity: Outward-Sensitivity Redux

It was noted above that the absence of allomorphic vacillation is something that globalist theories have no trouble in modeling. Thus, the argument is not that globalist theories are incapable of accounting for the attested facts. Rather, the point is that the strongest predictions of such theories do not appear to be borne out; moreover, the attested patterns of allomorphy are accounted for in a localist theory like that of part I.

One way of sharpening the line of argument from the last section is by considering what kinds of factors could rule out allomorphic vacillation in a globalist framework. The most obvious way of doing this would be in terms of PARADIGM UNIFORMITY: a constraint (or set of constraints) that ensures that a Root shows consistent allomorphy throughout its set of surface forms. It could be argued, for example, that the reason that -s-allomorph-taking *augēre* does not switch from -s to -u in the 1pl is that the constraints enforcing uniform realization of Asp[perf] outrank the constraints responsible for driving allomorph selection prosodically. Assuming that something like PARADIGM UNIFORMITY could produce the correct results, there are two points to be made.

The first point was stressed above: it might be possible for a globalist theory to appeal to PARADIGM UNIFORMITY, but what the paradigmatic constraints do, in effect, is rule out the cases in which the strongest predictions of a globalist system can be seen. Thus, while the resulting theory might make globalist assumptions, it is certainly not an argument for those assumptions. In the absence of any other arguments for global interaction, there is no reason to have a theory that is global but restrained by PARADIGM UNIFORMITY in the first place. However, if paradigms always are uniform, then the arguments of the last section about allomorphic vacillation might lose some of their force. If this type of vacillation is universally ruled out, then the absence of vacillation cannot argue against globalism.

These considerations lead up to the second point, which connects the predictions of the C_1-LIN theory with this discussion. The idea sketched above, appealing to PARADIGM UNIFORMITY, can be taken to the limit: if the uniformity constraints always dominate the constraints that would force a change of allomorphs for phonological reasons, there should never be "outward-looking" paradigmatic vacillation. At this point, it is important to recall that there *is* outward-sensitive allomorphy. This was seen in chapter 2 in cases like the Hungarian plural/possessive interaction repeated in (46), and in chapter 3 with the suppletive Latin verb *esse* 'be', repeated in a condensed form in (47):

(46) Hungarian plural/possessive (Carstairs 1987, 165)

Singular	Singular–1sg Poss	Plural	Plural–1sg Poss	Gloss
ruha	ruhá-m	ruhá-k	ruha-ái-m	'dress'
kalap	kalap-om	kalap-ok	kalap-jai-m	'hat'
ház	ház-am	ház-ak	ház-ai-m	'house'

(47) Allomorphy of Latin *esse* 'be'

	Present	Imperfect	Perfect
1sg	su-m	er-a-m	fu-ī
2sg	es	er-ā-s	fu-istī
3sg	es-t	er-a-t	fu-i-t
1pl	su-mus	er-ā-mus	fu-i-mus
2pl	es-tis	er-ā-tis	fu-istis
3pl	su-nt	er-a-nt	fu-ērunt

The Hungarian plural morpheme and the Latin v_{be} head that is 'be' each show outward-sensitive contextual allomorphy and thus "nonuniform" paradigms. As discussed in chapters 2 and 3, these effects are conditioned by adjacent nodes, not by phonological properties of entire words.

The fact that nonuniform paradigms are found, but in a way that shows sensitivity to local factors, is important. Many well-known cases of suppletion have the same general properties seen with Latin *esse*. If all cases of suppletion (and outward-sensitive allomorphy in general) are conditioned locally, as seems to be the case, then PARADIGM UNIFORMITY cannot be invoked to rescue the globalist theory.

There is at least one case in which it has been claimed that "outer" or surface phonology conditions stem suppletion. The example is the verb *andare* 'go' in Italian. Carstairs (1988) and others have followed traditional discussions of Italian by describing the alternation between *and-* and *va(d)-* in phonological terms. The pattern is that the stem is *va(d)-* when under stress, and *and-* otherwise:[24]

(48) Forms of *andare*

P/N	Present indicative	Present subjunctive
1sg	vádo	váda
2sg	vái	váda
3sg	vá	váda
1pl	andiámo	andiámo
2pl	andáte	andiáte
3pl	vánno	vádano

For Burzio (1998), among others, the correlation between stress and suppletion in (48) implies causation in the synchronic grammar: Burzio argues that these facts support a globalist view, with surface phonological properties determining the choice between *va(d)-* and *and-*. While the description in terms of stress is correct, on the face of it, this cannot play a role in the analysis in the theory presented in part I, since the output phonology cannot determine earlier Vocabulary Insertion.

Since the suppletion can also be characterized in morphosyntactic terms (the default *and-* appears in 1pl and 2pl present indicative, subjunctive, and imperatives instead of *va(d)-*), an analysis in which ϕ-features trigger suppletion can be given. As a result, the basic distributional pattern seen in (48) can be stated in either type of theory.[25] An important point is that there appears to be no way to look at predictions of the stress-based account beyond the facts in (48): in Standard Italian, there is no way to shift the stress in these forms to create forms in which allomorphic vacillation is predicted to occur.[26] As a result, there is no possibility of really testing the hypothesis that the surface position of stress drives stem choice; any claim to the effect that surface stress must be referred to in deriving the allomorphic pattern can be based only on conceptual arguments. Thus, this case is clearly analyzable with globalist assumptions, but it provides no arguments for a framework of that type.[27]

The conclusions to be drawn from this review of outward sensitivity and nonuniform paradigms are significant. There are cases in which constraints like PARADIGM UNIFORMITY do not apply; that is, changing allomorphs is not ruled out across the board. In cases where allomorphs do change, the strong predictions of globalist theories, with nonlocal factors determining allomorphic selection, should therefore be seen. Critically,

though, the attested cases of outward-sensitive allomorphy show sensitivity to local nodes, in the way predicted by the C_1-LIN theory. When allomorphic vacillation does occur, the vacillation is not triggered by the
global phonological context. The strong predictions of global-MP are
not found; appealing to PARADIGM UNIFORMITY does not help.

Overall, then, the point is not that outward-sensitive allomorphy does
not occur; it does. However, the conditions under which it occurs are not
those predicted by a globalist theory. Another way of putting this is that
paradigmatic vacillation does exist. However, it operates in ways that reflect the cyclic and linear restrictions of the theory developed in part I: it
is driven by local morphemes, not by the phonology of outer morphemes,
nor by the phonology of the whole (output) word.

6.5 Summary

The empirical predictions of globalist theories are straightforward. If such
theories are correct, there should be cases in which allomorph selection
is determined by global phonological properties, in a way that cannot be
stated in a localist theory.

As a general point, theories with even limited amounts of global interaction between morphology and phonology predict over- and underapplication in allomorphy. In empirical test-cases like the Latin perfect and -io
verbs, the theory that surface phonology drives allomorphy predicts allomorphic vacillation with certain "outer" morphemes. This is not found.
One possible response to this would be to attribute the nonvacillation to
paradigm uniformity effects. However, in cases where stem suppletion or
outward-sensitive allomorphy is found, (i) paradigm uniformity does not
hold, but (ii) there is still no evidence for the predictions of globalism over
localism.

The conclusion that must be drawn from these arguments is that there
is no evidence for the strong predictions of the globalist framework. In
the cases that have been studied in the literature, the patterns that are
found are those expected from a localist, cyclic point of view. It is significant to note that these cases are not arguments for "hybrid" theories like
cyclic or stratal OT; rather, such theories predict that global interaction
should occur within a given stratum, and there is no evidence that this is
correct.

7 Discussion

The $\mathbb{C}_1$-LIN theory developed in part I of the book is a localist theory that makes explicit predictions about how (morpho)syntax and (morpho)-phonology interact; these are developed with reference to contextual allomorphy, which constitutes the central empirical focus of the book. I chose this topic because this area provides significant insight into the relationship between syntax, morphology, and phonology, and because allomorphic interactions in language are highly restricted. The core proposal of the $\mathbb{C}_1$-LIN theory is that possible patterns of allomorphy in language are constrained by interacting cyclic and linear notions of locality. The predictions of this theory are defined and elaborated in numerous examples analyzed in chapters 2 and 3.

The predictions of the $\mathbb{C}_1$-LIN theory (and of localist theories in general) contrast sharply with those made by theories with even a limited amount of global interaction between morphology and phonology. Allomorphy—and phonologically conditioned allomorphy in particular—provides an important test-case for comparing localist and globalist grammatical architectures, because precisely this phenomenon allows us to determine whether global properties of the phonology determine morphology.

The argument in part II of the book identifies a number of phenomena that could in principle constitute evidence for globalism and against localism, and it shows that there is no evidence for the strong predictions of globalist theories. The argument has two components. First, as detailed in chapter 5, there appears to be little motivation for Phonological Selection—the idea that output phonology is crucial for allomorph selection—when systems of allomorphy are analyzed in detail. This point emerges from a number of case studies, including detailed analyses of case affixes in Djabugay and Yidiɲ. The second—and more important—

line of argument, advanced in chapter 6, shows that globalist theories predict interactions of a type that cannot be formulated in a localist theory: *NL-application*, where the factors determining allomorph choice are not local to the node undergoing insertion, and *allomorphic vacillation*, where allomorphs chosen for a particular Root change depending on the shape of outer, nonlocal morphemes. In case studies where these predictions could be manifested, as in different types of Latin verbal morphology, these effects are not found. Instead, the key cases show patterns that are expected on the more restrictive localist view.

The attested effects could, of course, be modeled in a globalist theory; but since there are no cases in which the strong predictions of globalism are found, restraining such theories by imposing additional constraints to produce the correct results is missing the point. The fact that allomorphic interactions do not show global interaction between morphology and phonology, instead behaving as predicted by the localist theory, argues that the localist view of the grammar is correct.

These results clearly have implications for how morphology and phonology interact. Although the point is less direct, they also have implications for phonology proper. Globalist theories of phonological interactions are competition-based; crucially, they involve competitions among complex objects, something that is ruled out in the localist theory of morphology and syntax developed in part I. Interface areas like allomorphy, where the relationship between morphology and phonology can be examined in detail, show the behavior predicted by localist theories. What does this mean, then, for approaches to phonology that employ globalist assumptions in order to implement competition? It is possible to consider different kinds of hybrid theories as a response to the results presented in this book. However, the type of phonological theory that fits most naturally with the no-competition theory of morphosyntax is a phonological theory with no competition among complex objects—that is, one in which the sound forms of complex expressions should be inextricably related to the generative procedure(s) responsible for constructing them in a localist and serialist fashion.

The following sections outline further implications of the arguments presented in this book, concentrating first on programmatic implications of the two main parts of the book in sections 7.1 and 7.2. Section 7.3 returns to the theme broached immediately above: what it might mean to have a morphosyntax and a morphophonology that differ fundamentally in their organization.

7.1 The Program I: Competition, Localism, Cyclicity

As stressed several times in the preceding chapters, a main point of tension between localist and globalist architectures is their stance on competition. A grammar that generates multiple potential competitors to express a given meaning is required in order for forms to be compared in terms of optimization of phonological or other properties. Competition among complex expressions is thus a fundamental component of how Optimality Theory implements globalism. The theory advanced in Embick and Marantz 2008, which looks primarily at morphosyntactic phenomena, holds that there is no competition among complex expressions. All other things being equal, the conclusions of this theory should extend to morphophonology as well. The facts revealed and analyzed in the study of allomorphy in parts I and II of this book strengthen the conclusions of the no-competition theory further.

The specific no-competition theory advanced in part I, the C_1-LIN theory, holds that cyclic derivation determines when nodes are potentially capable of influencing the form of other nodes and that linear adjacency is also required for nodes to interact with each other. These proposals must serve as the foundation for additional crosslinguistic work, so that the overall picture of possible allomorphic patterns can be elaborated further.

What it means for syntactic structure to be spelled out cyclically for both the sound (PF) and meaning (LF) interfaces has not yet been worked out in detail, and stands as a topic for further research. While the theory of part I makes explicit claims about aspects of cyclic derivation at PF, an important topic that remains to be worked out is whether the cyclic domains required for syntax, semantics, and phonology are the same. This would certainly be the best result for a cyclic theory. The study of allomorphic interactions provides a window on this larger set of questions, where the C_1 theory of cyclicity makes one set of assumptions about cyclic domains; one clear question for further study is how C_1 cyclicity lines up with the cyclic domains that are motivated on syntactic or semantic grounds.

The results of this book also provide a foundation for other questions that can be asked about the PF computation. First, exactly how does cyclic derivation play a role in other aspects of PF, and in phonology more generally? Second, for any of these further domains in PF, is there something like the linear condition seen in allomorphic locality? A related question concerns the "hybrid" nature of the C_1-LIN theory. The linear component of the theory interacts with the cyclic component so as to restrain possible allomorphic interactions within a cyclic domain to nodes that are adjacent. In a sense, the linear condition "overrides" the cyclic considerations in a limited way, to restrict possible interactions within a given cyclic domain. Whether linear override shows up in other aspects of PF computation, and whether analogues to the linear effect are found in domains outside of PF, are questions of great interest for cyclic theories.

I take questions like those just outlined to constitute natural extensions of the research program presented in part I of this book.

7.2 The Program II: Patterns in the Data

Localist theories like the one presented in part I and globalist theories of the type considered in part II differ in terms of what they try to explain in the grammar. The former type provides a theory of formal interactions in terms of the mechanics and architecture of derivations. It does not refer to the ultimate outputs of any of these computations. Most if not all globalist studies of morphophonology begin with the claim that the explanatory dimension of grammatical theory must be expanded to include a theory of the properties of outputs; this desideratum is then implemented in a way that requires competition among complex objects, and a globalist architecture.

The difference in explanatory orientation manifested in these opposing approaches is significant. The localist theory presented here stands or falls on its empirical predictions, which derive from its formal properties and from their emphasis on locality and ordering. This type of theory does not make any profound claims about the surface properties of the various phenomena that happen to exist in the languages that happen to exist. Put slightly differently, it provides a mechanical account of a system that generates sound-meaning connections; beyond placing formal conditions on what languages *could* exist in this way, it does not specify a theory of the outputs that it derives.

The arguments in part II of this book have direct implications for the view that the grammar must refer to properties of surface forms. A theory with the capacity to say that surface well-formedness in the phonology drives morphology makes the predictions about global interaction that are central to part II of this book. The argument of chapter 6 in particular is that the strong predictions made by globalist architectures—*NL-application* and *allomorphic vacillation* in particular—are not found. This is an argument against placing the explanation of surface patterns in the grammar. That is: a theory that is capable of satisfying "putative loss of generalization" makes strong empirical predictions about global interactions in grammar, yet these predictions are not supported by the data. It should be concluded from this that trying to account for surface generalizations in the grammar in the first place is the wrong idea. To the extent that there are things to say about surface patterns, these generalizations must be accounted for by other parts of the theory of language.

Situating the explanation of surface patterns outside of the grammar is a strong conclusion: it amounts to the claim that grammatical theories that refer to output forms in the grammar are misguided. The conclusions in this book must, of course, be limited to morphology-phonology interactions, and to patterns of allomorphy in particular. This specific case is clearly part of a larger set of questions about where, in the theory of language broadly construed, different types of generalizations should be accounted for. It can be concluded from the work presented here (i) that questions of this type must be addressed empirically, and not at the level of conceptual arguments, and (ii) that in one key domain, the surface-based view is incorrect. At the very least, these results call for a careful examination of other areas in which it is claimed that the grammar itself must account for generalizations about the properties of surface forms.

Regarding such (putative) generalizations, it is important to stress that none of the arguments in this book are directed against the idea that the distribution of allomorphs exhibits patterns in the first place. In many of the examples studied here, it is clear that the attested distributions could be seen as systematic in some sense and that the surface patterns could be understood in terms of phonological properties. According to the view argued for above, if there are important generalizations about why patterns of (phonologically conditioned) allomorphy produce certain patterns of surface forms (and not others), these generalizations must be accounted for in terms of the theory of diachrony, acquisition, phonetics, and so on. The programmatic conclusion is that careful study of the dynamics of language must be undertaken to see to what extent global concerns actually play a role in the historical developments that shape languages. This is an empirical question, and it could be answered in either direction. It could turn out that cases of putative global interaction in diachrony are epiphenomenal, or it could be that such interactions are crucial to explaining how languages develop. Either of these claims is worth pursuing in its own right, as long as it is recognized that considering a (limited) role for global interactions in diachrony falls far short of positing a globalist architecture for the synchronic grammar.

7.3   Epilogue: Phonology without Morphology/Syntax?

This book makes arguments that are based on the behavior of allomorphic interactions. It does not examine all predictions of globalist theories of phonology, only those related to the specific question of how morphosyntax and morphophonology interact in one crucial case study.

One conceivable response to these arguments is that globalist-oriented research in phonology is not affected by arguments that bear on morphology, or morphology-phonology interactions. In my view, this kind of response would be a grave error; it represents a failure to understand the depth of what is at issue. Globalist theories of phonology cannot really abandon morphology. This follows from the fact that in such theories, the inputs to any nontrivial competition are complex objects; that is, they consist of more than one piece. To the extent that syntactic theories of morphology like the one advanced in part I are correct, the complex objects that are the input to phonology are constructed in the syntax. In a globalist framework, this expands the set of predictions concerning global interactions, since the phonological constraints are predicted to interact with the syntax in the same way they are predicted to interact with morphology. There is no way to avoid the conclusion that a theory of phonology must account for how sound forms relate to the system responsible for creating complex objects.

Globalist theories predict that the constraints regulating the position, combination, and allomorphy of complex expressions should interact with the constraints determining its surface phonological form. If, as argued here, these interactions are not found, then one must ask why not; that is, at a minimum, one must ask if (some part of) phonology operates differently from syntax. Any other move, such as hypothesizing that morphological constraints invariably outrank phonological constraints, constitutes a tacit admission that the globalist architecture does not make the correct predictions as it stands. The same conclusion extends to cyclic or stratal versions of Optimality Theory, in which globalism is restrained, since there is no evidence for global interaction even within a restricted computational domain (i.e., one stratum).

In short, it appears that even a limited amount of global interaction between morphology and phonology leads to incorrect predictions about allomorphy, and that developing localist theories must be at the center of current research. My hope is that the theory presented in part I of this book provides a foundation for future research along these lines.

Notes

Chapter 1

1. In the broader background, it is worth noting that this sort of tension has been discussed from the reverse perspective; see Bromberger and Halle 1989.

2. As discussed in chapter 3, these allomorphs are better treated as *-ui* and *-si*. While this point plays a role in the discussion of chapter 3, it has no bearing on the main point here.

Chapter 2

1. It is assumed here that Roots possess a phonological underlying form and that they are not subject to Vocabulary Insertion in the way that functional morphemes are. There are reasons to think that phonological properties alone do not suffice to uniquely identify a Root in all cases. For example, the existence of homophonous Roots (e.g., *bank* 'financial institution' and *bank* 'side of a river') indicates that Roots must be distinguished from each other by something other than phonology, such as abstract indices.

2. In the approach taken in Halle 1990, functional nodes contain a dummy phonological matrix Q, which is replaced by the phonological exponent of the VI. Other formalizations of this process are conceivable. Beyond the addition of an exponent to a node, another possible effect of Vocabulary Insertion would be, for example, the deletion of the features that condition insertion, although this is contentious (some comments on this point appear in the case study from Latin perfect agreement endings in chapter 3).

3. See Kroch 1994 for pertinent observations about putative cases of "vocabulary-specific" linearization.

4. For present purposes, it does not matter whether the DP's PF properties are computed in a separate cycle, as might be the case in a theory with cyclic Spell-Out.

5. For example, it might not be necessary to have distinct *- and $\frown$-operators in linearization statements; this depends on whether these operators are *typed*. See Embick 2007b for some discussion.

6. This of course does not imply that there is only one type of phonological interaction in such objects.

7. Some intermediate copies of moved elements have been removed for simplicity.

8. Of course, this does not mean that M-Words and Subwords are linearized in the same direction with respect to one another. As is well-known, heads may differ in their position in complex heads versus phrases. In the view advanced here, these differences are reducible to the structural difference between M-Words and Subwords.

9. This does not, of course, mean that the notion of "paradigm" has no utility elsewhere in the study of language—for example, in the study of diachronic patterns, or of acquisition, or even in processing. The point is that the system responsible for the generation of grammatical forms does not use paradigmatic information.

10. These are not necessarily the only phases in the theory; phases implicated in the work of Chomsky (2000, 2001) and others—for instance, C and D—could be part of this type of theory as well. There is a question as to whether category-defining heads and heads like C and D have the same status, however. Some points along these lines are advanced in chapter 3, in a discussion of French prepositions and determiners.

11. For instance, in a structure like $[x \ [Z \ \sqrt{\text{Root}}]]$, where x is category-defining and Z is not, x counts as Root-attached.

12. There are some additional cases like *color-iz-ation* where an exponent other than *-ing* appears in an outer domain as well. See chapter 3 for discussion.

13. See Embick 1996 for an early formulation of such a theory.

  Beyond the "typical case" of Root-attached category-defining heads x, the $\mathbb{C}_0$ allows noncyclic heads in the inner domain to show Root-determined allomorphy.

14. At least, this interaction is ruled out if readjustment rules are subject to the same cyclic locality conditions as instances of contextual allomorphy; see chapter 3 for discussion.

15. Questions of this type are also touched on in Aronoff 1976, in a way that influenced other early work on cyclic interaction, such as the Adjacency Condition of Siegel (1978) and Allen (1979), and works like Williams 1981 and Scalise 1984.

16. It is possible that this potentation is restricted to the "potential" adjective head that is realized as *-able*.

17. With the Root $\sqrt{\text{Atroc}}$, the n affix that is pronounced *-ity* yields the noun *atrocity*. When this Root is merged with a, the a head is pronounced *-ous*, to yield *atrocious*. With *curiosity*, the Root is $\sqrt{\text{Curious}}$. This accounts for the lack of "truncation" in the latter case. See Embick and Marantz 2008 for discussion.

18. This definition connects with definitions of *phase impenetrability*, as explored in Chomsky 2000, 2001, and related work.

  Note that while elements become inactive in the sense defined in the text, the phonological matrix associated with such elements still might interact with later stages of the derivation; see section 3.4.2.

19. The idea expressed here appears in earlier theories as well; see, for example, Carstairs-McCarthy's (1992, 67) discussion of Siegel's (1978) and Allen's (1979) Adjacency Condition.

Lieber (1992) discusses a set of constraints on the percolation of features that restricts how much information is available to outer nodes in a way that is similar in some cases to what is proposed here: the visibility of features at "outer" morphemes is regulated by principles of percolation that stop features from moving up beyond category boundaries. The difference between cyclic and noncyclic nodes posited here builds on this important insight of Lieber's theory. At the same time, a detailed comparison of percolation versus cyclicity-plus-adjacency is beyond the scope of the present discussion.

20. As noted earlier in the text, there is perhaps noncyclic functional structure between v and outer n. This does not bear on the immediate discussion but is relevant when certain other cases are taken into account. These points are discussed in chapter 3.

21. The importance of considering both inward- and outward-looking allomorphy is stressed in Carstairs 1987.

22. Carstairs (1987) concentrates on an additional point: the idea that the externally sensitive form does not vary according to the specific features of outer morphemes, but is consistent across different person/number combinations (also Carstairs-McCarthy 2001, 2003). Carstairs-McCarthy proposes that sensitivity to node type (and not the feature content of a node) is a general property of outward- but not inward-sensitive allomorphy. This asymmetry is not predicted by the account I have presented in the text. However, there are instances of person/number-driven suppletion in verbs that might falsify the "node type but not content" generalization; these are discussed in section 3.2.2.

23. There are other types of cases that are not necessarily covered by the two categories outlined in sections 2.5.1 and 2.5.2. For example, Jonathan Bobaljik (pers. comm.) notes that Chung (2007) discusses what looks like stem suppletion conditioned by honorification in Korean, operating in a way that is nonlocal from the perspective of the theory advanced in the text. One question to ask is whether the honorific examples involve actual suppletion (i.e., contextual allomorphy) or are instead instances of different Roots.

Chapter 3

1. The pluperfect subjunctive contains two such pieces, -s and -sē.

2. This rule might have to be restricted so that it applies in derived environments; it appears to apply only before /r/'s that are the result of the Rhotacism rule discussed later in the text.

3. Invisibility might be a more general property of T[pres] in Latin, which does not appear in the nonperfect system either (see Embick and Halle, in preparation, for discussion).

4. Some additional complications—for example, the fact that the 1sg Agr has an -m allomorph in addition to -ō—are ignored in (11).

5. Note further that the contextual effect of Asp[perf] requires reference to the "abstract" form of this morpheme. As noted in the text, this head has three allomorphs, -*vi*, -*si*, and -*i*. The same special forms of Agr are selected with all of these allomorphs:

(i) Forms for all perfects

*Perfect-1*SG	*Gloss*
a. amā-v-ī	'love'
b. scrip-s-ī	'write'
c. ven-i-ī	'come'

Sensitivity to the features of Asp[perf] and not to the exponents that are inserted into that node follows directly if there is no "discharge" or "erasure" of features that are already spelled out by earlier applications of Vocabulary Insertion. The discharge of features with insertion may be required under other circumstances, as discussed in Noyer 1997; see also Bobaljik 2000.

6. Oltra-Massuet (1999) generalizes this claim to other functional heads such as T in her analysis of Catalan, a move that might be motivated for Latin as well (for similar suggestions, see Buck 1933; Williams 1981; Aronoff 1994). Whether or not this extension is compatible with the linear theory of allomorphy is not clear. See Embick and Halle, in preparation, for some discussion.

7. Alternatives would be to copy the features of the Root onto the *v*, via a sort of "concord" operation, or to simply have the *v* or the Th node acquire features like [IV] in the context of certain Roots.

8. Descriptively, *fused* affixes express two different types of features. I will make it clear when I am using *Fusion* for a structural operation that combines the contents of two nodes; see below.

9. The theory does not, however, prevent cyclic heads from ever being involved in Fusion. In principle, it is possible for a cyclic head to undergo Fusion with, say, its noncyclic edge[+] heads.

10. The class with -Ø in the transitive shows some differences in stem phonology in the intransitive. The -*aa*-affixed transitives also show a kind of vowel reduction process in the stem.

11. A small class of verbs that apparently have nothing in common shows variation in the indirect causative, with -*aa* being possible along with -*v-aa*. Evidently, the two forms are identical in meaning. All of these are verbs that take the -Ø allomorph in the transitive form.

12. It is assumed that Roots are visible for insertion at the inner Voice[ag] head because the *v* head in this configuration is pruned.

13. The head that appears in indirect causatives is a different type of passive head from the head found in passives that are not embedded in causative structures. Hindi passives are formed analytically, with the verb 'go' functioning as an auxiliary. The main verb is in a participial form, with an Aspectual head that has the exponent -*aa*. The verbs that show -*aa* and -Ø for Voice[ag] in transitives show the same exponents in passives, followed in each case by an additional -*aa* morpheme for the above-mentioned Asp head (the sequence /aa-aa/ is pronounced with an epenthetic glide):

(i) Passive forms

Intransitive	Transitive	Passive
$\sqrt{\text{Root}}$-v	$\sqrt{\text{Root}}$-v	$\sqrt{\text{Root}}$-$v^{\dagger}$-Asp
bāṭ-Ø	bāāṭ-Ø	bāāṭ-Ø-aa
bach-Ø	bach-aa	bach-aa-aa

In other words, there is in these cases no difference between the Voice exponents in the active and the passive. See Bhatt and Embick 2003 for additional discussion.

14. The most salient is the fact that not all cases that are called *suppletive* in traditional descriptions are necessarily cases of contextual allomorphy. Some of these might actually involve *defective* patterns of Root distribution.

15. Whether this works empirically for all cases classified as suppletion is another question (see, e.g., Corbett 2007 for a survey of the phenomenon). See, however, the qualification about what might count as suppletion in note 14.

16. A further question is whether this type of analysis extends to the present subjunctive, where v_{be} shows an *s*- stem as well.

Beyond this particular example, there are serious questions about the factors that constrain suppletion triggered by valued ϕ-features. In a worked-out theory of suppletion triggered by features from Agree, features on T must be restricted to be visible to v only with particular types of light verbs. Specifically, it appears that only intransitive light verbs show suppletion based on the person and number of the subject. In familiar patterns of suppletion in transitives, it is features of the object that trigger the different alternants (see, e.g., Hale, LaVerne, and Pranka 1990).

17. Although larger objects like CP are not addressed here, there is evidence from phrasal phonological interactions for cyclic Spell-Out in this domain. See the discussion in Pak 2008.

18. Certain aspects of (35a) are simplified for expository convenience. For instance, the formulation of (35a) does not take into account similar cases (such as those with prepositions, like *d'argent*). For further points about (35b), see Embick 2007b.

19. The way this analysis works, the *n* heads are the same, and what distinguishes them allomorphically is the type of structure they attach to. Another possibility is, of course, that different types of *n* are involved, so that, for instance, the *n* realized as -*ness* would be featurally distinct from the *n* realized as -*ing*.

20. For a discussion of the first of these points, see Embick and Halle 2005, where comparisons are made with theories that allow the storage and selection of "stems."

21. Thanks to Don Ringe for bringing this example to my attention.

22. The point about foot boundaries leads to a particularly strong set of predictions in metrical theories with single brackets, such as the theory developed in Idsardi 1992 and subsequent work: phonologically conditioned allomorphy associated with footing should be possible only at the particular points in the representation where a foot boundary appears.

23. Pak (2008) presents evidence suggesting that the linearization procedure that is responsible for dealing with such structural configurations has some special properties, and that these can be detected in patterns of (phrasal) phonological interaction.

24. In reality, the sequence /o-i/ compresses to /u/, which is what appears in the orthography (*ulbalə?*, *ulbasə?*, etc.).

25. One implication of this analysis is that there is more than one sense of "infixation." When the units involved are syntactic—Subwords and M-Words—operations like Local Dislocation may infix a morpheme by interpolating it. On the other hand, there are operations in the phonology that do something that is similar in the abstract, but that function in terms of a different set of primitives (i.e., syllabic or metrical units, not Subwords and M-Words).

On this general theme, Blevins (1999) and Yu (2004) discuss cases of "phonological" infixation where the predictions of certain globalist models of morphology and phonology are not borne out. Like others in this area, however, these works do not go far enough in terms of asking whether there is evidence for any aspect of the globalist architecture; see part II for discussion.

Chapter 4

1. For arguments centered on the predictions of P≫M for infixation, see Blevins 2004 and Yu 2007.

2. The possibility exists that patterns of irregular allomorphy, while not determined phonologically, are associated with particular phonological neighborhoods, as has been studied extensively in the context of the English past tense. At the same time, there is no reason to think that such calculations play a role in the synchronic grammar of the language, whatever role they might play in the acquisition of lists.

3. A further point is that in order for the syllable structure constraints to play the dominant role here, it must be assumed that DEP and MAX are ranked higher than ONSET and NOCODA; otherwise, various "fixes" with deletion or epenthesis could win. This point is important in some of the case studies in chapter 5.

4. Of course, in this type of case an analysis with competing allomorphs might not be warranted. It would be possible to posit one allomorph (e.g., -*nun*), along with a morphophonological rule that deletes the initial /n/ with C-final stems. Since these concerns are irrelevant to the overall point, I put them to the side here.

Chapter 5

1. This morpheme also appears in contexts that are not typically associated with determiners. However, these syntactic complications do not affect the general points about allomorphy that are considered in the text.

2. Moreover, there are no general reasons for positing rules or constraints that delete intervocalic /l/; see Klein 2003 for discussion.

3. Another point noted by Paster (2006) and Bye (2008) is that the distribution of allomorphs is rendered *opaque* by glide insertion, since underlyingly glide-final nouns take the *-la* allomorph, not the *-a* allomorph. The important questions raised by opacity are taken up in chapter 6.

4. McCarthy (2002, 154) considers something similar to this, noting that "the constraints responsible for allomorph selection may be only emergent and not otherwise active in the language under study." Again, it is hard to see how cases of this type could provide evidence for Phonological Selection. If the phonological analysis does not extend beyond a single case of allomorph selection, then the only argument in favor of such a treatment over one with ordered VIs would be conceptual, that is, based on putative loss of generalization.

5. There are some discrepancies between Patz's and Hale's descriptions of the form of the genitive morpheme. Hale (1976c, 239) gives the "short" genitive allomorph as *-:n* (i.e., with lengthening of the preceding vowel): *bama* '(Aboriginal) man' is given with genitive *bama-:n*. Patz (1991) and others who use this source do not indicate this length. Dixon (1977a, 136) cites the morpheme as *-:n* like Hale, and I assume this form to be correct.

   In writing Djabugay words, I use *ḓ* for Patz's (1991) *dj* and Hale's (1976c) *tʸ*. The digraph *rr* is used for a trill.

6. Regarding the status of this constraint, affixation can produce what look like complex codas word-internally in the language (e.g., *baḓigal* 'turtle', ergative *baḓigal-ndu*). If, however, Djabugay treats homorganic nasal-stop sequences as prenasalized stops, the codas are not actually complex. Nash (1979) proposes this for Yidiɲ (see below for some discussion).

7. One could ask whether, given this formulation, *-Ø* allomorphs should always win when they are available, given that they are (i) minimal and (ii) unlikely to create phonological problems. Kager does not consider this possibility. Similarly, one could ask about cases in which the competing allomorphs are of the same size, as far as segment counting goes. There seems to be little reason to dwell on these details, however.

8. The noun *bama* '(Aboriginal) man' takes the ergative affix *-lu*. This exponent is not found elsewhere in the language, although there are instrumental/locative forms with *-la* that are related to it.

9. An alternative would be to posit a *-da* allomorph in (10f) so that it is the stem-final /n/ that surfaces in the inflected form. While this move eliminates this particular case of opacity, little seems to be gained by it.

10. Dixon (1976) describes the basic historical pattern for ergative as typically assimilating *-du* with C-final hosts and *-lu* or *-ŋgu* with V-final hosts; the same takes place in locatives but with *-a* instead of *-u* (see also Hale 1976b). Djabugay has no *-ŋga* locative. The diachronic theory of the cases has been refined in various ways since these early proposals (see Dixon 2002 for summary), but the basic connection between ergative and locative cases stands.

11. Other cases exist as well, but these do not add much to the discussion beyond what can be learned from (14), so I will concentrate on ergative, inst/loc, genitive, and dative below.

12. The patterns in (21d) show some variation, as do those in (21e). Deletion of final rhotics is obligatory with even-syllabled stems and optional for odd-syllabled stems (Dixon 1977a, 127). The pattern of deletion with /y/-final stems appears to be less systematic.

13. That is, the expected locative+ of *buṛi* is **buṛi:l*. It turns out that there are five disyllabic nouns in which the final /l/ that is expected by the phonology does in fact surface. For example, Dixon (1977a, 50) gives *ḍugi* 'tree', with locative+ *ḍugi:-l*. The normal case can be treated as involving a rule of /l/-deletion, with the nouns that show final /l/ being an exception to this.

14. Deletion with stem-final rhotics is obligatory with even-syllabled stems and optional with odd-syllabled stems (Dixon 1977a, 129). With /y/-final stems, omission of the final consonant is reported to be variable (recall the ergative).

15. In the Comitative case of *mabi*, the surface *mabi:* results from a rule applying to *mabi:-y* to delete the final glide.

16. Long vowels affect stress placement. The interaction of stress with the placement of long vowels in Yidiɲ words is extremely complex, and, to a first approximation, looks "conspiratorial," in a way that excited Dixon's description and some analyses following his overall perspective (e.g., McCarthy 2002 and references cited there). The interaction of length with foot construction and stress assignment presents a number of challenges, as recognized by Halle and Vergnaud (1987). I leave a fleshed-out theory of stress in Yidiɲ for later work.

17. Dixon calls the affixed form of *maḍinda* a "dative subordinate"; this reduces by FSD, unlike the regular dative, which is an exception to this rule.

18. Another possible take on why *-gu* does not delete in *biɲḍi:n-gu* could be based on some notion of *contrast* from the base or "unmarked" form *biɲḍin*. It could be argued, for instance, that deletion of *-gu* is banned because the resulting form **biɲḍi:n* would be "too similar" to the base *biɲḍin*. This analysis would fail in the comitative case, for example, where the stem *mabi* 'kangaroo sp.' surfaces as *mabi:*. In the analysis with PL and FSD, the expected case allomorph *-yi* reduces to /y/ by FSD, following lengthening of /i/, to yield /mabi:-y/. Then /i:y/ is simplified to /i:/. The surface form differs from the "base" form only in terms of vowel length, exactly as **biɲḍi:n* does. Thus, unless the approach based on contrast is to be stipulated on a case-by-case basis, it appears to be on the wrong track.

19. This way of formulating the rule requires that in (e.g.) *-ŋgu*, the ŋ component must not be syllabified. Thus, if homorganic nasal-stop sequences behave as prenasalized stops (i.e., as a single consonant), as proposed by Nash (1979), this syllabification must take place subsequent to FSD.

20. In the final line of *mulariŋgu*, the idea is that the /ŋ/ of the ergative case morpheme is resyllabified as a coda. For a discussion of some cases in which it appears that there are prenasalized stops in Yidiɲ, see Nash 1979.

21. The second verb here is derived from *gali* 'go' with the comitative affix *-ŋa* and the *-l* conjugation suffix.

22. Some of the details of the VIs could be modified slightly, without changing the overall picture. For example, it might be possible to posit an additional erga-

tive morpheme -*Cu*, where the C is a stop that undergoes assimilation in place to left-adjacent consonants. Then -*ŋgu* would be inserted after vowels and the semi-vowel /y/, and -*Cu* would be inserted otherwise. It is not clear that this modification would add much to the discussion, however.

23. I put to the side constraints that would favor assimilated affixes like -*du* for the ergative over nonassimilated forms.

24. Moreover, PL as part of the phonology fares much better in cases in which nouns bear more than one affix. This is seen in the phenomenon of "Suffixauf-nahme," where, in possessive contexts, the case of the head noun appears after a genitive morpheme on nonheads, yielding Noun-GEN-ERG for a possessor in an ergative DP. So, to set the stage for this doubly affixed form, *guda:ga* 'dog' has the genitive *gudaga-ni*. The "morphological" treatment of vowel length would put this noun in the class that shows long vowels only in unaffixed forms. However, when nouns like this are further affixed with ergative "Suffixaufnahme," long vowels appear where the phonological analysis predicts: in the case at hand, the form is *gudaga-ni:-ŋ*, where the ergative morpheme appears after the genitive morpheme. Once the addition of the ergative morpheme creates the appropriate phonological conditions (an unfooted final syllable), lengthening occurs. A "morphological" account misses this effect. A similar point is made with *buɲa:-n* 'woman-GEN', *buɲa-nu-ŋgu* 'woman-GEN-ERG'. This stem does not simply show a long stem vowel whenever genitive is present, as the second form illustrates; it shows a long stem vowel only when the phonological context is appropriate. Treating vowel length as something other than the result of PL simply does not work very well.

Chapter 6

1. It is for this reason that in this and other cases, many OT analyses have moved toward *paradigmatic* resemblance with other morphological forms. That is, if there are no phonological reasons why a form should be as it is, then the reasons must be morphological in nature. As noted in chapter 1, such theories are clearly incompatible with the localist theory of morphosyntax argued for in part I. See also Bobaljik 2002, 2008.

2. This is one way of putting it; it would also be possible to say that the notion of local conditioning environment is immaterial, or derivative, or epiphenomenal, or the like, in such theories.

3. The rule is simplified, in that it actually applies only with certain affixes; see Inkelas and Orgun 1995 for discussion.

4. An alternative is to posit a single VI with the exponent -*sɪ*, and some additional rules to delete the consonant under specific circumstances; see below.

5. Here and below, matters related to the vowel component of -*(s)ɪ* are ignored.

6. In Turkish', the effects of Velar Deletion would be seen only with morphemes that have no C-initial allomorphs.

7. So if Z were an Agr node, Z_1 and Z_2 would represent different combinations of person/number features, for example.

8. Fulmer (1997) reports that certain affixes behave similarly in Afar.

9. There are other combinations about which the same type of point could be made. For example, consider an odd-syllabled host that takes both the passive affix and one of the alternating agreement morphemes: Root-PASS-AGR. An even-syllabled output could be derived by inserting the (locally unconditioned) disyllabic passive affix, then a monosyllabic outer affix. As far as I am aware, this does not occur.

10. In this section, I refer to the perfect allomorphs with -u and -s, as in Mester's discussion. In section 6.3.2, I refer to them as -vi and -si, as in chapter 3.

I am putting aside Reduplication, along with various stem-changing processes that apply in the perfect. These cases can be treated as taking the -i exponent of Asp[perf], in which there is, in addition, action in the form of readjustment rules.

11. Mester (1994, 47) excludes from consideration verbs that he classifies as "denominal," which do not take the allomorph expected on prosodic grounds alone. For example, albēre 'be white' has a heavy stem, but shows the -u- perfect alb-u-ī.

12. Here, I put aside initial trapping—representations in which the initial syllable is unfooted—although see below.

13. Mester also considers "marked" trochees where σ̆σ̆ is footed as [σ̆σ̆] instead of as [σ̆]σ̆. In the latter type of approach, the trimoraic trochee is what is avoided when possible.

14. The forms in (32) include three distinct entries for 3pl because three different agreement endings—namely, -ērunt, -ēre, and -erunt—were in variation in this context. In principle, something about optimization could be learned from -erunt; compare monuerunt σ̄[σ̆σ̆]⟨σ̄⟩ with augserunt [σ̄]σ̆⟨σ̄⟩. See Sommer 1914, 579, for correlations between perfect allomorph and 3pl agreement endings that might be worth looking into in the context of Latin historical phonology.

15. Mester uses an argument based on putative allomorphic vacillation in his second case study from Latin -io verbs; see below in the text. The failure of perfect allomorphs to vacillate is not addressed.

16. For this type of "uniform exponence" approach to work properly in this particular case, the allomorph found in the perfect would have to be preferred to the one favored on metrical grounds in the pluperfect, presumably something that could be accomplished in terms of making the former less marked.

17. This analysis draws in part on joint work with Morris Halle, most of which (with the exception of Embick and Halle 2005) has not been published.

18. With the exception of the theme vowel in conjugation III, given here as /-i-/, this is more or less uncontroversial (recall the comments in chapter 3). Verbs in this conjugation show an -i- theme vowel in certain person/number forms (e.g., dūc-i-t 'he/she leads'), but, unlike with the conjugation III(i) type verbs, this vowel does not appear in 1sg forms such as dūc-ō. There are other options for the vowel here that have been explored in the literature (e.g., Lieber 1980). Since this particular assumption does not play a role in the analysis of the perfect, I will not say anything more about it.

19. For conjugation I, the verb *iuvāre* 'help' has the perfect *iuvī*, which looks like an *-i-* perfect. The stem-final /v/ in *iuvāre* makes this case, an apparent instance in which a verb of conjugation I takes an *-i-* perfect, questionable at best. Conjugation II has some apparently thematic perfects: for example, *flēre, flēvī* 'weep'. Aronoff (1994) argues (as does Ernout (1952/1989) that these verbs are not actually in conjugation II. Rather, they happen to end in /-ē-/. The argument is based on the fact that Roots are minimally CV. The suggestion is attractive in that it allows for a cleaner statement of the rules concerning the presence or absence of themes in these verbs in perfect and participial forms, which are then always athematic (though there are some /i/ vowels in participles; e.g., *mon-i-tus* for *monēre*).

Another pattern I am not taking into account here involves apparent "conjugation change." For instance, *petō* 'seek', with infinitive *pet-e-re*, seems on the basis of these two forms to be conjugation III, like *dūcō*; likewise for conjugation III(i) *cupiō* 'desire', with perfect *cup-ī-v-ī*. However, the perfect form is *pet-ī-v-ī*, evidently with the *-ī-* theme vowel that characterizes conjugation IV verbs like *aud-ī-re*. There are a handful of verbs that behave this way, all showing conjugation III or III(i) behavior in the present system and the *-ī-* of conjugation IV in the perfect.

Finally, in line with the exclusion of stem-changing processes, I have not included Reduplication as a separate class here, on the assumption that the reduplicated perfects are a subcase of the *-i*-affixed perfects.

20. See Aronoff 1994 for discussion of the fact that the perfect shows many systematic patterns, regarding in particular Lieber's (1980) claims about the irregularity of the system of perfect formation.

21. There are some exceptions to the light-stem pattern. Light-stem verbs that end in liquids are in conjugation IV, not III(i).

22. Another prediction is that verbs like *venīre* that have a long theme despite having a light root syllable should show a short theme when these verbs have a heavy prefix. There are two problems here. The first is that Mester offers no explanation for why these verbs should ever surface with *-ī-* instead of *-i-* in the unprefixed forms in the first place. The second is that this additional prediction is not verified.

23. It is true that there are many cases in Latin where theme vowels differ in prefixed and unprefixed verbs: examples are *pellere* 'push', *compellāre* 'summon'; *spernere* 'remove', *aspernārī* 'reject'; *capere* 'take', *occupāre* 'seize'; *specere* 'look at', *suspicārī* 'mistrust' (Sommer 1914, 507ff.). These differ in themes and deponency, and they raise questions about when two forms may be said to contain the same Root, as well as other questions about morphophonology. But whatever there is to say about such cases, they offer no support for a globalist theory of morphology and phonology.

24. Carstairs (1987, 179ff.) looks at some additional cases of allomorphy that are putatively "outward-sensitive" to phonological properties. These cases do not appear to be fully suppletive; that is, it looks like the majority involve morphophonological rules, not competition for insertion, and thus are not directly relevant to the issue at hand.

The central cases (Carstairs 1987, 185ff.) come from Fula and are based on work by Arnott (1970) and McIntosh (1984). One case involves affixes that differ between "short" and "long" forms: anterior *-noo/-no*, relative past passive *-aa/-a*, and relative past middle *-ii/-i*. The factor conditioning the alternation is phonological, and the alternation itself is clearly not suppletive. The other case is found with the habitual imperative singular suffix, which is typically *-atay*. In the first person singular, this morpheme surfaces as *-at*. While there are some phonological correlates of this (the 1sg affix follows the habitual imperative morpheme and is the only vowel-initial agreement morpheme), the alternation is not necessarily suppletive; moreover, it can be stated with reference to the 1sg features, so that the phonological effect is incidental.

25. The same pattern of features is required elsewhere in the language's verbal system. As Carstairs (1988, 1990) discusses, the morphosyntactic pattern seen in (48) is found with other verbs, where it conditions, for example, insertion of the "infix" *-isc-* (e.g., the verb 'finish' has 1sg *fin-isc-o* but 1pl *fin-iámo*): on the face of it, *-isc-* does not appear with stressed affixes.

Maiden (2004) presents a detailed study of such stem alternations in Romance, concentrating on whether particular patterns of paradigmatic distribution of "stems" call for a morphological (versus, say, phonological) treatment. Looking at patterns like that seen in Italian, he presents arguments (2004, 159ff.) against the view that surface placement of stress must be referred to in these patterns of stem allomorphy. See also Corbett 2007, 22, for related discussion.

26. I thank Andrea Calabrese for discussion of this and related points.

27. The need to look for vacillation in this system is touched on by Kiparsky (1996, 25), who cites comments by Wolfgang Dressler in a discussion period (see also Maiden 2004, 161). It appears that the word *àndiriviéni* 'coming and going', where secondary stress appears on *and-*, does not conform to an analysis in which stress drives allomorphy. However, this form might not be probative, since it is not clear what its synchronic relationship to *va(d)-/and-* is.

In some dialects of Italian, stress shift can be induced by encliticization. As far as I am aware, there is no evidence that stem suppletion with 'go' vacillates in such cases.

References

Adger, David, Susana Béjar, and Daniel Harbour. 2001. Allomorphy: Adjacency and Agree. Paper presented at the 23rd GLOW Colloquium, Braga, Portugal.

Adger, David, Susana Béjar, and Daniel Harbour. 2003. Directionality of allomorphy: A reply to Carstairs-McCarthy. *Transactions of the Philological Society* 101:1, 109–115.

Alexiadou, Artemis. 2001. *Functional structure in nominals*. Amsterdam: John Benjamins.

Allen, Margaret. 1979. Morphological investigations. Doctoral dissertation, University of Connecticut.

Anderson, Stephen. 1992. *A-morphous morphology*. Cambridge: Cambridge University Press.

Andrews, Avery. 1990. Unification and morphological blocking. *Natural Language and Linguistic Theory* 8:4, 507–557.

Aranovich, Raúl, Sharon Inkelas, Orhan Orgun, and Ronald Sprouse. 2005. Opacity in phonologically conditioned suppletion. Paper presented at the Thirteenth Manchester Phonology Meeting.

Arnott, David Whitehorn. 1970. *The nominal and verbal systems of Fula*. Oxford: Oxford University Press.

Aronoff, Mark. 1976. *Word formation in generative grammar*. Cambridge, MA: MIT Press.

Aronoff, Mark. 1994. *Morphology by itself: Stems and inflectional classes*. Cambridge, MA: MIT Press.

Bachrach, Asaf, and Michael Wagner. 2006. Syntactically driven cyclicity vs. output-output correspondence: The case of adjunction in diminutive morphology. Paper presented at the Penn Linguistics Colloquium.

Bergsland, Knut. 1976. *Lappische Grammatik mit Lesestücken*. Wiesbaden: Otto Harrassowitz.

Bhatt, Rajesh, and David Embick. 2003. Causative derivations in Hindi. Ms., University of Texas and University of Pennsylvania.

Blevins, Juliette. 1999. Untangling Leti infixation. *Oceanic Linguistics* 38:2, 383–403.

Bobaljik, Jonathan David. 1999. Implications of Itelmen agreement asymmetries. In Steve S. Chang, Lily Liaw, and Josef Ruppenhofer, eds., *Proceedings of Berkeley Linguistics Society 25*, 299–310. Berkeley: University of California, Berkeley Linguistics Society.

Bobaljik, Jonathan David. 2000. The ins and outs of contextual allomorphy. In Kleanthes K. Grohmann and Caro Struijke, eds., *Proceedings of the Maryland Mayfest on Morphology 1999*, 35–71. University of Maryland Working Papers in Linguistics 10. College Park, MD: University of Maryland, Department of Linguistics.

Bobaljik, Jonathan David. 2002. Syncretism without paradigms: Remarks on Williams 1981, 1994. In Geert Booij and Jaap van Marle, eds., *Yearbook of morphology 2001*, 53–85. Dordrecht: Kluwer.

Bobaljik, Jonathan David. 2008. Paradigms (optimal and otherwise): A case for skepticism. In Asaf Bachrach and Andrew Nevins, eds., *Inflectional identity*, 29–54. Oxford: Oxford University Press.

Bobaljik, Jonathan David, and Susi Wurmbrand. 2002. Notes on agreement in Itelmen. *Linguistic Discovery 1*.

Bonet, Eulàlia. 1991. Morphology after syntax: Pronominal clitics in Romance. Doctoral dissertation, MIT.

Bonet, Eulàlia, Maria-Rosa Lloret, and Joan Mascaró. 2007. Allomorph selection and lexical preference: Two case studies. *Lingua* 117:9, 903–927.

Bresnan, Joan. 2001. Explaining morphosyntactic competition. In Mark Baltin and Chris Collins, eds., *Handbook of contemporary syntactic theory*, 1–44. Oxford: Blackwell.

Bromberger, Sylvain, and Morris Halle. 1989. Why phonology is different. *Linguistic Inquiry* 20:1, 51–70.

Buck, Carl Darling. 1933. *Comparative grammar of Greek and Latin*. Chicago: University of Chicago Press.

Burzio, Luigi. 1998. Multiple correspondence. *Lingua* 104:1–2, 79–109.

Bye, Patrik. 2008. Allomorphy: Selection, not optimization. In Sylvia Blaho, Patrik Bye, and Martin Krämer, eds., *Freedom of analysis?*, 63–92. Berlin: Mouton de Gruyter.

Carstairs, Andrew. 1987. *Allomorphy in inflexion*. London: Croom Helm.

Carstairs, Andrew. 1988. Some implications of phonologically conditioned suppletion. In Geert Booij and Jaap van Marle, eds., *Yearbook of morphology 1988*, 67–94. Dordrecht: Foris.

Carstairs, Andrew. 1990. Phonologically conditioned suppletion. In Wolfgang Dressler, Hans Luschützky, Oskar Pfeiffer, and John Rennison, eds., *Selected papers from the Third International Morphology Meeting*, 17–24. Berlin: Mouton de Gruyter.

Carstairs-McCarthy, Andrew. 1992. *Contemporary morphology*. London: Routledge.

Carstairs-McCarthy, Andrew. 2001. Grammatically conditioned allomorphy, paradigmatic structure, and the Ancestry Constraint. *Transactions of the Philological Society* 99:2, 223–245.

Carstairs-McCarthy, Andrew. 2003. Directionality and locality in allomorphy: A response to Adger, Béjar, and Harbour. *Transactions of the Philological Society* 101:1, 117–124.

Chomsky, Noam. 1970. Remarks on nominalization. In Roderick Jacobs and Peter Rosenbaum, eds., *Readings in English transformational grammar*, 184–221. Waltham, MA: Ginn.

Chomsky, Noam. 1993. A minimalist program for linguistic theory. In Kenneth Hale and Samuel Jay Keyser, eds., *The view from Building 20: Essays in linguistics in honor of Sylvain Bromberger*, 1–52. Cambridge, MA: MIT Press.

Chomsky, Noam. 2000. Minimalist inquiries: The framework. In Roger Martin, David Michaels, and Juan Uriagereka, eds., *Step by step: Essays on minimalist syntax in honor of Howard Lasnik*, 89–156. Cambridge, MA: MIT Press.

Chomsky, Noam. 2001. Derivation by phase. In Michael Kenstowicz, ed., *Ken Hale: A life in language*, 1–52. Cambridge, MA: MIT Press.

Chomsky, Noam, and Morris Halle. 1968. *The sound pattern of English*. New York: Harper and Row.

Chung, Inkie. 2007. Ecology of PF: A study of Korean phonology and morphology in a derivational approach. Doctoral dissertation, University of Connecticut.

Corbett, Greville G. 2007. Canonical typology, suppletion, and possible words. *Language* 83:1, 8–42.

Dixon, R. M. W. 1976. Rapporteur's introduction. In R. M. W. Dixon, ed., *Grammatical categories in Australian languages*, 313–314. Canberra: Australian Institute of Aboriginal Studies.

Dixon, R. M. W. 1977a. *A grammar of Yidiɲ*. Cambridge: Cambridge University Press.

Dixon, R. M. W. 1977b. Some phonological rules of Yidin^y. *Linguistic Inquiry* 8:1, 1–34.

Dixon, R. M. W. 2002. *Australian languages*. Cambridge: Cambridge University Press.

Dolbey, Andrew. 1997. Output optimization and cyclic allomorph selection. In Brian Agbayani and Sze-Wing Tang, eds., *Proceedings of the 15th West Coast Conference on Formal Linguistics*, 97–112. Stanford, CA: CSLI Publications.

Embick, David. 1996. Causativization in Hupa. In Janice Johnson, Matthew Juge, and Jeri Moxley, eds., *Proceedings of the Berkeley Linguistics Society 22*, 83–94. Berkeley: University of California, Berkeley Linguistics Society.

Embick, David. 1997. Voice and the interfaces of syntax. Doctoral dissertation, University of Pennsylvania.

Embick, David. 2000. Features, syntax, and categories in the Latin perfect. *Linguistic Inquiry* 31:2, 185–230.

Embick, David. 2003. Locality, listedness, and morphological identity. *Studia Linguistica* 57:3, 143–169.

Embick, David. 2004a. On the structure of resultative participles in English. *Linguistic Inquiry* 35:3, 355–392.

Embick, David. 2004b. Unaccusative syntax and verbal alternations. In Artemis Alexiadou, Elena Anagnostopoulou, and Martin Everaert, eds., *The unaccusativity puzzle*, 137–158. Oxford: Oxford University Press.

Embick, David. 2007a. Blocking effects and analytic/synthetic alternations. *Natural Language and Linguistic Theory* 25:1, 1–37.

Embick, David. 2007b. Linearization and local dislocation: Derivational mechanics and interactions. *Linguistic Analysis* 33:3–4, 303–336.

Embick, David, and Morris Halle. 2005. On the status of *stems* in morphological theory. In Twan Geerts, Ivo van Ginneken, and Haike Jacobs, eds., *Romance languages and linguistic theory 2003*, 59–88. Amsterdam: John Benjamins.

Embick, David, and Morris Halle. In preparation. *The Latin conjugation*. Ms., University of Pennsylvania and MIT.

Embick, David, and Alec Marantz. 2008. Architecture and blocking. *Linguistic Inquiry* 39:1, 1–53.

Embick, David, and Rolf Noyer. 2001. Movement operations after syntax. *Linguistic Inquiry* 32:4, 555–595.

Ernout, Alfred. 1952/1989. *Morphologie historique du latin*. 4th ed. Paris: Klincksieck.

Flora, Marie Jo Ann. 1974. Palauan phonology and morphology. Doctoral dissertation, University of California, San Diego.

Fulmer, Sandra Lee. 1997. Parallelism and planes in Optimality Theory: Evidence from Afar. Doctoral dissertation, University of Arizona.

Golla, Victor. 1970. Hupa grammar. Doctoral dissertation, University of California, Berkeley.

Hale, Kenneth. 1976a. Dja:bugay. In R. M. W. Dixon, ed., *Grammatical categories in Australian languages*, 321–326. Canberra: Australian Institute of Aboriginal Studies.

Hale, Kenneth. 1976b. On ergative and locative suffixal alternations in Australian languages. In R. M. W. Dixon, ed., *Grammatical categories in Australian languages*, 414–417. Canberra: Australian Institute of Aboriginal Studies.

Hale, Kenneth. 1976c. Tʸaˈpukay (Djaabugay). In Peter Sutton, ed., *Languages of Cape York*, 236–242. Canberra: Australian Institute of Aboriginal Studies.

Hale, Kenneth, Jeanne LaVerne, and Paula Pranka. 1990. On suppletion, selection, and agreement. In Carol Georgopoulos and Roberta Ishihara, eds., *Interdisciplinary approaches to language*, 255–270. Dordrecht: Kluwer.

Halle, Morris. 1990. An approach to morphology. In Juli Carter, Rose-Marie Déchaine, Bill Philip, and Tim Sherer, eds., *Proceedings of North East Linguistic Society (NELS) 20*, 150–184. Amherst: University of Massachusetts, Graduate Linguistic Student Association.

Halle, Morris. 1997. Distributed Morphology: Impoverishment and fission. In Benjamin Bruening, Yoonjung Kang, and Martha McGinnis, eds., *PF: Papers at the interface*, 425–449. MIT Working Papers in Linguistics 30. Cambridge, MA: MIT, MIT Working Papers in Linguistics.

Halle, Morris, and William J. Idsardi. 1995. General properties of stress and metrical structure. In John Goldsmith, ed., *The handbook of phonological theory*, 403–443. Oxford: Blackwell.

Halle, Morris, and Alec Marantz. 1993. Distributed Morphology and the pieces of inflection. In Kenneth Hale and Samuel Jay Keyser, eds., *The view from Building 20: Essays in linguistics in honor of Sylvain Bromberger*, 111–176. Cambridge, MA: MIT Press.

Halle, Morris, and Alec Marantz. 1994. Some key features of Distributed Morphology. In *Papers on phonology and morphology*, ed. by Andrew Carnie, Heidi Harley, and Tony Bures, 275–288. MIT Working Papers in Linguistics 21. Cambridge, MA: MIT, MIT Working Papers in Linguistics.

Halle, Morris, and K. P. Mohanan. 1985. Segmental phonology of Modern English. *Linguistic Inquiry* 16:1, 57–116.

Halle, Morris, and Bert Vaux. 1998. Theoretical aspects of Indo-European nominal morphology: The nominal declensions of Latin and Armenian. In Jay Jasanoff, H. Craig Melchert, and Lisi Oliver, *Mír curad: Studies in honor of Calvert Watkins*, 223–240. Innsbruck: Institut für Sprachwissenschaft der Universität Innsbruck.

Halle, Morris, and Jean-Roger Vergnaud. 1987. *An essay on stress*. Cambridge, MA: MIT Press.

Hargus, Sharon. 1993. Modeling the phonology-morphology interface. In Sharon Hargus and Ellen M. Kaisse, eds., *Studies in Lexical Phonology*, 45–71. San Diego, CA: Academic Press.

Harley, Heidi. 2005. On the causative construction. Ms., University of Arizona.

Hayes, Bruce. 1982. Metrical structure as the organizing principle of Yidin^y phonology. In Harry van der Hulst and Norval Smith, eds., *The structure of phonological representations*, 97–110. Dordrecht: Foris.

Idsardi, William J. 1992. The computation of prosody. Doctoral dissertation, MIT.

Idsardi, William J. 2000. Clarifying opacity. *The Linguistic Review* 17:2–4, 337–350.

Inkelas, Sharon. 1993. Nimboran position class morphology. *Natural Language and Linguistic Theory* 11:4, 559–625.

Inkelas, Sharon, and C. Orhan Orgun. 1995. Level ordering and economy in the Lexical Phonology of Turkish. *Language* 71:4, 763–793.

Jacobsen, Wesley M. 1992. *The transitive structure of events in Japanese*. Tokyo: Kurosio.

Josephs, Lewis S. 1975. *Palauan reference grammar*. Honolulu: University Press of Hawaii.

Josephs, Lewis S. 1990. *New Palauan-English dictionary.* Honolulu: University of Hawaii Press.

Kager, René. 1996. On affix allomorphy and syllable counting. In Ursula Klein-henz, ed., *Interfaces in phonology,* 155–171. Berlin: Akademie Verlag.

Kager, René. 1999. *Optimality Theory.* Cambridge: Cambridge University Press.

Kenstowicz, Michael. 1996. Base-identity and uniform exponence: Alternatives to cyclicity. In Jacques Durand and Bernard Laks, eds., *Current trends in phonology: Models and methods,* 363–393. Salford: European Studies Research Institute.

Kiparsky, Paul. 1982. Lexical Morphology and Phonology. In Linguistic Society of Korea, ed., *Linguistics in the morning calm: Selected essays from SICOL-1981,* 3–91. Seoul: Hanshin.

Kiparsky, Paul. 1996. Allomorphy or morphophonology? In Rajendra Singh and Richard Desrochers, eds., *Trubetzkoy's orphan,* 13–31. Amsterdam: John Benjamins.

Kiparsky, Paul. 2000. Opacity and cyclicity. *The Linguistic Review* 17:2–4, 351–366.

Kisseberth, Charles. 1970. On the functional unity of phonological rules. *Linguistic Inquiry* 1:3, 291–306.

Klein, Thomas B. 2003. Syllable structure and lexical markedness in creole mor-phophonology: Determiner allomorphy in Haitian and elsewhere. In Ingo Plag, ed., *The phonology and morphology of creole languages,* 209–228. Tübingen: Niemeyer.

Kornfilt, Jaklin. 1997. *Turkish.* London: Routledge.

Kratzer, Angelika. 1994. The event argument and the semantics of voice. Ms., University of Massachusetts, Amherst.

Kratzer, Angelika. 1996. Severing the external argument from its verb. In Johan Rooryck and Laurie Zaring, eds., *Phrase structure and the lexicon,* 109–137. Dor-drecht: Kluwer.

Kroch, Anthony. 1994. Morphosyntactic variation. In Katharine Beals et al., eds., *CLS 30: Papers from the 30th Regional Meeting of the Chicago Linguistic Society.* Vol. 2, *The Parasession on Variation and Linguistic Theory,* 180–201. Chicago: University of Chicago, Chicago Linguistic Society.

Lapointe, Steven. 1999. Stem selection and OT. In Geert Booij and Jaap van Marle, eds., *Yearbook of morphology 1999,* 263–297. Dordrecht: Kluwer.

Lewis, Charlton T., and Charles Short. 1969. *A Latin dictionary.* Oxford: Oxford University Press.

Lewis, Geoffrey. 1967. *Turkish grammar.* Oxford: Oxford University Press.

Lieber, Rochelle. 1980. The organization of the lexicon. Doctoral dissertation, MIT.

Lieber, Rochelle. 1992. *Deconstructing morphology.* Chicago: University of Chi-cago Press.

Łubowicz, Anna. 2005. Opaque allomorphy in OT. In Donald Baumer, David Montero, and Michael Scanlon, eds., *Proceedings of the 25th West Coast Conference on Formal Linguistics*, 261–269. Somerville, MA: Cascadilla Press.

Maiden, Martin. 2004. Morphological autonomy and diachrony. *Yearbook of Morphology 2004*, 137–175.

Marantz, Alec. 1984. *On the nature of grammatical relations.* Cambridge, MA: MIT Press.

Marantz, Alec. 1988. Clitics, morphological merger, and the mapping to phonological structure. In Michael Hammond and Michael Noonan, eds., *Theoretical morphology*, 253–270. San Diego, CA: Academic Press.

Marantz, Alec. 1995. A late note on late insertion. In Young-Sun Kim et al., eds., *Explorations in generative grammar*, 357–368. Seoul: Hankuk.

Marantz, Alec. 1997. No escape from syntax: Don't try morphological analysis in the privacy of your own lexicon. In Alexis Dimitriadis, Laura Siegel, Clarissa Surek-Clark, and Alexander Williams, eds., *Proceedings of the 21st Penn Linguistics Colloquium*, 201–225. Philadelphia: University of Pennsylvania, UPenn Working Papers in Linguistics.

Marantz, Alec. 2001. Words and things. Handout, MIT.

Marantz, Alec. 2007. Phases and words. In Sook-Hee Choe, ed., *Phases in the theory of grammar*, 199–222. Seoul: Dong In.

Marlett, Stephen, and Joseph Stemberger. 1983. Empty consonants in Seri. *Linguistic Inquiry* 14:4, 617–639.

Marvin, Tatjana. 2002. Topics in the stress and syntax of words. Doctoral dissertation, MIT.

Mascaró, Joan. 2007. External allomorphy and lexical representation. *Linguistic Inquiry* 38:4, 715–735.

McCarthy, John. 2002. *A thematic guide to Optimality Theory.* Cambridge: Cambridge University Press.

McCarthy, John. 2005. Optimal paradigms. In Laura Downing, Tracy Alan Hall, and Renate Raffelsiefen, eds., *Paradigms in phonological theory*, 170–210. Oxford: Oxford University Press.

McCarthy, John. 2008. The serial interaction of stress and syncope. *Natural Language and Linguistic Theory* 26:3, 499–546.

McCarthy, John, and Alan Prince. 1993. Prosodic Morphology I: Constraint interaction and satisfaction. Technical Report #3. New Brunswick, NJ: Rutgers University Center for Cognitive Science.

McCarthy, John, and Alan Prince. 1995. Faithfulness and reduplicative identity. In Jill Beckman, Suzanne Urbanczyk, and Laura Walsh Dickey, eds., *Papers in Optimality Theory*, 249–384. University of Massachusetts Occasional Papers in Linguistics 18. Amherst: University of Massachusetts, Graduate Linguistic Student Association.

McIntosh, Mary. 1984. *Fulfulde syntax and verbal morphology.* Boston: Kegan Paul.

Meiser, Gerhard. 1998. *Historische Laut- und Formenlehre der lateinischen Sprache.* Darmstadt: Wissenschaftliche Buchgesellschaft.

Meiser, Gerhard. 2003. *Veni vidi vici: Die Vorgeschichte des lateinischen Perfektsystems.* Munich: C. H. Beck.

Mester, R. Armin. 1994. The quantitative trochee in Latin. *Natural Language and Linguistic Theory* 12:1, 1–61.

Miyagawa, Shigeru. 1994. *(S)ase* as an elsewhere causative and the syntactic nature of words. In *Program of the Conference on Theoretical Linguistics and Japanese Language Teaching,* 61–76. Tsuda University.

Nash, David. 1979. Yidiny stress: A metrical account. In Edwin Battistella, ed., *Proceedings of North East Linguistics Society (NELS) 9,* 112–130. Amherst: University of Massachusetts, Graduate Linguistic Student Association.

Niedermann, Max. 1908. Une loi rythmique proéthnique en latin. In *Mélanges de linguistique offerts à M. Ferdinand de Saussure.* Librairie de la Société de Linguistique de Paris. Geneva: Slatkine Reprints edition, 43–57.

Noyer, Rolf. 1993. Mobile affixes in Huave: Optimality and morphological well-formedness. In Erin Duncan, Donka Farkas, and Philip Spaelti, eds., *Proceedings of the Twelfth West Coast Conference on Formal Linguistics,* 67–82. Stanford, CA: CSLI Publications.

Noyer, Rolf. 1997. *Features, positions and affixes in autonomous morphological structure.* New York: Garland.

Noyer, Rolf. 1998. Impoverishment Theory and morphosyntactic markedness. In Steven Lapointe, Diane Brentari, and Patrick Farrell, eds., *Morphology and its relation to syntax and phonology,* 264–285. Stanford, CA: CSLI Publications.

Odden, David. 1993. Interaction between modules in Lexical Phonology. In Sharon Hargus and Ellen M. Kaisse, eds., *Phonetics and phonology 4: Studies in Lexical Phonology,* 111–144. San Diego, CA: Academic Press.

Oltra-Massuet, Isabel. 1999. On the notion of theme vowel: A new approach to Catalan verbal morphology. Master's thesis, MIT.

Oltra-Massuet, Isabel, and Karlos Arregi. 2005. Stress by structure in Spanish. *Linguistic Inquiry* 36:1, 43–84.

Orgun, C. Orhan, and Andrew Dolbey. 2007. Phonology-morphology interaction in a constraint-based framework. In Gillian Ramchand and Charles Reiss, eds., *The Oxford handbook of linguistic interfaces,* 103–124. Oxford: Oxford University Press.

Pak, Marjorie. 2008. The postsyntactic derivation and its phonological reflexes. Doctoral dissertation, University of Pennsylvania.

Paster, Mary. 2006. Phonological conditions on affixation. Doctoral dissertation, University of California, Berkeley.

Patz, Elizabeth. 1991. Djabugay. In Barry J. Blake and R. M. W. Dixon, eds., *The handbook of Australian languages*, vol. 4, 245–347. Oxford: Oxford University Press.

Pesetsky, David. 1979. Russian morphology and lexical theory. Ms., MIT.

Poser, William J. 1992. Blocking of phrasal constructions by lexical items. In Ivan Sag and Anna Szabolcsi, eds., *Lexical matters*, 111–130. Stanford, CA: CSLI Publications.

Prince, Alan, and Paul Smolensky. 1993. Optimality Theory: Constraint interaction in generative grammar. New Brunswick, NJ: Rutgers University Center for Cognitive Science.

Pylkkänen, Liina. 2002. Introducing arguments. Doctoral dissertation, MIT.

Scalise, Sergio. 1984. *Generative morphology*. Dordrecht: Foris.

Siegel, Dorothy. 1978. The Adjacency Constraint and the theory of morphology. In M. J. Stein, ed., *Proceedings of North East Linguistic Society (NELS) 8*, 189–197. Amherst: University of Massachusetts, Graduate Linguistic Student Assocation.

Smyth, Herbert Weir. 1920. *Greek grammar*. Cambridge, MA: Harvard University Press.

Sommer, Ferdinand. 1914. *Handbuch der lateinischen Laut- und Formenlehre*. Heidelberg: Carl Winters Universitätsbuchhandlung.

Sproat, Richard. 1985. On deriving the lexicon. Doctoral dissertation, MIT.

Svenonius, Peter. To appear. Spatial P in English. In Guglielmo Cinque and Luigi Rizzi, eds., *The cartography of syntactic structures, vol. 6*. Oxford: Oxford University Press.

Vaux, Bert. 2003. Syllabification in Armenian, Universal Grammar, and the lexicon. *Linguistic Inquiry* 34:1, 91–125.

Wagner, Michael. 2005. Prosody and recursion. Doctoral dissertation, MIT.

Williams, Edwin. 1981. On the notions *lexically related* and *head of a word*. *Linguistic Inquiry* 12:2, 245–274.

Wolf, Matthew. 2008. Optimal interleaving: Serial morphology-phonology interaction in a constraint-based model. Doctoral dissertation, University of Massachusetts, Amherst.

Yu, Alan. 2004. The morphology and phonology of infixation. Doctoral dissertation, University of California, Berkeley.

Index

Linguistic Inquiry Monographs
Samuel Jay Keyser, general editor